11-22-60

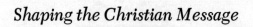

Shaping the Christian Message

THE MACMILLAN COMPANY
NEW YORK · CHICAGO
DALLAS · ATLANTA · SAN FRANCISCO
LONDON · MANILA

IN CANADA
BRETT-MACMILLAN LTD.
GALT, ONTARIO

Shaping the Christian Message

ESSAYS IN RELIGIOUS EDUCATION

EDITED BY

Gerard S. Sloyan

Head of the Department of Religious Education
The Catholic University of America, Washington, D.C.

.

CONTRIBUTORS

André Boyer   John A. Hardon, s.j.

Joseph Colomb, P.S.S.   Johannes Hofinger, s.j.

François Coudreau, P.S.S.   Josef A. Jungmann, s.j.

J. D. Crichton   J. J. Maguire

Georges Delcuve, s.j.   Pierre Ranwez, s.j.

F. H. Drinkwater   Gerard S. Sloyan

Gustave Weigel, s.j.

New York

THE MACMILLAN COMPANY

1958

Nihil obstat:
Robert Paul Mohan, S.S.
Censor Deputatus
Imprimatur:
Patrick A. O'Boyle
✠ Archbishop of Washington

The *nihil obstat* and *imprimatur* are official declarations that a book or pamphlet is free of doctrinal or moral error. No implication is contained therein that those who have granted the *nihil obstat* and the *imprimatur* agree with the content, opinions or statements expressed.

July 30, 1958

First Printing

Library of Congress catalog card number: 58-11545

The Macmillan Company, New York
Brett-Macmillan Ltd., Galt, Ontario

Printed in the United States of America

Grateful acknowledgment is hereby made to the following publishers for permission to quote: from THE VIRTUES AND STATES OF LIFE, by A.-M. Henry, copyright 1957 by Fides Publishers, Fides Publishers, Chicago, Ill.; from BIOGRAPHIA LITERARIA, by Samuel Taylor Coleridge, E. P. Dutton & Co., Inc., New York, N. Y. and J. M. Dent & Sons, Ltd., London, England; from JESUS CHRIST, by R. P. de Grandmaison, Vol. II, copyright 1934 by Sheed and Ward, Sheed and Ward Inc., New York, N. Y.; from THE LIFE AND TIMES OF BISHOP CHALLONER by Edwin H. Burton, Longmans, Green & Co. Ltd., London, England; from LYRICAL BALLADS by William Wordsworth edited by George Simpson, copyright 1950 by Methuen and Co., Methuen & Co., Ltd., London, England; from ELIZABETHAN RECUSANT PROSE, by A. C. Southern, copyright 1950 by Sands & Co., Sands & Co., Ltd., London, England; from THE BIBLE AND THE LITURGY by Jean Daniélou, S.J., copyright 1956 by University of Notre Dame Press, University of Notre Dame Press, Notre Dame, Ind.; from ANCIENT CHRISTIAN WRITERS, Newman Press, Westminster, Md.; from FATHERS OF THE CHURCH, Fathers of the Church, Inc., New York, N.Y.

The Scripture quotations are in the translation of Monsignor Ronald Knox, Copyright 1944, 1948, 1950 by Sheed and Ward Inc., New York, N. Y.

The Right Reverend William H. Russell

These essays are a tribute of affection from two groups: The Kerby Foundation, Catholic laymen dedicated to promoting the concept of the spiritual basis of American democracy, and the teachers of religion and students who felt the warmth of Monsignor Russell's personality and the depth of his charity. The former have made the book possible; the latter will know best why there should have been such a volume.

Not every development in the field of religious education is represented here. There are many lacunae. An attempt was made to produce a book which would reflect certain ideals in the service of which Monsignor Russell spent a lifetime.

A word of profound appreciation is in order here to the late Mr. Fenton Moran, Executive Secretary of the Kerby Foundation, who was so intimately concerned with the production of this memorial volume. May the eternal light shine upon him.

Introduction

Complaining against children's catechisms is an old business. It can be a tiresome one. Yet every Christian has the freedom to work for the improvement of a situation in the Church provided he has the needed knowledge and can bring his reforms to the attention of those who have jurisdiction. If it is they who take initiative in the task, as with the *Catechismus Romanus* of 1566, so much the better. It is worth while observing that the right to be heard on any question must be won. No one automatically deserves to challenge a present situation, thought by many to be praiseworthy, until he first knows all the reasons for the favorable judgment. The man of good will may oppose criminal action and moral wrong with all vigor. When, however, he sets about the reform of some social situation or institution, or theological monument (like the child's catechism), he may be heard effectively only when he knows how that thing came to be, and came to be approved.

There does not exist in English a large body of writing on the roots of the catechism as a handbook of faith. Informative summaries are not lacking, but neither are they numerous. What they summarize is the drift of things: the catechumenate as an institution, the great names in patristic preaching and teaching, the emergence of the creeds, and all subsequent use of the question-answer technique. The essay which follows immediately has no different goal, but it does employ as its means selections of some length. This is a field that is not crowded, any more than patristic and medieval writings in English generally can be said to embarrass by their profusion.

The first two studies in this book establish two things: that the special needs of children were not attended to in any special way, in a context either of liturgy or of formal pedagogy; and that because believing Christians multiplied consistently for the fifteen or so centuries under discussion, the family, the Sunday Eucharistic assembly, and sacrament preparation must have sufficed somehow. How effectively we cannot say.

What we can do about effectiveness is surmise. A pedagogy in-
attentive to child nature cannot be good for children. The evidence
is that it was not good because it was not so attentive. What we may
do is to make a general act of faith in parents and pastors of those
early times, and conclude that the riches of the great bishops of
Jerusalem and Hippo and the others were ideally adapted and
transmitted to children by adult hearers. It *may* have been so; that
is history's strongest verdict.

Yet history's verdict also is that if the oral catechesis reflected
even partially the written corpus from those times, children were
reared in a world of biblical beauty and doctrinal firmness. Good
teaching provided to adults cannot but do good to children, ultimately. It is a slower process because indirect. But it is a surer
process than mediocre teaching provided to young and old alike.
There follows, then, some fine gold of good education which cannot
have become all dross when it was dispensed to the young.

The temper of pre-Reformation Germany and Austria, the bold
response of recusant England, catechetical practice in Paris of the
seventeenth through nineteenth centuries, all provide us with categories of thought for attending to the modern situation. We are
hampered from clear thought, though, until we have got some
sound notion of the complexity of child nature. A further hindrance
to fruitful catechetical action is ignorance of the profound inroads
made by "dechristianized" modes of thought. Here the American
reader is well aware of certain differences from the European situation. Danger for him lies in his going jauntily unaware of the great
elements of likeness.

Like criticism of the catechism, unkind remarks about pulpit
catechesis and the college study of doctrine are standard practice
among Catholic adults. Both questions receive their merited attention in this collection.

Yet the supreme blunder would be to forget that all religious edu-
cation is primarily the work of the Holy Spirit, "the interior Master."
Consequently, His is the final word, as it was the first on Pentecost
Day.

GERARD S. SLOYAN

Contents

PART II
RELIGIOUS EDUCATION
Some Theological and Scientific Considerations

PART III
RELIGIOUS EDUCATION
Practical Considerations

PART I

RELIGIOUS EDUCATION

An Historical Perspective

1.

Religious Education:
From Early Christianity to Medieval Times
.
Gerard S. Sloyan

In reading the conciliar legislation of pre-Tridentine Europe, one
has the feeling that life was a good deal simpler in days when
bishops could insist on enough Latinity in their clerics to have them
recite Pater, Ave, Credo and read the text of Mass and the other
sacraments. The faithful had only to know the Lord's Prayer and
Creed in their own tongues; these their priests were required to be
able to expound in the vernacular of the place.[1] This public instruction delivered to adults and children indiscriminately on the occasion of the celebration of the Eucharistic liturgy is the oldest form
of catechetical presentation. Nothing can be expected to supplant it
in importance, though a myriad of devices can and should be
worked out to meet the special needs of the young.

One such device is the catechism. In concept, the catechism is a
doctrinal handbook prescribed by bishops as a guide to their clergy
in providing a pulpit catechesis. It has inevitably made its way into
the hands of children as both the first outline of faith presented to
them (in abridged form, i.e.) and the last summary many of them
see of religious knowledge. This is a development no more than
four centuries old, that each child should have a summary of
doctrine in the form of a handbook for his own use. Yet when
Martin Luther brought out his *kleine Katechismus* in 1529, following late-medieval practice already well-established, he set a pattern

---

[1] See A. Boyer, "Catéchisme," *Catholicisme, Hier, Aujourd'hui, Demain*, dir.
G. Jacquemet, II (Paris: Letouzey et Ané, 1949), 646 ff.; C. Hézard, *Histoire
du catéchisme* (Paris: Librairie des Catéchismes, 1900); E. Mangenot, "Catéchisme," *Dictionnaire de Théologie Catholique*, dir. Vacant, Mangenot, Amann,
II (Paris: Letouzey et Ané, 1905), 1895–1906.

that is with us still and gives promise of being so for many years to come.

The earliest non-canonical handbook of instruction we have and our "sole ancient source on the matter of the catechesis"[2] is the *Didaché* or *Teaching of the Twelve Apostles,* sixteen brief chapters, possibly of multiple authorship, stemming from Egypt, Syria or Palestine sometime between the years 60 and 90. A few put it as late as 130 and fewer still place it in the third century as a Montanist document.[3] Very likely it is a compilation of materials from various periods. It echoes the decrees of the Apostolic Council (Acts 15, 28 ff.) in its prescription to abstain from meat offered to idols (6, 3). In general, its primitive status is not seriously questioned by scholars. Leclercq reviews the arguments concerning its Hebraic character which incline some to think that large parts of it are pre-Christian in origin, the Christian elements being interpolated.[4] There is no professedly dogmatic instruction in the *Didaché* but only Christian morality, an outline of liturgical conduct (baptism, Eucharist, public confession, fasting), and some indications as to authority and the various ministries in the early Church. There is every reason to consider it a faithful mirror of apostolic teaching methods. An interesting matter is the simple, catechism-like division at the outset between the two Ways leading to Life and Death, basically an Old Testament pattern. Further on, Christ's command to love God and neighbor is coupled with the Golden Rule in negative form as the one means to blessedness. The Lord's precepts from the Sermon on the Mount are woven in beautifully with the ten commandments and with St. Paul's spirit of clear admonition to the churches. There are warnings against infanticide and killing a fetus by abortion (2, 2), and some stirring phrases about open-handed generosity. Preachers must be honored

[2] G. Bardy, "Catéchèse," *Catholicisme,* II, 645.

[3] James A. Kleist, *Ancient Christian Writers,* ed. J. Quasten and J. Plumpe, No. 6 (Westminster, Md.: Newman Press, 1948), 3–15.

[4] H. Leclercq, "Catéchèse," *Dictionnaire d'Archéologie Chrétienne et de Liturgie,* 2 (Paris: Letouzey et Ané, 1925), 2530–34. See also J.-P. Audet, *La Didachè* (Paris: Gabalda, 1958), pp. 61, 101 ff., who argues that a late interpolation in the present text made a pre-baptismal catechesis of what had originally been designed as post-baptismal.

as the Lord (4, 1). The trinitarian formula of baptism (by triple pouring if immersion in running or other water is impracticable) is followed by the Lord's Prayer (7 and 8). The latter is to become a constant in all catechetical instruction. In the *Didaché* it is commanded to be said with its concluding doxology ("for Thine is the glory and the power for evermore") three times a day (8, 2–3). "As regards your prayers and alms and your whole conduct, do exactly as you have it in the gospel of Our Lord" (15, 4), is a phrase which seems to presuppose a written gospel. There is no use made of Bible incidents in the *Didaché*, but phrases from both Testaments are used with all naturalness throughout: "In every place and time offer only a pure sacrifice; for I am a mighty king, says the Lord" (Mal. 1, 11–14). . . . "You do not know the hour in which Our Lord is coming" (See Mt. 24, 42).

When the Alexandrian Jew Apollos arrived at Ephesus, speaking with fervor of whatever had to do with Jesus, he was described (Acts 18, 25) as *katēchēménos*—"instructed" in the way of the Lord from the fact of his having learned from a living voice. The sound specified the act.[5] *Katēchéthēs* meant for St. Luke the fact of having been taught about Christ (Lk. 1, 4); to give the instruction, *katēchésō*, that led to understanding was Paul's ambition much more than "ten thousand words in a tongue" (I Cor. 14, 19). A man instructed, *katēchoúmenos*, should share all good things with his teacher, *katēchoûnti*, according to Gal. 6, 6. The fact that oral instruction was the normal means of knowledge about Christ made the term "catechesis" come to mean either the act of teaching or the message taught. Private instruction was the primitive form, of course. Subsequently, groups were prepared for reception into the Church, and by the late third century "catechesis" commonly described what was transmitted in the "catechumenate" or sessions preparatory to baptism.[6]

[5] See J. P. Christopher's instructive note on *katēcheîn* (literally "to echo") as derived from ancient sing-school methods, in his St. Augustine, *The First Catechetical Instruction*, 2 (ACW, 1946), 93, n.4. The first use of the verb *catechizare* is ascribed to Tertullian, *De cor. mil.*, 11; *catechismus* to Augustine, *De fide et operibus*, XIII, 9.

[6] See D. dePuniet, arts. "Baptême" and "Catéchumenat," *Dictionnaire Apolo-*

Origen speaks of the books of Esther, Judith, Tobias and Wisdom and other biblical extracts effective in inculcating moral conduct as suitable for the preparation of those "beginning the study of divine things." [7] From him and Tertullian we learn of the practice of infant baptism and therefore conclude that instruction was somehow in the parents' hands. The "church order" of Hippolytus of Rome known as the *Apostolic Tradition* describes, around the year 215, the moral stringency with which prospective candidates were screened and the form if not the subject matter of the primitive catechumenate.[8] Origen's homilies are our first clear indication of the presence of the catechumen at Mass. Inducted into the catechumenate, after lengthy proof of good will, by the sign of the cross on his forehead and salt on his tongue, an imposition of hands and a breathing on his brow, the candidate did his subsequent learning from Old

---

getique de La Foi Catholique; Bardy, *loc. cit.,* and "L'enseignement religieux aux prémiers siècles," *Revue Apologetique,* 66 (1938, I), 641–55; 67 (1938, II), 5–18. Cf. also J. A. Jungmann, *Katechetik* (Vienna: Herder Verlag, 1953), pp. 5–12. These references are especially helpful because no attempt is made in the present essay to describe the development of the catechumenate.

[7] *PG* 12, 780, *In Num. hom.,* 27, 1. Origen (†254?) came after Tertullian (†230?) who in his *De Baptismo* writes as if to catechumens, in the first extended work on Christian initiation after I Peter.

[8] "XVI. 1. Those who come forward for the first time to hear the word shall be brought to the teachers before all the people come in.

"2. And let them be examined as to the reason why they have come forward. And those who bring them shall bear witness for them whether they are able to hear. . . .

"XVII 1. Let a catechumen be instructed for three years (but if earnest, his reception should come sooner). . . .

"XX   1. . . . . If those who bring them bear witness that they have lived piously, 'honored the widows,' fulfilled every [good work] let them hear the gospel. . . . 3. [and] be exorcised daily. . . .

"XXI 1. And at the hour when the cock crows they shall first [of all] pray over the water. . . . 4. And they shall baptize the little children first. . . . if they cannot [answer for themselves], let their parents answer or someone from their family."—Gregory Dix, *The Apostolic Tradition of St. Hippolytus of Rome* (London: S.P.C.K., 1937), pp. 23, 28, 30 ff. Hippolytus also gives the Roman rite of baptism which contains this creed, a combination of trinitarian and christological formulas (the latter developed in the *praefatio* of the eucharistic liturgy): "I believe in God the Father Almighty, and in Jesus Christ the Son of God, who was born of the Virgin Mary by the Holy Spirit, was crucified under Pontius Pilate, died, and was buried. He arose on the third day living from the dead, ascended into heaven, sits on the right hand of the Father; He will come to judge the living and the dead. And in the Holy Spirit and holy Church and resurrection in the flesh."

and New Testament readings and sermons during the fore-part of
the Mass.

In the late second century, Clement of Alexandria (†ca. 215)
paints a charming picture of Christ as the Educator of little ones
(all who follow Him) in his *Pedagogue*. Clement's career as an instructor in doctrine is marked by the transition within his lifetime
from an earlier, simpler, catechetical pattern to a more complex
theological one. His students in the Alexandrian school of Pantaenus,
whom he succeeded as head, were mostly well-to-do Greeks—therefore neither children nor the unlettered nor catechumens in the
pre-baptismal sense. The presentation in *Paidagōgós* is philosophic
and apologetic. "The all-loving Word," he writes, "anxious to perfect us in a way that leads progressively to salvation, makes effective
use of an order well adapted to our development; first He persuades,
then He forms, and after that He instructs." [9] Clement's *Protreptikós*,
the first volume of his trilogy, is usually translated as *Exhortation to
the Greeks;* then comes his *Paidagōgós* (in the sense of molder of
character rather than intellectual instructor); finally the doctrinal
course known as the *Strómata* or *Tapestries*. The Word Himself
sings a new song to charm with its beauty ears that have been
given over to paganism. All the philosophic inconsistency and
moral crudity of pagan ways are to be dislodged by the knowledge
of the justice and goodness of God, by the utter transcendency of
Christianity.[10] Christ lays in the soul the foundation stone of noble
persuasion. He has one proper title:

Educator of the little ones, an Educator who does not simply follow
behind, but who leads the way, for his aim is to improve the soul, not
just to instruct it; to guide to a life of virtue, not merely one of knowledge. Yet that same Word does teach. It is simply that in this work we
are not considering Him in that light.[11]

It is evident from this that the early Church grasped the twofold
role of Christ as revealer and ruler of hearts. The distinction is im-

---

[9] *PG*8, 251 f., I, 1 (9). An English translation is available as *Christ the
Educator,* Simon P. Wood (New York: Fathers of the Church, 1954). See p. 5.
[10] A. de la Barre, "Clement d'Alexandrie," *DTC*, 3, 146. See *PG*8, 60 ff.
[11] I, 1 (6). Cf. Wood, *op. cit.,* p. 4.

portant for all religious education: it must proclaim (*kerýssein*) a rule of divine love or salvation accomplished, and elucidate (*didáskein*) the terms of life in the kingdom.[12]

Clement's style is rambling, but his mind is beautifully furnished. It has been said that he never came to write his treatise on Christ the Teacher because of the order it would have held him to. In philosophy he is a Stoic, in theology an allegorist of Scripture. Chapters 5 and 6 of *Paidagōgós* wring all the sap from the concept of childlikeness before the loving instructor God, as it is developed in the two Testaments. The puffed-up mentality of the Gnostics is the great enemy. Quoted above is his catechetical principle on spiritual formation as a legitimate end in teaching. Here is the way Clement states his commitment to simplicity of approach. It was Christ's way of teaching, and presumably it should be ours:

In war there is need for much equipment, just as self-indulgence claims an abundance. But peace and love, simple and plain blood sisters, do not need arms nor abundant supplies. Their nourishment is the Word whose leadership enlightens and educates, from whom we learn poverty and humility and all that goes with love of freedom and mankind and the good.[13]

The third-century Syriac treatise called *Didaskalía* or *The Teaching of the Twelve Apostles* indulges in the fiction of having the several apostles speak up as the authors. It is a moral and disciplinary document from Syria or Palestine, not extant in its Greek original. The sole catechetical directive in the section on states in life is a charge to the bishop to nourish the people with the word as with milk, dispensing to each according to his need:

You then (O bishops) are to your people . . . receivers of the word, and preachers and proclaimers thereof, and knowers of the Scripture and of the utterances of God, and witnesses of his will. . . . you are they who have heard how the word strongly threatens you if you neglect and preach not God's will.[14]

[12] Cf. David M. Stanley, S.J., "Didachē as a Constitutive Element of the Gospel-Form," *Catholic Biblical Quarterly*, XVII (April, 1955), 216–28.

[13] I, 12 (21) f., col. 369. Cf. Wood, *op. cit.*, p. 88.

[14] R. Hugh Connolly, *Didascalia Apostolorum*, the Syriac Version Translated and Accompanied by the Verona Latin Fragments (Oxford: The Clarendon Press, 1929), ch. 8, p. 80.

There is very little in this absorbing treatise that is directly doctrinal, but the Old Testament is extensively used to illustrate the virtues proper to various states.[15] When the author claims to be St. Matthew he is somewhat embarrassingly handicapped in quoting from the gospel according to St. John, which presumably had not been written yet.[16]

Irenaeus, Bishop of Lyons in the late second and early third centuries (†202?), met his obligation to teach with the treatise *Proof of the Apostolic Preaching*.[17] It is more apologetic than catechetical in intent, being a statement of the case against Gnosticism and for the acceptance of the divine mission of the Church, yet its net effect is instruction for Christians rather than a polemic against their enemies. In orientation the work is biblical. Its proof of the truth of the Gospel lies in establishing that the Gospel is the fulfillment of Old Testament prophecy.[18] Irenaeus contributes two important ideas to the catechetical question, one concerned with content and the other with method. He provides a basic creed in three articles (ch. 6), which foreshadows all the creeds that are to follow:

God, the Father, uncreated, beyond grasp, invisible, one God, the maker of all; . . . the Word of God, the Son of God, Christ Jesus, Our Lord . . . at the conclusion of ages, for the recapitulation of all things, is become man . . . in order to abolish death and bring to light life (2 Tim. 1, 10) and bring about the communion of God and man; . . . the Holy Spirit, through whom the prophets prophesied . . . who . . . has been poured forth in a new manner upon humanity over all the earth, renewing man to God.[19]

---

[15] Thus, there are admonitions to married men, married women, bishops, transgressors who repent, etc. E.g., "Hear then, you bishops, and hear, you laymen: I will judge between ram and ram, and between ewe and ewe; that is, between bishop and bishop and between layman and layman: whether layman loves layman, and whether again the layman loves the bishop and honors and fears him as father and Lord. . . ." Connolly, *op. cit.*, ch. 7, p. 60.

[16] *Ibid.*, p. 103.

[17] Joseph P. Smith, ACW 16, p. 20 ("Introduction"), translated from an Armenian MS first discovered in 1904. Eusebius refers to the work as (*Lógos*) *'eis tēn epídeixin toû 'apostolikoû kērýgmatos*. It is frequently referred to simply as *Epídeixis*.

[18] *Op. cit.*, p. 43.

[19] *Op. cit.*, p. 51. For a history of the Apostles' Creed, its provenance and

The baptism of our rebirth comes through belief in these three articles on the three Persons, since the Father confers incorruptibility on those presented to Him by the Son, who in turn were led to that Word by the Spirit. As to method of presentation, Irenaeus' treatise is not far advanced (ch. 11, eight modern pages), before he begins with the creation narrative and retells the bulk of the Old Testament very succinctly. His recapitulation figure of Adam and Christ (virgin earth; virginal disobedience and virginal obedience; cross and tree) is the beginning of a restrained search for types of our Lord through the patriarchal period and the periods of Moses and the prophets. He employs the narrative method with considerable effect and sets the stage for all subsequent attempts to see in Christ the summing-up of humanity, typified by the Jews who awaited God's revelation. In general his technique is the simple quotation of Old Testament prophecy and its fulfillment by Christ, literal wherever possible. Because of its distinct typology, a brief "chapter" —one of one hundred such (all are short but this one is exceptionally brief)—may be worth quoting:

> 77. Again, He says in the twelve prophets (Osee 10, 6) [according to the Septuagint text]: *and they brought Him bound as a present to the king.* For Pontius Pilate was Procurator of Judaea, and was at that time on bad terms with Herod, king of the Jews. Now, therefore Pilate sent Christ . . . bound, to Herod . . . having found in Christ an apt occasion for reconciliation with the king.[20]

Coming down to religious instruction more professedly, the magnificent course given by Cyril, Bishop of Jerusalem, to the catechumens of his flock in Lent and Easter Week of 348(?), is outstanding of its kind. It is known as *Katēchēseis phōtizoménōn, Instruction for Those About To Be Illumined.*[21] The chief thing to bear in mind about St. Cyril's lessons in Christian belief is that

---

general acceptance at Rome, cf. J. N. D. Kelly, *Early Christian Creeds* (London: Longmans, Green & Co., 1950), ch. 13.

[20] *Op. cit.*, p. 97.

[21] *PG*33, 331–1128; for the last five given after Easter ("mystagogic"), see F. L. Cross, *St. Cyril of Jerusalem's Lectures on the Christian Sacraments* (London: S.P.C.K., 1951). Le Bachelet discusses the work in *DTC*, 3, 2533 ff. The authenticity of the last five is in some doubt, the credit often going to Cyril's successor, Bishop John.

such homilies woven into the fabric of liturgy were for centuries the sole mode of religion teaching for young and old alike. Forty days of catechetical training were evidently given in eighteen lectures to those inscribed for holy baptism (already called "the faithful," as if more a part of the Church than the simple inquirers in the catechumenate).[22] These talks to the *competentes* or *electi*, as they were known in Rome, went concurrently with prescribed ascetical practices. After baptism on Holy Saturday night, five instructions to the *neophyti* followed. These dealt with the sacraments of baptism, confirmation, the Eucharist, and the new obligations of Christian life as outlined in I Peter 2, 1–23.

St. Cyril is a simple and clear teacher who does not multiply theological terms. His method is in part apologetic in that he includes the teachings of heretics, Jews, Samaritans, and pagans, and coaches his hearers on how to respond. The first three catechetical talks are by way of (1) introduction, (2) a consideration of sin, the devil, repentance, remission, and (3) holy baptism. A dogmatic summary follows in the fourth catechesis: belief about God, Christ, the virgin birth, Christ's crucifixion and burial, resurrection, His return as judge, the Holy Spirit; then about man, his soul and body, corporeal resurrection, and man's final end as known from the Scriptures. This done, Cyril has a fifth instruction on faith, and with his sixth begins thirteen distinct catecheses on the Creed as mid-fourth century Jerusalem recited it. The rule of secrecy (*disciplina arcani*) forbade its presentation in any one place before baptism, but it can be pieced together from the fact that the numbered catecheses are essentially a paraphrase and exposition of a "symbol" composed of these articles: belief in (6) one God who is a (7) Father, (8) all-powerful, (9) Creator of the heavens and earth and of all things visible and invisible; and in (10) Jesus Christ, (11) the only Son of God, begotten by the Father before all ages, through whom everything was made, (12) Incarnate, that is, made Man of the Virgin and the Holy Spirit, (13) crucified and buried; (14) He rose on the third day, ascended into heaven to sit on the Father's right hand, (15) will come in glory to judge the living and

[22] Le Bachelet, *op. cit.*, c. 2560.

the dead, with no end to his reign; and in (16–17) one Holy Spirit Who has spoken through the prophets, (18) in one only Church, Holy and Catholic; in the resurrection of the body and life without end. A penultimate phrase in this Palestinian creed concerns belief in one baptism of repentance for the remission of sins, but St. Cyril has discussed this article in his first three catecheses.[23]

He is not accounted theologically rich or complex in the manner of his contemporaries Athanasius, Hilary or Basil, but there is in him an echo of Christian doctrine as presented in the fourth century at its best and clearest.[24] Cyril resembles Christ in his fusion of dogmatic and moral elements when he presents the Gospel. His sermons are parochial preaching of a high order. He is as fond of paradoxes as Augustine is, and when he hits his stride they come tumbling at the hearer:

Christ came to be baptized and to sanctify baptism, to work miracles such as walking on the water. Before His coming in the flesh, the sea saw and fled and the Jordan was turned back. Because of this the Lord assumed a body so that the water might see Him and receive Him, the Jordan embrace Him unafraid. . . .

When men deserted God, they made likenesses of the human form and this lying likeness they worshipped as a god; but God became man to dispel the lie. . . . The Lord assumed our likeness so as to grant salvation to our nature. He took it with the purpose of conferring on it a greater grace than the defect it had suffered, of making a sinful human nature participant in God.[25]

Gregory of Nyssa's *Katēchéseos lógos* or *Great Catechetical Discourse* is another treatise of the same period (usually dated somewhat prior to 385), but a controversial manual much more philosophical than its name would imply.[26] The great dogmas are expounded—Trinity, Incarnation, Redemption—and the sacraments of baptism and the Eucharist. This, however, is done in a way suited more to masters of the catechumenate than to the catechumens

---

[23] *Op. cit.*, c. 2540.
[24] *Op. cit.*, c. 2575.
[25] PG33, 741. Cat. 12, *De Christo incarnato.*
[26] PG45, 9–106. Translated by J. H. Srawley, *The Catechetical Oration of St. Gregory of Nyssa* (London: S.P.C.K., 1917), pp. 123.

themselves, and the subtitle, "against pagans, Jews, and heretics," is indicative of this fact. St. Gregory attended to individual differences in his recommendation of various approaches to persons who had believed either in many gods, or in one God but not in Jesus as the Christ, or in God but not as one in three persons (the Arians, for example). He advises instructors in religion to profit by intermediate concessions to listeners so that they may be brought to the possibility of belief in the Church. Thus:

But it may happen that the Greek, with the help of his general ideas, and the Jew, with his Scriptures, will not dispute the existence of a Word of God and a Spirit. But the design of God the Word exhibited in His becoming man will be rejected by both of them equally as being incredible and unfit to be attributed to God. We shall adopt, therefore, a different starting point in order to induce our opponents to believe in this.[27]

The proper "starting point" is surely basic to all catechetical discussion.

St. Gregory is speculative throughout. He relies on biblical data for his argument on a limited number of occasions. There is one instance, for example, where he reviews the evil perpetuated by Cain, the Sodomites, Assyrians, and Herod the Great to prove that God the healer waited until every form of human evil had been explored before He applied a cure to the disease.[28]

The lectures of St. Cyril to his catechumens described above, because of their wide diffusion, resulted in a whole series of interpretations of the creed over the next five or six decades.[29] Note-

[27] Srawley, *op. cit.,* pp. 33 f. ch. 5.
[28] *Ibid.,* p. 88, ch. 29.
[29] Thus, for example, the *Hermēneía toû symbólou* or *Interpretation of the Creed* of Gelasius of Caesarea (†395); a *libellus,* one of six in the *Libelli instructionis* of Niceta, Bishop of Remesiana (late 4th century), for which see A. E. Burn, *Niceta of Remesiana, His Life and Works* (Cambridge: University Press, 1905); the *Explanatio symboli ad initiandos* (PL17, 1155–60), probably based on notes from a lecture of Ambrose; and four sermons of Augustine, numbered 212–15, addressed to baptismal candidates as they were first given the creed (*traditio symboli*) and later rehearsed it before the bishop (*redditio*), (PL38, 1058–76). The information above is given in J. N. D. Kelly, *Rufinus . . . A Commentary on the Apostles' Creed,* ACW, 1955, No. 20, p. 94, nn. 18–22. Cf. also the same author's *Early Christian Creeds,* esp. ch. 13.

worthy among these is the *Commentarius in Symbolum Apostolorum* of Rufinus of Aquileia, usually dated around the year 404. There are numerous borrowings in it from the treatises on baptismal creeds which are common in his day and from St. Gregory of Nyssa's *Catechetical Discourse,* but Cyril's influence is preponderant. The main body of Rufinus' work has even been described as a "rather free, drastically abbreviated presentation in Latin of St. Cyril's teaching in the Catechetical Lectures, notably Catecheses 13–18." [30] Rufinus' chief service is that he enlightens us as to the composition of Western creeds, of which until his time only fragments were known from the writings of Tertullian, Cyprian, and the threefold questioning at immersion quoted in Hippolytus' *Apostolic Tradition* (see Note 8 above). Rufinus is not precisely a pioneer in Latin, for the Illyrian Bishop Niceta of Remesiana (335?–415?) had produced an admirable short treatise on the creed entitled simply *De Symbolo* which gives us substantially the same articles as those of the Apostles' Creed.

Niceta has a laudable succinctness of style but a certain polemical air as he warns his flock against the "meshes" of heretics, pagans and Jews. He devotes the last three pages of what comprise eleven in a modern book to a defense of the possibility of bodily resurrection.[31] A brief example of his style should suffice:

> Our faith, therefore, is that He who was born of the Virgin is God with us, God from the Father before all ages, a man born of the Virgin for the sake of men. He was truly born in the flesh, not in mere seeming. Certain heretics, erroneously ashamed of the Mystery of God, say that the Incarnation of the Lord was effected in a phantom. . . . This is far indeed from God's truth. For if the Incarnation is unreal, the salvation of men will be an illusion.[32]

To return to Rufinus, the point should be made that his catechetical teaching is directed to extremely thoughtful adults, despite his

[30] Kelly, *op. cit.,* p. 11.

[31] Gerald G. Walsh, Niceta of Remesiana, *An Explanation of the Creed* (New York: Fathers of the Church, Inc., 1949), pp. 43–53. Migne wrongly attributes this and other works to Nicetas of Aquileia, *PL*52, 865–71, an error corrected by Burn, *q.v.,* pp. 38–54.

[32] Walsh, *op. cit.,* p. 45 (4).

protestations about a "brief word" directed to "little ones in Christ and mere novices." (ch. 1) He passes along the already deep-rooted tradition that the Apostles' Creed was composed by the contribution of one article by each of the Twelve before they dispersed finally to preach to the ends of the earth.[33] There is in his pages a modicum of allegorical interpretation of the Old Testament. In the main, however, Rufinus provided his contemporaries with a most enlightening handbook of apologetics and doctrine. It is closer in spirit to the dogmatic explanations which the modern adult Catholic is used to than most of the patristic writings that went before it. Thus, in his commentary on the article "the forgiveness of sins" he writes:

Pagans habitually make fun of us, saying that we deceive ourselves if we imagine that mere words can wipe out offences which have actually been committed. "Is it possible," they say, "for one who has committed murder to be no murderer, or for the perpetrator of adultery to be represented as no adulterer? How then is someone who is guilty of misdeeds like these going to be suddenly made holy?" [34]

Rufinus is far from devoid of the gift of biblical usage to make his points. When he writes of the article The Holy Church,[35] for example, he describes it as "without spot or wrinkle" (Eph. 5, 27). The prophet's comment (Ps. 25, 5) on Marcion, Valentinus, Ebion, Mani and Arius is said to be, "I have hated the assembly of the malignant, and with the wicked I will not sit." But the Spirit says of our Church in the Canticle (6, 8), "One is my dove; one is she; and perfect unto her mother." The "council of vanity" and "doers of unjust things" (Ps. 25, 4) denote Marcion's assembly, Ebion's Judaizing, and the teaching of Mani in those places where he proclaims himself the Paraclete.[36] Rufinus employs the Old Latin version of the Scriptures so frequently that he becomes a substantial witness to its text. Taken all together, we begin to have in

[33] Kelly, *op. cit.*, pp. 29 ff., ch. 2.
[34] *Ibid.*, pp. 77 f., ch. 40.
[35] "Catholic" appears in St. Cyril's creed (*Cat.* 18, 23), and although implied in Tertullian's question in *De Bapt.* 6 (*CSEL* 20, 206), first appears in a Western creed in Niceta of Remesiana. Cf. Kelly, *op. cit.*, p. 141, n. 238, and Walsh, *op. cit.* (10), p. 49.
[36] Kelly, *op. cit.* (39), p. 74.

his credal catechesis (it covers some eighty-seven printed pages in English) a core instruction basic to the theology and preaching of the West. He devotes a lengthy section to the mode of generation in divine Persons as contrasted with human, and says in connection with the Passion:

No doubt, inspired as you are by loving devotion to the Sacred Scriptures, you will protest to me that these facts ought to be corroborated by convincing Scriptural evidence. . . . On the assumption, however, that my argument is addressed to people familiar with the Law, I am deliberately passing over a whole forest of evidence for the sake of brevity.[37]

His "passing over" can be called an omission only by some elusive standard, for he immediately begins to multiply biblical references despite the assumption he has just made. Rufinus employs the New Testament in what we would call a strict theological sense, though for the Old he indulges in every shade of typology and accommodation.

St. Ambrose's *De Mysteriis* (almost certainly authentic) is a colorful exposition in nine brief chapters which conveys to the newly baptized (*neophyti*) the idea of the change the Spirit has wrought in them through the bath of rebirth, the seal in chrism as they emerge from the waters, and the spiritual food of Christ's Body. In a sense doctrine is not so much taught as assumed. The credal explanation of the catechumenate days just before Easter is totally available to them, and the writer does no more than reword its elements with the illustrative aid of both Testaments. He goes from Pentateuch to prophets, epistles to gospels indiscriminately. Here in classic form is the oldest catechetical assumption: that the Bible or the oral teaching based upon it is the source-place of all doctrine for Christians.

For Ambrose, the baptizing bishop who preaches the kingdom of Christ and life eternal is none other than the priest of the old Law, God's visible messenger (Mal. 2, 7).[38] Naaman the leprous Syrian is the soul in need of baptism, and the slave girl of Israel who knows that healing power is from her God and not from rushing

---

[37] *Ibid.* (18), p. 52.
[38] *PL*16, 391, ch. 2; *CSEL* 73 (1955), 91.

rivers stands for the unredeemed Gentile nations who yet will be a grace-enlivened Church; [39] Christ nourishes His Church with sacraments which are like the breasts of the spouse in the Canticle, the honey on her lips, the fragrance of her garments; like a garden enclosed the Christian mysteries must be kept inviolate by the faithful, unadulterated by evil speech or deeds.[40] Baptismal regeneration is described in terms of the flood and its signs of abatement (Gen. 7 and 8), the branch brought back by the dove being the wood of Christ's cross and the raven a figure of sin which departs never to return.[41] In another place, Christ's cross is the staff of Moses turning bitter waters sweet by its regenerating effect on the natural water of a stream, and so on. Ambrose's catechesis is a pedagogic marvel, but it leaves in some doubt the way in which the earlier learnings had been conveyed. In the language of modern pedagogy, it is a "culminating lesson" so successful that it makes the onlooker wonder about the many hours of "drill." This question suggests itself about all the early centuries of catechesis. What were the nonlenten and non-festal Sundays of instruction like? Did the general level of instruction approach that of the great patristic landmarks summarized by Daniélou at the close of his introduction to *The Bible and the Liturgy?*

All the evidence available (or better, the lack of it) indicates that it was left to Christian parents and godparents to instruct their offspring in the truths of faith. No treatise directed to parents or children exists. There is, in fact, but one piece of early Christian writing addressed to adult heretics and pagans while they still had the status of inquirers (*accedentes*). This is St. Augustine's famous *De Catechizandis Rudibus*, written about 405.[42] A *rudis* for him was a person untaught in Christianity, not by any means a rough fellow. Deogratias, a deacon of Carthage, had asked Hippo's famous bishop for some hints on the task of catechizing, and received by way of response a full-scale *enarratio* (exposition of sacred history), along with a second, briefer one. The first of these model catecheses runs to ten chapters, the latter, a masterpiece of effective com-

[39] *PL*16, 394, ch. 3.
[40] *Ibid.,* 407, ch. 9.
[41] *Ibid.,* 392, ch. 3.
[42] Christopher, *op. cit.,* p. 5.

pression, one and one-half. Before he gives these two instructions, which have as their purpose leading the *rudes* toward the cate- chumenate, Augustine has devoted fifteen chapters to a discussion of the proper subject matter, the motivations of candidates, and various techniques of address. The treatise is pedagogical in a classic sense. It does not often descend to the particulars of doc- trinal presentation, which are saved for the two catecheses them- selves. Augustine suggests how best to deal with the supercilious, the half-educated, the weary, the bored. A serialized discourse is contemplated (or under the pressure of time a single one); ques- tions are to be used as a periodic check on the learner's grasp of things rather than as a teaching device. The catechist must labor to keep his enthusiasm alive despite the repetitive nature of his task and the elementary knowledge conveyed. The picture of the in- comparable Augustine methodically laying siege to the mind of some heavy-lidded Punic laborer is sheer balm for the theologians and catechists of the ages who have put in endless hours with the very simple or the very young.

No one, actually, who teaches religion can afford to be unfamiliar with Augustine's uncanny analysis of this apostolate. His insights into the characters of teacher and taught are beyond price, and yet his specifications for the content of the preliminary catechesis need careful evaluation. The Augustinian method is usable today only if catechists are determined to restore to their pupils a full-scale familiarity with the Bible. There is no question of where Augustine's emphasis lies. He is an apostle of divine love whose success lies in his having put emphasis on the Decalogue as perfectly summarized in the command to love God and neighbor. Augustine observes (ch. 4, par. 7) that in all human experience, nothing invites love more than a lover who takes the lead in loving:

If . . . Christ came chiefly for this reason, that man might learn how much God loves him, and might . . . love his neighbor at the bidding and after the example of Him who made Himself man's neighbor by loving him . . . then it is evident that on these two commandments of the love of God and the love of our neighbor depend . . . the whole law and the Prophets.[43]

[43] *Ibid.*, p. 23.

Augustine maintains that all divine Scripture written before Christ was written to foretell His coming, and that the whole purpose of any subsequent writing is to tell of Christ and to counsel love. "Therefore, in the Old Testament the New is concealed, and in the New the Old is revealed." [44] No understanding of Augustine is possible without a grasp of this simple exegetical and pedagogic principle. He attacks all portions of both Testaments in search of Christ, and because they contain Him, Augustine is not disappointed.

His longer catechesis has as its preliminary a discussion of the contrast between the peace assured by a good Christian conscience and the mad pleasures of life which any little fever could carry off. The "void and wounded conscience . . . shall find in Him a severe Lord whom it scorned to seek and love as a gentle Father" (par. 25). Augustine describes the lover of God, on the other hand, as one who shudders at offending by sin, not so much because he deserves punishment thereby, but because he forfeits the chance to be forever with Him whom he loves. After thus dividing the whole race into men of these two states of heart, the Augustinian catechesis proceeds to examine the opening pages of Genesis. The Lord's rest on the Sabbath after creation is no sooner told than it is used to illustrate the world's seventh age—that of repose in the peace of Christ. The Fall in Paradise becomes immediately the vehicle for a justification of that good-out-of-evil which God is always able to achieve, whether the disruption of order be angelic or human.

The good and the wicked on the earth, the wheat and the chaff, are Augustine's great preoccupation. His treatment of the deluge and of Abraham reveal what a transcendent spiritual sense the least Scriptural detail can bear in his handling. All the patriarchs and prophets were like limbs emerging from a womb before the infant's head, for example (par. 33), Christ being head of the universal body. The Easter Vigil liturgy of baptism as we know it is contained in Augustine's exposition of the Red Sea escape, the rock struck by Moses' rod and the account of the exodus. The catechesis touches on the levitical precepts and King David's earthly Jerusalem and Jeremiah's prophecy of release after seventy years of captivity.

[44] *Ibid.*

Nowhere does Augustine satisfy himself with the mere Old Testament telling; with him all is type and foretelling: "In that land of promise many things were done for a type of the Christ to come and of the Church; and these you will be able to learn gradually in the holy books." [45]

An important cue for modern catechetics lies here. St. Augustine is making Christianity attractive by means of an interpretation of a Bible which the *rudes* will spend a whole subsequent lifetime growing familiar with in liturgical worship. His plan is effective only because there is a full-scale exposition of the sacred books in prospect. Otherwise the Bible becomes a tantalizing conundrum without historical context or literal sense of its own. He uses the Scripture narratives in his initial instruction to whet spiritual appetites, but the technique is valid only so long as the appetite has a chance of being later satisfied. Otherwise the candidate will receive nothing but an incomplete and garbled ladling out of biblical information.

Augustine names the five ages of humanity from creation down to Christ (marked off by Adam, Noe, Abraham, David, and the Babylonian migration). The sixth age is our Lord's earthly life, which he tells of in a sustained paradox which must qualify as one of the great passages in all the history of rhetoric: "Christ the Lord, made man, despised all the good things of earth that He might show us that these things are not to be despised; and endured all earthly ills . . . so that neither might happiness be taught in the former nor unhappiness be feared in the latter. . . . He hungered who feeds all, He thirsted by whom all drink is created. . . . He was bound who has freed men from the bonds of their infirmities. . . . He was crucified who put an end to our torments" (ch. 22, par. 40).

Augustine's conclusion in this longer of the two proposed catecheses is much of a piece with the whole product: incredibly fine writing which never scruples to reach the heart, and which always starts from some observed phenomenon of daily life. The terrible silence of the dead, or the untrustworthiness of man, or human longing for a surfeit of power, wealth, prestige—these are the

[45] Ch. 20, par. 36; *op. cit.*, p. 67.

starting points of Augustine's defense of God and His love. Although it is perhaps not fair to let this simple, short treatise preparatory to the salt and sign of a catechumen's status stand for his entire catechesis, there is enough of it here to bear the weight. Augustine stands for beauty of language in religion teaching, emotional appeal based on the most intellectual considerations, and a "spiritual" reading of the data of revelation. This sentence from chapter 49 should be a death blow (of course it has been nothing of the sort) to the idea that catechisms must be written dully: "But it is one thing to love man, another to put your trust in man; and so great is the difference that God commands the former but forbids the latter." The new German catechism which concludes each lesson, "For my life" or "From the teachings of the saints," attempts to convey the sap of great teachers like Augustine in brief and memorable phrases like the above.

Tracing the decline of the catechumenate as an institution is not an easy matter, though it is sure that this decline set in toward the end of the fifth century. The assumption is that the infant baptism of the offspring of Christians was much on the increase during the period, and the practice of deferring the regenerating sacrament until high maturity or until one's deathbed, much in decline. The catechumenate became the training ground for reduced numbers of converts; primarily it became an institution for parents and godparents, in their children's interest. In other words, the instructional situation went from pre-baptismal to post-baptismal.[46] There are scattered sixth century references to the continuance of the catechumenate in Africa, Gaul and Spain. St. Isidore of Seville (†636) required instruction of the *competentes* in the creed and rule of faith at baptism, chrismation and the imposition of hands.[47] His six brief chapters are a valuable compendium. Yet, with all his speed and compression of treatment, anointing must begin with Moses and Aaron (ch. 26, 2).

An extant poem of St. Avitus (†526) is entitled *De mosaicae*

[46] H. Leclercq, "Catéchèse—Catéchisme—Catéchumène," *Dictionnaire d'Archéologie Chrétienne et de Liturgie*, 2 (Paris: Letouzey et Ané, 1925), 2566 f.
[47] PL83, 814–26, *De officiis*, 1. 2., chs. 21–27.

historiae gestis libri quinque. In it, Satan is "callidus Draco" and "lethi magister." The poem recalls St. Augustine's historical approach to catechetics in that the topics treated are creation, original sin, the expulsion from paradise, the deluge, the crossing of the Red Sea.[48] The sermons attributed to St. Caesarius of Arles (†542) show us that the distribution of catechetical material was proceeding as customarily.[49]

It was the apostolic activity of men like Ss. Patrick, Columban, Augustine of Canterbury, Eligius (Eloi), Gall, Willibrod and Boniface that required in the fifth through the eighth centuries a recasting of the whole concept of religious instruction. The challenge of apostolic times was back upon the Church in this period of expansion, and although nothing essential was sacrificed a simplicity of approach succeeded the highly organized catechumenate days. None of the catechetical sermons of these men has survived, busied as they were with a round of exposition in vernacular tongues foreign to them. We must assume that they achieved products modeled on the Latin discourses (with Cyril and Methodius it would be Greek) they were accustomed to from youth, rough-hewn to meet the challenge of idolatrous paganism. Pope Boniface V's letter to Edwin of Northumberland while the king was not yet a Christian (624) outlines this catechetical program: the futility of idol worship; the need to believe in God who is the Creator, in His Son sent for our salvation; the need to accept the Gospel, signified by baptism.[50]

The recital of sacred history as given by St. Augustine in his *enarratio* continues to be normative for most Christian teachers.[51] Among the Germans and Anglo-Saxons especially there seems to have been carried over the catechumenate practice of requiring the Creed and Pater to be memorized by the candidates and expounded by the bishop or priest during the Lenten season preceding their baptism.[52]

---

[48] *PL*59, 323–68.
[49] *PL*39, Serm. 6, 6; 168, 3; 237; 267.
[50] See *PL*80, 438, Epist. II.
[51] *PL*87, 13–26, sermon of St. Gall on the occasion of the consecration of John as Bishop of Constance.
[52] St. Bede wrote to Egbert, Bishop of York in 734 (the closing year of Bede's

With what amounts to a monotony of solicitude the conciliar legislation of the Carolingian period tries to see to it that the clergy explain the Lord's prayer and the Apostles' or Nicene Creed both regularly and adequately.[53]

Alcuin of York (†804), the teacher of Charlemagne, is credited with having introduced the question-and-answer method of catechetical instruction, but the attribution seems to be faulty. What he actually did was compose 281 separate queries for his biblical commentary *Interrogationes et responsiones in Genesin*.[54] Perhaps as a result, the authorship of a manuscript dating to the year 900 is likewise ascribed to him. Entitled *Disputatio puerorum per interrogationes et responsiones*, it runs to a dozen chapters of the most amazing information, philological and otherwise.[55] Large sections are compiled directly from the writings of Origen and Isidore of Seville. Usually the questions are short and to the point, less frequently the answers. But we do find this brevity: "Can the soul have any other likeness to the Trinity?" "Yes, it can." "How, then?" "Well, in the first place, just as God exists, lives and knows, so too does the soul exist, live and know, after its own fashion." [56] The soul's three

---

life) detailed instructions as to how the rural areas are to be taught the deeper meaning of the Apostles' Creed and Lord's Prayer by their priests: in Latin for the few who can handle it; otherwise, *"Ipsa sua lingua dicere, ac sedule decantare facito."* The idea of singing them recurs in the passage; also memorization: *"Memoriae radicitus infigere cures,"* he admonishes (*PG*94, 659).

[53] E.g. Cloveshowe under Cuthbert of Canterbury (747), a national council, in which a vernacular "spiritual" exposition of the prayers of "Mass, baptism and other ecclesiastical functions carried on before the people" is required, can. 10 (J. D. Mansi, *Sacrorum Conciliorum . . . Collectio*, Florence: A. Zatta, 1766), 12, 398; Frankfurt in 794, can. 33 (Mansi 13, 908); Arles (813), can. 19 (Mansi 14, 62), put responsibility on parents and sponsors; Mainz (813) did the same and recommended school attendance, cans. 45, 47 (Mansi 14, 74). To St. Boniface of Mainz are credited canons 25 and 26 of a Synod at Leipzig (743) requiring godparents to know Creed and Pater, "that they may be saved by faith and prayer" (*PL*89, 822). Charlemagne was responsible for similar legislation in 802 (*PL*97, 247, nn. 14, 15), and also instructed priests to have lists of the greater and lesser sins at hand, to aid their people in avoiding the devil's snares (*PL*97, 326). For the Emperor's role as catechist supreme, cf. Joseph Lecler, *The Two Sovereignties* (New York: Philosophical Library, 1952), pp. 55 f.

[54] *PL*100, 515–66.

[55] *PL*101, 1099–1144.

[56] *Ibid.*, 1101.

faculties of intellect, will and memory are alleged as a further human similarity to the Trinity (since memory depends on the former two somewhat as the Spirit proceeds from Father and Son). Occasionally a "question" will serve more as a Socratic means to retain the inquiry form, and little else. Thus:

> *Inter.* I should like to hear more on this same topic from you.
> *Resp.* And I shall continue explaining in proportion as I know.

The answerer then returns to his briefly interrupted argument, using phrases much like the soul-body analogy employed by the Athanasian Creed to teach the Incarnation, though in this case it is the Trinity which is being illustrated.

An early chapter describes the days of creation, though it turns out to be chiefly a defense of six as a perfect number. Then comes a lesson in human nature: corporeal, spiritual and etymological (the temples beneath the cranium are called such because they move at intervals—*tempora . . . tempora*). A third chapter describes the three kinds of spirits: pure, mixed (that is, human) and brutish. Some highly questionable Hebrew philology follows on the ten Old Testament names of God, but the discussion of the divine attributes is the traditional one. His impassibility, simplicity and immensity as described in the *Disputatio* are in much the same form as they have come to us through the medieval *summae*. Ever since Christ's coming we are in the sixth and last age of the world (ch. 5), while chapter 6 discusses the concept and divisions of time.

Once this preliminary work has been done, Sacred History proper begins. Chapters 7 and 8 describe the contents of each of the books of the two Testaments. The authorship of Esther is attributed to Esther, but this spirit scarcely characterizes the work as a whole; for example, the possibility of the non-Pauline authorship of Hebrews for vocabulary and stylistic reasons is referred to, Barnabas and Clement being cited as likely composers. It is, in all, a surprisingly good summary of factual information and is almost without exhortatory material. A ninth chapter discusses sacred orders in the Church (a fifth minor order, psalmist, is included), and under "deacon" there is a digression to establish why Matthew is correctly understood to be symbolized by the man of Isaiah, Mark by the lion, Luke by the heifer and John by the eagle. It is typical of the *Disputatio* that the etymology of *presbyter* and *sacerdos* should suffice to define the priesthood, at the conclusion of the chapter, while surprisingly the episcopate is not discussed.

Chapter 10 is on the Mass (explained as a word taken from the dismissal of the catechumens as the offertory came on). *Dona et munera* refer respectively to gifts which are God's and obligations proper to men; a *donum* is bought with money, a *sacrificium* effected in blood. In somewhat unsettling fashion we are told the meaning (frequently a supposed derivation and no more) of *immolatio, libatio, victima, hostia*. There are listed seven chief prayers of the Mass, an early echo of the number seven in the whole catechetical process. They are the (1) *Dominus vobiscum* and *Oremus*, (2) Collect, (3) prayer for the living offerers or the faithful departed in the interest of whose pardon the sacrifice is being offered. (4) *Sursum corda* to *per Christum Dominum nostrum* of the Preface, described as a prayer for peace and reconciliation, (5) *Per quem majestatem tuam* to *Osanna in excelsis*, an invitation to all the creatures of heaven and earth to worship, (6) *Te igitur*, a plea for the conformity of the visible species to the body and blood through the action of the Spirit, and (7) the *Pater noster*. The seven petitions of the "Our Father" are then analyzed, three describing God's attributes and four the needs of men.

Chapter eleven is on faith. It employs a careful scrutiny of the phrases of the Apostles' Creed and is much in the manner of the modern catechism—though there is time to pause and explain that the "judge in Judaea at that time" was called Pontius because of his birthplace. "What does Catholic mean?" "Universal, that is, spread over the whole earth. I believe that there is for me a communion of saints, that is to say holiness and fellowship with them if I hold fast to the faith and serve by works." The password used by Jepte and his Galaadites, "shibboleth" (Jgs. 12), is described at length to illustrate why the twelve apostles thought it important to compose a symbol or sign of the faith Christians held, before they departed on their separate evangelical missions. Then the anonymous author gives the first article as composed by Peter, the second as by Andrew, after them James, John, Philip, and so on. Matthias, although a latecomer, contributes the double article "the resurrection of the body and life everlasting." The twelfth and concluding chapter has the questioner checking back to see whether the petitions of the Lord's Prayer were committed to memory. He is always gentle; until now it had been "my dear brother," but now we find, "Tell me, I beg you." This the cooperative *puer* does, even to pointing out that we do not ask to be freed of temptations, since we all need trial, but only those we cannot endure.

The spirit and influence of the *Disputatio puerorum* are such that the space devoted to it here seems justified. It was analytical to the point of pedantry, a theologian's work or even an encyclopedist's, but endowed with the specious cast of a student's handbook. In it the Bible is taught about rather than taught from. Philosophical terms are given full credit in this exposition of religion, and the makings of textbook catechetics are already on the horizon: orderly, exhaustive, removed from the spirit of Christ's preaching, slightly repellent to the youthful mind.

A truncated manuscript is in existence dated 841–43, twelve brief chapters of the seventy-two originally written by a good mother named Dodena (Duodena, Dhuoda), wife of Bernard of Septimania, to her son William (a page to Charles the Bald) and his little brother. This *Liber manualis* is a very warm document which disappoints only by its abbreviated condition. We have her thoughts and admonitions on loving God but not her chapters "On the Holy Trinity" or "On Faith, Hope and Charity." Other attractive but missing titles concern the respect due to priests, the fleeing of pride, and a proposed list of trials and means to their avoidance, for example, persecution, need, illness. The mother's stated purpose is that her sons will have a mirror-image of her near when she is separated from them. Dodena's manual happens to be addressed to youth, but it is of a literary type with Alcuin's *De virtutibus et vitiis* (addressed to Wido of Marca Britanniae around 800, on

Christian perfection for the soldier),[57] and Paulinus of Aquileia's *Libellus exhortatorius.*[58]

It must be remembered that the function of the episcopal schools was largely to prepare a clergy rather than Christian youth generally. A canon (7) of the Council of Béziers in 1246 is more to the point in connection with religious ignorance with its requirement that,

parish priests see to it that they explain to the people on Sundays the articles of faith in simple and clear fashion so that no one may claim a veil of ignorance. . . . Children too from seven upwards, brought to Church by their parents on Sundays and feasts, shall be instructed in the Catholic faith, and parents shall teach them *Mary's Salutation, Our Father* and *Creed.*[59]

At Albi in 1254 the same wording is repeated, with the suggestion that what the bishop cannot accomplish in his own person he should enlist "other reliable and prudent persons" to aid him in doing.[60]

The eleventh century treatises of Fulbert of Chartres [61] and Bonizon of Plaissance [62] on the sacraments are catechetical in the remote sense. The same is true of Abelard's short expositions of the Lord's Prayer, Apostles', and Athanasian creeds.[63] They are more for the information of the clergy or the pious reading of the learned —though all three are simple and direct. With the twelfth century comes the *Elucidarium* attributed to Honorius, head of the school of Autun, a prolific writer of whose life nothing is known.[64] More likely an unknown disciple of St. Anselm was its author. Again, it is a theological summary, not a child's handbook, but the question-answer form places it in the catechetical stream. A distinguishing feature which should recommend it to modern youth is that

[57] *PL*101, 613–38.
[58] *PL*99, 197 ff.
[59] Mansi, 23, 693.
[60] *Ibid.*, 836 f.
[61] *PL*141, 196–204.
[62] *PL*150, 857–66.
[63] *PL*178, 611–32.
[64] *PL*172, 1109–1176. Cf. Y. Lefèvre, *L'Elucidarium et les Lucidaires: Contribution, par l'histoire d'un texte, à l'histoire des croyances religieuses en France en moyen-âge* (Paris: De Bocard, 1954), pp. 543.

discipulus asks the questions while *magister* answers them. The influence of this work on medieval piety is incalculable. It was translated into many languages, including the Welsh, and flourished for several centuries.

The *Elucidarium* has a distressingly modern ring to it in dozens of places. Surely it marks the death and burial of the patristic tradition in catechetics, just as it brings to the fore the theological answer-man who, while he says he deals in mysteries, does not seem to be aware of any. There is a certain censorious tone to this work with its author's calm settlement of who shall likely be damned. Tradesmen have little hope, being cheats; soldiers will almost surely be lost, as will craftsmen and public penitents—evidently a bad lot in those days. (On who shall be saved he does not seem to possess as exact information, though farmers will in large part make it because they live simply.) And yet there are many ways in which it is attractive, notably the brevity of its responses and its directness. The dialogue is in three books, the first of which is dogmatic (progressing from the nature of God to the efficacy of the sacraments, with a lengthy concluding section on evil priests and prelates); the second is concerned with sin, concupiscence, the number of the elect, and the influence of angels and demons; the third has to do with the last things, especially the respective statuses of the blessed and the damned. This "summary of all Christian theology," as its subtitle describes it, uses quotations from Scripture for purposes of proof and hole-stopping rather than by way of any attempt to elucidate the sacred text. An extended quotation should convey the technique best:

Discipulus. What was the cause of the world's creation?
Magister. The goodness of God, so that there might be those on whom to confer His grace.
D. How was it done?—*M*. "He spoke and all things were made." (Ps. 22, 9)
D. And did He use words?—*M*. For God, to speak is to create all things by His Word, that is, in the Son; which is why we read, "In wisdom have you done all things." (Ps. 103, 24)
D. Was there any delay in the act of creating?—*M*. In the twinkling

of an eye, which is to say as quickly as one could open his eye, or rather as the surface of the opened eye could perceive light.

D. Did He create successively?—*M.* He made everything but once and at the one time: "He who endures forever created all things simultaneously." (Eccles. 18, 1)

All this sounds extremely familiar to the modern ear. It could get past most theological censors. There are, however, nine choirs of angels for the Trinity's sake (being thrice three). Satan, who did not forsee his downfall, wanted to improve his lot and tyrannize over others. And for his pride? (*"Quid tunc?"*) "M. Ejected from the palace and thrust into prison, he who had been brightest in splendor was pitched in deepest darkness; once the foremost in fame, he is now the most hateful in horror." Such is the pattern of the treatise: an alternation of sound doctrine with poetic theology and occasionally barely defensible surmise or even legend.

Its author is especially hard on the evil lives of clerics and religious, with a certain boldness and balance one does not come upon in most anti-clerical tirades. "Should the sons of priests be ordained?" he asks. By no means, for a poisoned strain flows in their veins, father to son. He is sound on their ability to "confect" true sacraments but weak in declaring that they do not receive the body of Christ but only eat and drink judgment to themselves. The section on the predestination of the elect and the reprobate is helpful toward understanding why St. Augustine was claimed by the reformers. ("Whatever the predestined do they cannot perish because all works together unto good for them, even their very sins.") One encounters in this handbook, "the mystical body of Christ, that is the Church," but enthusiasm is tempered by the discovery that Christ is the head, the eyes are the prophets and apostles, the ears the obedient, the mouth teachers in the Church, and the feet the farmers who feed it. The agricultural origins of this earnest schoolmaster are not hard to trace.

The *Elucidarium* is not a child's book (children could take little comfort from learning that all three-year-olds are saved whereas at five some are saved and some not). Nonetheless, it must have informed thousands of adults who in turn formed many children theologically. One has to admire the writer in the sweep of his knowledge—easy to lampoon but almost impossible to imitate. He knows no doubts; his is the ancient view that the last judgment will come in the middle of the night, and the bear who ate the wolf who ate the man will pose no problem for God at the resurrection. But through all this pyrotechnics there runs the salvation-theme in undisputed clarity. "The Father delivered up the Son and the Son delivered Himself out of charity, but Judas delivered him over out of avarice." He has an eye to beauty and to tradition. "Why did Christ die on a cross?" "To save all at the four corners of the earth." "What does it mean to say that Christ sits at the right hand of the Father?" "That his human nature is at rest in the glory of divinity." He grows lyrical at the lot of the blessed and what it is *discipulus* may expect ("the handsomeness of Absalom, the strength of Samson, the prestige of Joseph in Egypt, the love of friends like David's for Jonathan.") And yet the net effect of the *Elucidarium* is slightly depressing, for religious encyclopedism is well in the saddle and a cloud no bigger than a man's hand is on the horizon. It will burst when 483 distinct questions and answers have been assembled in one book. (In one national catechism the number is 700.) The technique is deadly because it lends itself to memorization so readily.

Another catechetical development followed when the question-and-answer method was already well rooted. This was the practice of teaching sacred truth by sevens. St. Augustine's *Sermon on the Mount* had given the lead to this technique, with its harmonization of the seven petitions of the Lord's Prayer and the beatitudes.[65] Bishop Joscelin of Soissons (†ca. 1099) remarks that he is familiar with the usage and does not particularly favor it.[66] It is to Hugh of St. Victor (†ca. 1119) that we owe it chiefly, in his four-page work *De quinque septenis seu septenariis*.[67] Hugh lists as his "five

---

[65] *PL*34, 1285 f.
[66] *PL*186, 1496.
[67] *PL*175, 406–14.

sevens" catalogues of the capital sins (pride, envy, anger, weariness of spirit, greed, gluttony and lust), the petitions of the Lord's Prayer, the gifts of the Holy Ghost (in reverse order from the Vulgate's translation of Isaias 11, 2 f.), the virtues (humility, meekness, compunction, desire for the good, mercy, cleanness of heart, peace), and beatitudes (that is, states of blessedness: the kingdom of heaven, the land of the living, consolation, one's fill of goodness, mercy, the sight of God, and the sonship of God). Having elaborated on the ways the chief vices destroy a man, he finds a parallel between each vice and one of the seven things Christ taught us to pray for. His treatment of the gifts of the Spirit is less choppily mathematical, yet taken all together the little work is abstract and even dull, except for one who has all the information beforehand and can marvel at the cleverness of the harmonization.

St. Thomas Aquinas follows the pattern of Hugh of St. Victor with regard to the numbering of petitions in his *opusculum* (7, *ed. Rom.*) on the Lord's Prayer. For example:

FOURTH PETITION

Give us this day our daily bread. It frequently happens that a person will become timorous as a result of great learning or wisdom. Then it is that he needs fortitude of spirit lest he grow weak at critical times. *It is he who gives the weary fresh spirit, who fosters strength and vigor where there is none.* Ez. 2, 2. . . . We must realize that in the first three petitions spiritual things are asked for which begin here in this world but are not made perfect except in life eternal. . . . For when we ask that the name of God be hallowed, we ask that the holiness of God be made known. Again, when we ask God's kingdom to come, we petition to be made sharers in eternal life. And when we pray that God's will be done, we ask that it be done in us. All of these things, even if they be begun in this world, cannot be had perfectly except in life eternal; therefore it is necessary to ask for some necessities which can be possessed perfectly in the present life. . . .[68]

This is taken from one of the fifty-seven reports of sermons which St. Thomas preached in the Church of St. Dominic in Lent

[68] St. Thomas Aquinas, "Opusculum XXXIV," *Opuscula Omnia,* coll. P. Mandonnet, IV (Paris: Lethielleux, 1927), 401 f.

of 1273, the last Lent of his lifetime.[69] He preached in Italian each evening to students and townsfolk, probably in three successive series: on the Apostles' Creed (fifteen short *collationes*), the Lord's Prayer (ten), and the Law (charity and the Decalogue—thirty-two).[70] His sermons never took longer than half an hour, some of them only fifteen minutes. Peter d'Andrea was his probable reporter.

The sermons are free of scientific language and argumentation, but they are extremely methodical. Kraus calls them "brisk and authoritative," and attributes to them the defects of a *reportatum*. One both marvels at the perfection of order in St. Thomas and is slightly worn down by it. Thus he will say, "Our debt to Him (as Father) is fourfold. Firstly we owe Him honor: *If I am Father, where is my honor?* (Mal. i, 6). This honor consists in three things. (*a*) In reference to God, by giving Him praise. . . ."[71] The other three things owed to God besides honor are imitation, obedience, and patience under chastening; under honor, purity of body and just judgment of our neighbor are required as well as formal praise, and so on. The Thomistic catechesis is largely non-speculative. He shows himself a master of sources, employing both Testaments of Scripture and the Fathers with ease and unerring appositeness. The sermons are a tapestry of quotations which, however, never seem forced. There is abundant illustration out of daily experience but it is never developed further than is required for immediate application. This technique is a familiar one from St. Thomas's theological writings. Thus, we pray "Thy will be done" in the manner of a sick man who, consulting a doctor, does not take medicine according to his own will (he would be a fool to do so), but in accord with the doctor's will.

These *opuscula* of St. Thomas became source works for much

[69] The writer is indebted in this section to James E. Kraus for the full text of his dissertation done at the Athenaeum Angelicum, Rome, under Angelus Walz, O.P., *The Catechetical Sermons of St. Thomas Aquinas*.

[70] *Ibid.*, p. 11.

[71] St. Thomas Aquinas, *The Catechetical Instructions*, trans. with a commentary by Joseph B. Collins, S.S. (New York: J. F. Wagner, 1939), p. 155; *The Three Greatest Prayers*, trans. Laurence Shapcote, O.P. (Westminster, Md.: Newman, 1956), p. 17.

medieval pulpit instruction, which is reason enough to consider them. An additional importance of the threefold catechesis (there is a fourth candidate for inclusion, a *commentariolus de Salutatione Angelica*, but it seems not to have been delivered on this occasion), is that it gives us the Saint's mind on what instruction the Christian man needs, and in what order. He himself speaks of the "three things necessary to man for salvation; namely knowledge of what to believe (*scientia credendorum*), what to wish for (*desiderandorum*), and what to do (*operandorum*). The first is taught in the Creed . . . The second in the Lord's Prayer, the third in the Law. . . ."[72] In other words, the catechesis takes its ordering from the message itself, in St. Thomas's view: the act of faith and the object of faith (which is God and the mystery of salvation); the sacraments, dealt with by him under the credal phrase *communionem sanctorum*, which he understands to mean a community of goods in the Church, or holy things shared by Christ the Head with His members;[73] prayer, both of praise and petition, which is most perfectly epitomized by the prayer Christ taught; and the commands of Christ, obedience to which He identified as proof of love for Him. The beauty of St. Thomas's treatment of divine love (thirteen and one-half pages in Mandonnet) before he attacks the commandments of the Decalogue individually is striking. One is led to wonder why the *Catechismus Romanus* of 1566 began its treatment with the first commandment and confines to a single sentence its treatment of the twofold law of the Gospel.[74]

In any case, it is an important question whether we have here the clear mind of St. Thomas on the optimum form a catechesis should take or whether it is just what he thought he could accomplish between Septuagesima Sunday and the Tuesday of Holy

[72] Mandonnet, *op. cit.*, "De duobus praeceptis charitatis et decem legis praeceptis," IV, 413.
[73] Collins, *op. cit.*, pp. 53–57. Mandonnet, *op. cit.*, IV, 381. The Roman Catechism has the same idea, I, 10, 24, where it speaks of the sacraments as holy chains binding us all to Christ in a union of spirit which is none other than membership in the one holy Church. Cf. *Catechismus ex Decreto Concilii Tridentini ad Parochos . . . Editus* (Romae: Typis Sacrae Congregationis de Propaganda Fide, 1845), p. 66.
[74] *Ibid.*, p. 221.

Week in a given year. About twelve years before, at the request
of the Archbishop of Palermo, he had written a little treatise on
the sacraments.[75] Does his very concise treatment of them here
under *sanctorum communionem* prove that he thought that this
much sufficed in relation to the rest of his exposition? Or was he
merely falling in with medieval practice by commenting on the
two prayers from the baptismal liturgy, plus the Christian rule of
life? In earlier times treatment of the sacraments—at least the
three of initiation—came after baptism at the Easter or Pentecost
Vigil. Perhaps on such an historical principle St. Thomas felt that
a full-scale treatment of them did not properly belong in a Lenten
framework.

We probably should not suppose that we have in these reported
sermons any definitive response to a question of total catechetical
theory. What they are is the richest kind of treasury of popular
exposition, on the basis of which much good pulpit material was
written in succeeding centuries.

John Gerson (1363–1420), Chancellor of the University of Paris,
surely requires mention as we come on to the period when the
catechism took shape as a child's book. Even while Chancellor he
taught catechism (1409–1412). The story is frequently told of his
having spent the last years of his life in Lyons despite the death
of his sworn enemy John the Fearless and his theoretical freedom
to return. Gerson engaged in works of priestly zeal in his last
years, among them catechizing the young at the Church of St.
Paul and writing the little book *On Drawing the Little Ones to
Christ.*[76] Taking as his text the words of Christ about letting the
little ones come to him, Gerson considers four matters in the field
of teaching; how needful it is to Christ and the Church that the
little ones come; types of scandal that can keep them off; the proper
zeal that should mark those who lead the little ones to Christ; and
a personal *apologia* against his detractors as to why, despite the
gap between his conduct and a child's, he nonetheless can bring

[75] Mandonnet, *op. cit., De Ecclesiae Sacramentis*, III, 11–18.
[76] Joannis Gersonii, "Tractatus de Parvulis Trahendis ad Christum," *Opera
Omnia*, III (Antwerpiae: Ellies du Pin, 1706), 278–91.

them to Christ. Gerson addresses himself here to the need for catechetics and the spirit that should mark its practitioners. He is strong for love and condescension in teaching the little ones, and he cannot abide turgid patterns of speech with them. His great fear is of the corruption of unchastity that may overtake them if they progress from youth to age uninstructed. When he comes to name the ways in which the young are led to Christ he lists: "Public preaching. Admonition in private. The disciplining proper to teachers. Finally, and most characteristic of the Christian religion, confession." [77] He is eloquent on the supreme efficacy of this sacrament as formative of Christian character, and he spends considerable time describing how to keep the trust and friendship of children even though, as their confessor, one comes to know their weaknesses and the dark places in their souls. 1132976

Gerson in a letter on the reform of theological studies (1400?) asked theological faculties to produce little treatises dealing with the main points of religion, the commandments especially, for the use of simple folk, just as the faculty of medicine had produced a little medicinal summary in a recent time of plague.[78] He did something of the kind himself in his *Opus tripertitum,* a treatise on the commandments, confession, and how to die well.[79] It was published widely and made mandatory reading for many clerics by their bishops (for example, Francis of Luxembourg, Bishop of Mans, in 1507). Gerson himself even proposed at the beginning of his book that it be divided up on tablets and posted in places where people gather, "parish churches, schools, hospitals, religious houses." He proposed at the beginning of the second section on confession that a *"tabula"* be made containing the number and kind of sins, which the uninstructed penitent could first inspect and then be quizzed on. Following his own suggestion, he then proposed his examination of conscience as a series of direct questions on the seven capital sins. This question-and-answer form underlay the printed *"libelli"* which penitents employed in the

[77] *Ibid.,* III, 283.
[78] *Ibid.,* I, 124.
[79] *Ibid.,* I, 426–50.

pre-Reformation period to prepare for their annual confession. The priest would quiz them on the chief prayers and points of doctrine before he would hear their sins and absolve them. Gerson's points of consideration for the Christian prince, written for Charles VII, indicates what form such *libelli* might take before dismemberment into sections.[80] Gerson also wrote a small, catechism-like book called *L'ABC des simples gens* not printed in his collected works.

The late fifteenth century witnessed all sorts of "mirrors" to help one live and die well which stressed the virtues, vices and commandments as aids to confessing properly. The Waldensians worked out a set of instructions in question form, *Interrogacions memors,* which the Bohemian brethren followed in writing their *Kinderfragen.* Luther was acquainted with the latter, and relied on it in 1523 for his earliest catechetical writings.[81] In 1526 he employed the Wittenberg translation of it done the previous year in high and low German, *Eyn Bökeschen vor de Leyen unde Kinder.* In 1529 his *Kurze Auslegung der Zehn Gebote* went onto charts; then, after the commandments, confession and the sacraments of baptism and the Eucharist. These formed the first edition of his catechism. In June of that year it appeared in Latin and in German as an *Enchiridion,* to be reedited six times by 1542.

Mention of this child's catechism about brings us to where we wished to be. Luther's little work is immediately recognizable as late medieval. It proceeds in the order: Ten Commandments, Creed, Lord's Prayer, Baptism, and Lord's Supper. Subsequent editions contain a treatment in questions and answers of the Order ("economy") of Salvation, another "systematical connection" of the same, and questions and answers for those who would prepare themselves for the Lord's Supper. "Historical catechisms" of both Testaments follow, then a "table of duties" for states in life, prayers, and hymns.

The smaller catechisms of Canisius and Bellarmine are not greatly unlike Luther's editorially. In them and that of the Spaniard Ripalda the pattern for the next four hundred years is set. The two

---

[80] *Ibid.,* III, 234 f.
[81] See L. Fendt, "Katechismus," *Evangelisches Kirchenlexicon,* 18/19 (Göttingen: Vandenhoeck and Ruprecht, 1957), 562 f.

chief prayers, the commandments, and the sacraments provide the framework. Lists of sins, virtues and vices complement this basic treatment. There is no attempt to derive instruction on the Christian life from the Story of Salvation as it is contained in the inspired Scriptures. Neither is there any attempt to "teach as Christ did," or "proclaim the good news of salvation" in the manner of the apostolic period. Scripture is used and used extensively, but not in a way the patristic period would be familiar with.

In brief, then, the efforts of men like Overberg, Hirscher, Pichler and the modern giants of the catechetical revival must be seen for what they are: a break clean away from fifteen centuries of pedagogic practice and a return to better, surer ways of teaching Christ, in a way suited to children, which is quite new. *Analysis* of prayers, commandments, sacred practices, had dominated the field. The great contribution of the "new catechetics" has been *synthesis:* the setting into place of each dogma and moral demand in a framework of God's saving action in biblical times, made present to us in every age in joyful liturgical celebration.

2.

Religious Education
in Late Medieval Times
·
Josef A. Jungmann, S.J.

The last half of the Middle Ages was without doubt one of the most flourishing periods in the history of the Catholic Church. The fact has to be admitted, even though this particular era of history no longer arouses in us that enthusiasm which began with the romanticists and persisted through the nineteenth century.

These centuries of the later Middle Ages did not owe their greatness solely to outstanding geniuses such as Dante or the authors of the theological *summae.* As we stand in admiration before the cathedrals and minsters found in every important town of western Christendom, it dawns on us that here we must reckon with something more than the mere product of a few talented architects whose names in most cases are not even known to us. What strikes us rather is that thousands of ordinary people played a part in building these lofty edifices, and that these products of their hands were but an outward expression of their innermost souls.

How did this great blossoming of Christian culture come about? How much of it was attributable to zeal on the part of those who had the care of souls? And—a question especially pertinent to our present purpose—what sort of religious instruction was being given in those ages capable of inspiring such living faith?

Many authors, in a superficial attempt to evaluate the type of catechetical instruction given in the Middle Ages, either describe a scene in which things are roughly comparable to what they were in early Christian times, or else they depict things as they are in our age. They give us the impression that those who had the care of souls in the medieval period were quite solicitous about religious instruction, and even about the catechetical instruction of children or the establishment of schools. They refer to the cathedral and the monastic schools, as well as to a certain number of parish schools. The actual historical records indicate, however, that there was usually only one cathedral school to a diocese, that the number of scholars in the average one was scarcely a dozen, and that the children who were catechized there were most often boys who were being prepared for the clerical state.

With the monastic schools it was pretty much the same. Schools for externs conducted in connection with a monastery for the sons of the nobility were very few in number. When it comes to parish schools, the tendency has been to confuse the ordinances laid down by Charlemagne with the actual state of affairs prevailing throughout the long centuries of the Middle Ages. At best the ordinances of Charlemagne were in effect for several decades only. Moreover, it is generally overlooked that a parish school in Charlemagne's day was for the most part an advanced course for acolytes, preparing them for their duties in the sanctuary. The pastor simply selected a certain number of mentally alert lads and taught them to read Latin and sing the psalms with him, hoping that one day he could present one or other of them to the bishop for ordination. Surely all this was a far cry from anything like a systematic catechetical course for children. Historical accuracy forces us to maintain that there was no such thing as a widespread study of catechism under ecclesiastical auspices.

Yet it is certain that throughout the Middle Ages there did exist a simple form of religious instruction for adults.[1] At the end of the homily on Sundays the priest along with the faithful recited the Creed and the Lord's Prayer, to which were added in the late Middle Ages the Hail Mary as well, and sometimes other formulas. In some instances the priest alone recited these prayers for the congregation. Over and above this, various synods legislated that these formulas should frequently be explained to the faithful. It was expected, moreover—as the Synod of Utrecht legislated in 1294 and again in 1310—that the ten commandments and the seven

[1] P. Göbl, *Geschichte der Katechese im Abendlande vom Verfall des Kate-chumenates bis zum Ende des Mittelalters* (Kempten: Jos. Kosel, 1880); E. Mangenot, "Catéchisme," *Dict. de Théol. Cath.*, II (Paris: Letouzey et Ané, 1932), 1899 f.

sacraments should be explained to the people in their mother tongue once a month or at least three to four times a year.

The formulas so presented to the faithful became more numerous toward the end of the Middle Ages, especially those that have some connection with the number seven: seven beatitudes, seven gifts, of the Holy Spirit, seven capital sins, seven works of mercy, and so on.[2] Other Christian truths were presented in a scale of ascending numerals: two chief commandments of love, three theological virtues, four sins that cry to heaven for vengeance, five senses, six works of mercy, and so on. It was sought to have all the faithful know by heart at least this minimum, and this was a concern not only of the Church but of the state as well from the time of Charlemagne on. In Nuremberg in 1476 a law was passed requiring beggars to know the Lord's Prayer, Hail Mary, Creed, and ten commandments if they wished to enter the town.[3]

In the late Middle Ages efforts were likewise made by the Church to provide catechetical instructions for children. Individual synods solicitous about improving the general state of religious instruction mention children in their statutes specifically. For instance, the Synod of Albi (1254) ruled that children of seven years and over must be brought along to instructions.[4] And a synod of Dublin in the year 1186 required priests—who evidently had been remiss—to catechize the children *ante fores ecclesiae*.[5] Still, any kind of systematic instruction for children must have been the rare exception before the Council of Trent.

A certain progress in this direction can perhaps be claimed for the later Middle Ages wherever there happened to be schools in the real sense of the word. From the time of the Crusades onward, commerce and industry began to spring up. This necessitated the

[2] E. Mangenot, *op. cit.*, 1899 f.

[3] *Historisches Jahrbuch*, V (München: Herder, 1884), 94, n. 2.

[4] J. Mansi, *Sacrorum Conciliorum . . . . Collectio*, XXIII (Venetiam: A. Zatta, 1779), 836 ff. Similar stipulations of the Synod of Tournai (1481); in the synodal statutes of Valencia (1255); in Germany at the Synod of Eichstadt (1447), Salzburg (1454), Passau (1470), Worms (1457). See R. J. Jansen, *Canonical Provisions for Catechetical Instruction* (Washington: The Catholic University of America Press, 1937), pp. 20–23.

[5] Mansi, *op. cit.*, XXII, 525, D.

ability to read and write, so that people could transact business in more distant places. Thus it happened that schools were established in all the larger towns and, for that matter, toward the end of the Middle Ages, even in a fair number of the villages. It goes without saying that at that time and as late as the early part of the modern era the representatives of the Church took over the supervision of such schools—in the episcopal sees in the person of the *magister scholarum,* elsewhere in that of the pastor.

Where such schools existed it was the responsibility of the teacher to impart Christian doctrine as well as to instruct the children in reading, writing, and arithmetic. The matter taught by him was in the main the same catechetical formulas drilled into the grown-ups. Only a minority of the children, obviously, was reached through these measures.

We would therefore be quite wrong if we were to attribute the flourishing Catholic life found in all lands of Christendom at the height of the Middle Ages to the state of catechetical instruction then prevailing. For the most part the latter consisted in a certain amount of memorizing of doctrinal formulas with emphasis on questions of morality, as is evidenced by the manuals of preparation for confession which were the forerunners of the catechism.

What the children assimilated of Christian doctrine and Christian morality they owed, in the main, not to the schools nor to indoctrination by the priests of the Church, but to the home and to the environment in which they grew up. Their training came from their surroundings, their milieu, their way of life or whatever one wishes to call it. It came from the formative influence of a world imbued with a Christian spirit in every least detail.

For this reason it should be worth while to give at least an over-all picture of this Christian world of the late Middle Ages. In the sketch attempted in the following pages we intend to make use almost exclusively of German sources. Conditions would have been practically the same, however, in France or England. Christian life was every bit as flourishing in these countries as it was on German soil, as any study will show. Nevertheless, it may interest American and other English-speaking readers to learn about conditions which prevailed in a part of Christendom which may not happen to be the land of their own origin.

In various devotional writings of the latter part of the Middle Ages, Christian family life is described as it ought to be ideally. Parents are admonished that the home must be the first school and the first church for tender youth.

Christian mother, as you hold your child made in God's image on your lap, make the Sign of the Holy Cross on his brow, on his mouth, and on his breast; and as soon as he is able to speak, pray with him so that he can pray after you, that is, repeat the words which you have uttered. You should bless your child, instruct him in the faith, and prepare him at an early age for confession, explaining to him everything that is necessary to make a good confession.[6]

One of the earliest catechisms in German, composed by Diedrich Coelde and first published in the year 1480, admonishes parents to teach their children "the Our Father, Hail Mary, the twelve articles of Christian faith, the ten commandments, as well as other points given in this book. . . . Each morning and evening they should bless themselves (with the Sign of the Cross), and in the evening get down on both knees and give thanks to God." [7] In another place it is recommended to parents that they take their children with them to divine worship on Sunday, and after the service that the father should question the children as to how much they noted of the sermon, and then add his own observations thereto.[8]

That such admonitions did not indicate merely wishful thinking but were actually carried out is testified to by a Protestant preacher, who is forced to admit from his own unhappy experience that matters were certainly better in the Catholic Middle Ages. "In those days," he acknowledged, "mothers were still the principal

---

[6] *Der Seelenführer* (Mainz, 1498), cited by Johannes Janssen, *History of the German People at the Close of the Middle Ages,* trans. M. A. Mitchell and A. M. Christie, I (St. Louis: Herder, 2nd rev. ed., 1905), 31. Passage above rendered from original text.

[7] Christoph Moufang, *Katholische Katechismen des sechszehnten Jahrhunderts in deutscher Sprache* (Mainz: Fr. Kirchheim, 1881), p. 42. Cf. Janssen, *loc. cit.*

[8] Janssen, *op. cit.,* p. 33.

resident chaplains and bishops," from whose lips the articles of faith and the commandments were learned.[9] It goes without saying that, in the matter of teaching catechism in the home, a systematic method was not the chief factor. Of much greater significance was a Christian way of life, a Christian atmosphere which enveloped the child on every side.

The very beginning of a young person's life came under the influence of the Faith. By no means did the people of that time regard baptism simply as a moral obligation. For them it was a matter of that utmost conviction that baptism freed a child from the power of the devil. So convinced were they of this that the Bretons made it a practice to have an old woman watch and pray beside the cradle during the night before baptism. And in other provinces of France the father himself, well armed, stood guard against the evil spirit in a corner of the room.[10]

The first act of a mother with regard to her new newborn child was to trace on its brow the sign of the cross. But she bestowed the first kiss on it only after it had been brought home reborn and sanctified in baptism. Until then it was considered a little heathen or, as the Spanish mothers said, a little Moor.[11] It was in baptism, moreover, that the child first received its name, its baptismal name or, as it is so aptly called in English, its Christian name, even though the practice of conferring a name at baptism did not come about through ecclesiastical legislation. As late as the ninth century it was not yet customary to give a child its name at baptism; and in Germany the name given was not yet at that date a saint's name but an old Teutonic name. Gradually, however, the Christian sentiments of the people led to the practice of combining the conferring of a name with baptism, and finally to the further step of naming the child after a saint.

A long time before any kind of synod concerned itself with the question of a baptismal name the name of John the Baptist, for example, was very widely used. Such was the case as early as the

[9] Georg von Anhalt, *Predigten* (Wittenberg: 1555), p. 189.
[10] Paul Doncœur, S.J., *Retours en chrétienté* (Paris: Bernard Grasset, 1933), pp. 17 ff.
[11] *Ibid.*, p. 48.

eleventh century, and soon after that time the names of all the apostles were chosen as baptismal names. Eventually names were taken from the entire litany of the saints and from the full list in liturgical books.[12] So much weight was attached to the conferring of a name at baptism that in the year 1374 the Council of Benevento had to forbid the practice of repeating the baptismal rite in a case where a name had been omitted in its original administration. How very popular it became to use the names of saints is also shown by the numerous surnames found among Western people toward the end of the Middle Ages, many of which are a derivation of baptismal names. It suffices to refer to modifications on the name John, such as Johnson, Jansen, Hansen, Grosjean, and so on.

High regard for baptism was also shown by the great reverence with which the holy chrism was treated, used in anointing the child in the concluding part of the baptismal rite as well as in later anointings. The spot that had received the chrism was protected by a headband (Latin: *mitra, mappa, chrismale*), which sometimes took the form of a little cap.[13] This was worn for several days, or eight days, or until the mother came to church with the child to receive the blessing after childbirth (*benedictio mulieris post partum*). The priest alone was allowed to remove it; in many cases he did this during the course of the Mass, at the same time wiping with cotton the place that had been anointed.[14] It became a custom too in many families to treasure this headband as a sacred heirloom.

Another living reminder of baptism was the godparent, just as later on in confirmation the godparent became a living reminder of that sacrament. The role of godparent in those days was not looked upon as a formality of the moment. Rather—and this is still true in my homeland of Tyrol—it was the foundation of a new

[12] J. B. Lehner, "Patrone," *Lexikon f. Theologie u. Kirche*, VIII (Freiburg: Herder, 1936), 1–5.

[13] Oftentimes in those days the anointing was made on the brow or just above the brow, and not as at present on the crown of the head. Cf. Alban Dold, *Die Konstanzer Ritualientexte* (Münster: Aschendorff, 1923), p. 26.

[14] Ludwig Andreas Veit, *Volksfrommes Brauchtum und Kirche im deutschen Mittelalter* (Freiburg: Herder, 1936), pp. 160 f. E. Martène, *De Antiquis Ecclesiae Ritibus*, I, 1, art. 15, no. 6, I (Antwerp: 1736), 148–50.

kind of relationship binding families together in closer Christian fellowship. These bonds were kept alive through precisely regulated visits which the godchild paid to the godparent, for instance on All Saints' Day and Easter. Prescribed also was an exchange of gifts, for example, Easter eggs on that feast day.

Acting in the capacity of godparent also helped people to bridge social inequalities. The rule in Brittany was that a nobleman select a peasant as godparent.[15] A similar thought lay at the basis of a practice in medieval Germany to the effect that a woman during the period of confinement had to be excused from paying the usual tax to her overlord, for example a hen or something of the sort.[16]

Just as with the beginning of life, so also the end of life was sanctified through various devout practices which for the most part persist today in Catholic provinces. Whenever a person seriously ill was to be fortified with the last sacraments, the whole village was acquainted with the fact by a signal from the "departure bell." Whoever was free to do so, and in any event a large group of children, formed an escort for the Blessed Sacrament. The occupants of the homes which lay along the route taken by the little procession knelt on the street and received the blessing. Count Rudolph of Hapsburg may serve as a typical example of the pious fervor of people of that age. While out hunting one day he met such a procession and immediately put his horse at the disposal of the priest.

The death of a member of a parish also was announced by the tolling bell in the tower, calling on the people to pray for the deceased. Moreover, as Durandus (d. 1296) relates, the manner of tolling indicated who had died: two strokes for a woman, three for a man, and for a cleric as many strokes as the orders he had received.[17] The body was carried to the cemetery to the accompaniment of prayers said aloud and the ringing of bells. Ever since the time of St. Boniface the rule had been that the cemetery should lie next to the church edifice. It served, we might say, as a courtyard

[15] Doncœur, *op. cit.*, p. 49.
[16] Veit, *op. cit.*, p. 158.
[17] Guilelmus Durantis (Durandus), *Rationale*, I, 4, 13 (Venetiam: Barnardinus de Vitalibus, 1519).

to the church. Whenever the faithful came to the house of God, they first had to pass through the place where the bodies lay buried in hallowed soil—"God's acre," *campo santo*. Before entering the church no doubt they first paid a visit to the grave of their beloved departed to offer a prayer and to sprinkle the grave with holy water. Death held no terror for them; it served rather as a reminder of the things of eternity.

The late medieval period was also the time of the "dance of death." The hymn *Media vita in morte sumus,* both in Latin and in the vernacular, was one of the most popular and beloved of hymns, in Germany at any rate.

The religious character of the Middle Ages was also expressed in the very arrangement of a town's buildings. This is still in evidence today in practically every old village and town. In the center of everything stands the house of God. All streets find their terminus at this point. It is here that the feast days are celebrated. This is the center of gravity; the community is held together by the pull it exerts on human lives. Even the everyday life of these people, these peasants, craftsmen and merchants, had the church edifice as its center and sanctuary, with the structure towering over all the other buildings and its steeple pointing up to heaven.

By the very expenditure involved in the construction of the house of God the Middle Ages made known how much its people esteemed it. We are struck with admiration at the sight of the Gothic cathedrals which, beginning with the twelfth and thirteenth centuries, sprang up in practically every city of France, Germany and England. They are in the main of tremendous proportions, far exceeding in size the demands of the cities of that time, especially when one reflects that there were so many other churches at hand; for even at the end of the Middle Ages cities with more than 10,-000 inhabitants were an exception. The city council deemed it important for the prestige of the city, however, to possess a magnificent church. Gladly did that age supply the wealth which had accrued from the flourishing state of commerce in its later period, as well as the full talents of artists and architects, to pay honor to God by means of outstanding church buildings.

At that time in rural areas too, at least in southern Germany and Austria, many village churches were being newly built. Their outlines dominate the countryside today. The steep towers that come from that era are still standing, provided there has not been any cover-up by a second architectural period dating from the age of Baroque.

Yet apart from the erection of churches that dominated village and city in those times, the landscape breathed holiness from other sources also. In the older Christian countries, significant are the many little shrines which everywhere dot valley and mountain. Near the manor house court stands a chapel where devotions were held on an evening or a Sunday afternoon. On wayside paths is found a cross with an image of the crucified, or in more conspicuous places a statue on a pedestal.[18] Leading to a church of pilgrimage on a height one finds a row of Stations of the Cross (toward the end of the Middle Ages they usually numbered seven), each one marked with a little framed picture or even its own chapel if they date from the Middle Ages. Well known are the Calvary groups which in many parts of France bear witness to the spirit of faith of earlier generations. Rightfully has this been called a "consecrated landscape."

Besides these outdoor shrines, it was the custom to hold processions on designated days, starting in church and progressing outdoors with prayer and song through the confines of the parish, so as to unite all of creation with the sanctuary of God's dwelling. Here we have a visible fulfillment of the text that occurs in the martyrology of Christmas Eve: namely, that Christ will consecrate the world by His grace-laden advent. All who grew up in such an environment knew that the world belonged to God.

Even secular life was religiously oriented in the late Middle Ages. Artisans were organized into guilds, and each guild chose for itself a heavenly patron, the choice being dictated by some attribute or legend that would apply in the particular case. The

---

[18] In most cases a cement shaft surmounted by a cube, the sides of which were ornamented with pictures. J. Weingartner, in his book, *Tiroler Bildstocke* (1948), describes more than 200 of these found in the tiny province of Tyrol, the majority of which date from the fifteenth and sixteenth centuries.

kettle-makers venerated St. Vitus, who was martyred in a caldron; the archers St. Sebastian; the miners St. Barbara because she had been locked up in a tower; the wagon-makers St. Catherine because of the wheel; the tailors St. Martin because of the mantle; the fishermen St. Peter, who also became the patron of locksmiths because of the keys.[19]

An image of the patron was employed on the banners of the guilds and also on their trademark. On the feast day of the patron a special service was held at which all members assisted and in which they made an offering in an offertory procession. The more important guilds in many cases had their own chapel in the church, or at least their own altar with an endowment of Masses. In religious processions the guilds marched separately, carrying their own banners and emblems and following a well-ordered procedure. In Munich, for example, in the year 1484, the order of procession provided for forty-three guilds, each one having a fixed rank of precedence before the Blessed Sacrament. The place of honor immediately before the Blessed Sacrament was reseved for millers and bakers because of their relationship to bread.[20]

When the guilds were at their best, their officers kept close watch to see that all members observed the precepts of the Church and led an honorable life. To give mutual aid was an obligation taken for granted by the members.

Oftentimes not only the guild as a whole but each house, each branch had its special patron, thus bringing into relief the relationship of the things of this world to the things of eternity. It was a commonplace for an inn to have not just any kind of name or sign to attract the passerby, but a biblical representation. This phe-

[19] See A. Bruder, *Ueber Wappen und Schutzpatrone der alten Zünfte* (Innsbruck, 1885), who lists the patron saints of fifty-eight different occupations. Some of these patrons have not yet been forgotten completely. Miners (not excluding the Socialists) still celebrate the feast of St. Barbara with a special service. On Nov. 25, 1944, in a village of lower Austria, I met a wagon-maker of my acquaintance dressed in his holiday best. When in my surprise I questioned him, I received the reply: "Well, today is the feast of St. Catherine."

[20] A. Mitterwieser, *Geschichte der Fronleichnamsprozession in Bayern* (München, 1930). In my home town in the south of Tyrol, even today the millers and the bakers march as separate groups in the Corpus Christi procession directly after the Blessed Sacrament, carrying large candles.

nomenon can still be noted in the older cities and villages. Out of respect for the Bible the innkeeper might choose one of the four Evangelists, and his inn would go by the symbolic title Inn of the Angel, Inn of the Ox, Inn of the Lion, Inn of the Eagle. Or the innkeepers would use one of the symbols that had to do with the journey of the Three Kings, the patrons of travelers, and called their establishments Inn of the Star, Inn of the Crown, Inn of the Three Crowns, Inn of the Elephant, Inn of the Steed, or Inn of the Ethiopian.

It was taken for granted that hospitals would take the name of a heavenly patron. Those restricted to lepers named themselves after Lazarus in the biblical parable, from which originates today's custom of calling such institutions lazarettos. From the twelfth century on it became more and more common to place hospitals under the protection of the Holy Spirit. The more ineffective the medicines of that time were in treating many illnesses, the more confidently did people have to look for help from above. The Holy Spirit is invoked as strength for healing in the hymn in His honor:

> Lava quod est sordidum,
> Riga quod est aridum,
> Sana quod est saucium.

If one walks along the streets of Vienna today and observes the numerous apothecaries, one cannot help noticing that the vast majority of them have religious names: Apothecary of the Blessed Trinity, Apothecary of the Angels, Apothecary of Mary, Apothecary of St. Martha, Apothecary of St. Leopold, and so on.

A special patron was associated with every necessity, every interest. Tobias was the patron of travelers, St. Anne the patron of expectant mothers. The various illnesses had each its special patron, until eventually they were limited to the fourteen most popular ones known as the "Fourteen Intercessors in Time of Need," or simply as the "Fourteen Saints." [21]

The village peasant, too, venerated the various patrons of his

---

[21] Consider the famous church of the "Fourteen Saints" in Oberfranken, Bavaria.

occupation. In his case they were holy hermits especially who, because of their rustic life, had some connection with the life of a peasant. To such patrons were credited all manner of legendary powers. Thus Wendelin and Leonard became patron saints of cattle. St. Antony the Hermit, in whose temptations and tribulations animals of all kinds play an important part, as the artists of the late Middle Ages were fond of depicting, was by no means the least of these patrons of farm life.[22]

Not only was it the common man of village and town who placed his life and his work under the protection of heaven, but also the knight, the count and the prince. They humbled themselves before God and accepted their respective offices as commissions from above. When the candidate for knighthood reached the proper age and was sufficiently practiced in the art of weapons, he received in solemn ceremony the order of knight or of squire, or for religious purposes, the consecration to knighthood. The Pontifical of Durandus contained a special rite used by the bishop in receiving the prospective knight into his particular rank.[23]

The above-mentioned rite took place in the course of the Mass. Before the Gospel, the bishop would interrupt the Mass and bless the sword, using a prayer consisting of two parts which appeared in a Pontifical of Mainz as early as the tenth century. "May this sword serve to protect the Church, the widows and orphans, and all who are in God's service. May it act as a deterrent against the fury of the heathen and against invisible enemies." Then he said a longer prayer over the candidate, imploring for him the virtues of Christian knighthood, with frequent references to prototypes found in sacred Scripture. Next he presented him with the sword, and after it had been stuck in the scabbard fastened it around the

---

[22] See F. v. S. Doyé, *Heilige und Selige der römisch-katholischen Kirche,* II (Leipzig: Vier Quellen Verlag, 1929), 890–905, for a reference to various authentic patron saints for certain occupations and circumstances, with consideration of the development up to the present. About 1,000 entries are listed.

[23] Michel Andrieu, *Le Pontifical Romain au Moyen-Age,* III (Civ. Vat.: Bib. Apost. Vaticana, 1940), 447–50, "De benedictione novi militis." This formulary is still included, with some modifications, in the official Roman Pontifical of today. See Emil Michael, S.J., *Geschichte des deutschen Volkes seit dem dreizehnten Jahrhundert,* I (Freiburg: Herder, 1897), 231–40.

waist of the young knight, who in turn drew the sword and brandished it three times in the air. Thereupon the new knight received the kiss of peace and also a light stroke on the cheek, like the ceremony in confirmation. What the bishop did here was in reality the dubbing formerly administered by a superior officer.[24]

In another familiar writing of an earlier date having to do with the consecration to knighthood in 1247 of the young Count William of Holland, we learn that the dubbing was administered by a cardinal in the course of the Mass. In this instance the ceremony began with an enumeration of a knight's duties, among which the first mention made was of the duty of assisting daily at Mass. Every castle had its chapel and wherever possible also its own chaplain. Following the reception into knighthood there was a joyous celebration.[25]

Even the act of ascending to the pinnacle of political rank, namely the dignity of being made king or emperor, was consecrated by an ecclesiastical ceremony. Nowadays we are accustomed to the fact that, in Europe at least, presidents and heads of state take over their office without much formality and without the least recognition of a supreme Power. And if, now and then, a royal coronation does take place such as we have lived to see with Queen Elizabeth II, most people regard it as a relic of former times which has no real significance, because they mistakenly believe that authority comes from the people. Things were far different in the centuries of the Middle Ages which demanded that the bearers of the highest honor of state give expression to the conviction that all authority is ultimately rooted in God. The coronation of a ruler by a representative of spiritual power is much older than the consecration to knighthood, even in the West. The list of royal coronations for which there is historical testimony opens with that of Aidan, King of Scotland, in 574, and among the Franks with that of Pippin by Boniface in 751. The list reaches its high point in the coronation of Charlemagne as emperor in the year 800.

[24] Michael, *op. cit.*, p. 236.
[25] *Ibid.*, pp. 237–41.

The coronation of the Emperor of "the Holy Roman and German Empire" by the Vicar of Christ opened with a ceremonial that grew richer and richer at time went on. First came the introductory prayers along with the anointing given by a cardinal. In the course of the papal Mass which followed, the Pope girded the emperor with a sword and so made him a Knight of St. Peter. Next he presented him with scepter and orb, and then placed the crown on his head. At the same time the emperor was made a Canon of St. Peter's with the rank of deacon. With this act he received the right to chant the Gospel in the Mass of Christmas Night clothed in the full vestments of his rank—a right which, by the way, was exercised.

Throughout the Middle Ages, and not in Germany only, the people held in greatest awe the consecrated majesty of the emperor. An example of this attitude can be seen in St. Francis Xavier who, when making his preparations for the mission in China, kept constantly referring to the "King of China." He refused to designate him an emperor because this title connoted a religious consecration.[26]

Since the life of Christians in the Middle Ages was permeated with a spirit of religion, it was to be expected that the very passage of time, the days and the years, would be dedicated in a special way to almighty God. Since such a thing as a clock was still a rare luxury in the latter part of the Middle Ages, church bells served to signal the periods of the day. From the bells in the tower the people were informed of the individual canonical hours. Not only in cathedrals, chapter houses and monastic churches were the seven canonical hours sung day after day, but in parish churches as well, where the pastor, if he himself were prevented, could arrange to have the duty fulfilled by his scholars.[27] Thus a special bell announced from day to day the hours of the Divine Office—early in the morning the hour of Matins (*matutinum:* our present Lauds); then later and with greater solemnity the hour of Terce, after which came Mass; and finally Sext, None and Vespers. In the hot climate

[26] J. Brodrick, *St. Francis Xavier* (New York: Wicklow Press, 1952), p. 500.
[27] See J. A. Jungmann, *The Mass of the Roman Rite* (*Missarum Sollemnia*), I (New York: Benziger, 1951), 212, n. 25.

of the south the stroke of the bell for Sext was at the same time
a signal for the noonday nap. This "old Spanish custom" was
gradually adopted by other countries, so that by the eighteenth
century we find even the Germans speaking about a siesta (Sext),
and so also other nationalities.

In England, on the other hand, the emphasis in the populai
mind was especially on the hour of None. From this we get the
English word "noon" which since the thirteenth century has designated not the ninth hour of the day (3:00 P.M.), but rather mid-
day, so that we have the expressions "forenoon" and "afternoon."
In England and elsewhere it has long been the custom to sing
None in the middle of the day.

In our day in Catholic provinces the solemn ringing of bells
ushers in and accompanies the observance of feast days or calls the
faithful to Mass each morning. This is a relic of medieval times.
The same is true of the Angelus bell as it rings out its peals morning, noon and night. Moreover, throughout the Middle Ages the
sound of the bell at Terce, Sext, None and Vespers was not merely
a time signal for the laity. Devout laymen really understood it as
a call to prayer. Devotional books and catechisms published even
as late as the first part of the modern era gave directions to the
faithful which told them how they could meditate on the respective
mysteries of Christ's passion at the various hours of the day. At
Prime and Terce they were to think of Christ standing before
Pilate and Herod and of the scourging He endured, and were to
offer their gratitude to Him for these mysteries of salvation. At
Sext they were to meditate on His crucifixion, at None on His
death.[28]

What was true of the sanctification of the day's cycle was equally
or more true of the year's cycle. The custom had not yet been instituted of reckoning days by the names of the months nor by the
numerals of each month as we do now, but rather by means of
the Church calendar. One simply said: on the day before Michael-

[28] See, for example, the many editions of *Christenspiegel* (*Speculum Chris-
tianorum*) which have appeared since 1480—brought out by the Franciscan
Coelde; cf. Moufang, *op. cit.*, pp. xxx ff.

mas, on the third day after St. Martin's, on the feast of St. Thomas the Apostle, and so on. Nor were these simply names; these feast days were really observed. In the book of ecclesiastical laws of the Middle Ages (twelfth to thirteenth centuries), forty holy days of obligation were prescribed in addition to the Sundays,[29] to which one must add the special feasts of individual dioceses and countries. Besides a long list of feasts in honor of the Blessed Virgin, there were among others the feasts of the Apostles—also the Conversion of St. Paul and St. Peter's Chains—and the anniversaries of the more renowned martyrs and confessors such as Stephen, the Holy Innocents, Sylvester, John the Baptist, Lawrence, Michael and Martin. In Germany as a general rule the anniversaries of Saints George, Nicholas, Mary Magdalen, Cecilia and Catherine were regarded as holy days of obligation also.[30]

Thus it happened that practically every week there occurred a holy day of obligation over and above the Sunday. The people then did not find these many feast days oppressive. The very opposite was true, so much so that when Cardinal Nicholas of Cusa (around 1450) was traveling through Germany in the capacity of papal visitator, he found it necessary to limit drastically the arbitrary introduction of new feasts, such as a day "against inclement weather," the Fridays after Ascension and Corpus Christi, and so on.

Social and economic life of that time was organized on a much different plan from that of the present. The entire domestic economy was geared toward making each family self-sufficient. One lived content with what one had. As a general rule men would not think of working in a factory or carrying on a business. The unliberated peasant at any rate felt a definite antipathy toward the practice. And so one was not stingy about time for the observance of the Church's feasts. It was taken for granted that on all Sundays and feast days all the faithful, with the exception only of those who were reasonably hindered, would be present at Mass which was celebrated at nine o'clock, and that they would attend their own parish church.

[29] *Decretum Gratiani*, III, I.
[30] Veit, *op. cit.*, p. 93.

It was only toward the end of the Middle Ages that the mendicant orders as a whole caused a breach in parochial organization, to the displeasure of both pastor and bishop. Yet their churches did afford the faithful the advantage of better preaching and more frequent opportunity of receiving the sacraments. In any case, divine worship on Sundays and feast days occupied a good share of the day. Nothing was further removed from the people's minds than to fulfill the Sunday obligation with a short Mass of a half-hour's duration, and then to be free to spend the rest of the day in relaxation and recreation.

It cannot be doubted that such an intensive devotional life had powerful formative value. It must have been deeply impressed on the people that the service of God was the first and the main duty of their lives. If the frequent and lesser holy days stirred the popular imagination of that day, much more was this so of the celebration of the Church's high solemnities. Interest was centered above all on the re-presentation or recurrence of the various mysteries by which the economy of Redemption had come to pass. These were given special prominence from the fact that each one was accompanied by a number of other festivals. The feasts that followed Christmas, for example, were without exception holy days of obligation. And as regards Easter, the whole of Easter week was required to be celebrated, according to the Decree of Gratian. If this was not enforced universally, in Germany at any rate both at Easter and at Pentecost five days, Sunday through Thursday, were kept as holy days.[31] Easter, the "solemnity of solemnities," was distinguished in yet another way; namely, by having it preceded and followed by a "closed season."

A similar thing was true of Christmas time. In the latter part of the Middle Ages it became less common to keep St. Martin's Lent before Christmas, which used to begin on November 11th and which at one time in France was comparable to the Lent that preceded Easter. Yet everywhere the time from Advent through Epiphany was observed as a "closed season" during which marriage could not be solemnized and married couples were supposed to abstain from the conjugal act. The latter was at least earnestly counseled.

[31] *Ibid.*, p. 93.

The same rule held true for the time from Septuagesima till Low
Sunday, as well as for the three weeks before the octave of Pentecost
and before the feast of St. John the Baptist.[32]

Nor was there any lack of special fast days. Of these about
sixty-five at that time were prescribed annually for the universal
Church, exclusive of those days which were simply days of absti-
nence and of those observed only in some places.[33] The forty days
before Easter marked Lent strictly so called. All worldly amuse-
ments were forbidden during this period. The images in church
were veiled and the altar concealed by the Lenten curtain—referred
to sometimes as the "hunger cloth." [34] Since Lent was taken seriously, being truly regarded as the time of penance, it was understandable that before it commenced a certain amount of gaiety
was permitted. The carnival was the last breathing spell previous
to the beginning of Lent. It is not a good sign that today we are
forced to admit that Lent is without significance to a great number
of our fellow men who give not the least thought to the question
of fasting.

How deeply the soul of the people was affected by the great
feasts of the Church can best be seen from the mystery dramas
staged during the Middle Ages.[35] The most important elements of
these mystery dramas grew out of the liturgy. For instance, the
question: "Whom seek ye?" contained in the last responsory of
Easter matins, and the answer given to it by the women, were the
point of departure first for a further developed dialogue between
the clergy and then for a dramatic presentation which, beginning
in the twelfth century, gradually moved from the church to the
cemetery or to the market place or even to the town hall. Done
initially in Latin, it was afterward translated into the vernacular.
Here we have the germ of the later Easter plays.

[32] Doncœur, op. cit., pp. 87–91.
[33] Veit, op. cit., pp. 121 f.
[34] See Herbert Thurston, S.J., "The Lenten Curtain," Lent and Holy Week
(London: Longmans, Green, 1904), pp. 99–105.
[35] The whole subject is treated by Karl Young, The Drama of the Medieval
Church, 2 vols. (Oxford: Clarendon Press, 1933). For a summary of the
mystery plays in Germany and elsewhere, see A. Dörrer, "Mysterienspiele,"
Lexikon f. Theol. u. Kirche, VII, 403 ff.

Similarly the Passion plays, some of which are still being performed, grew out of the ceremony of sepulture in part of the liturgy of Good Friday. From the liturgy of Christmas arose the Christmas plays which portrayed the events from the Holy Night itself up until the slaughter of the Holy Innocents. In the late Middle Ages the Corpus Christi plays developed from the Corpus Christi celebration. Consisting of a long series of living tableaux staged at various points along the route of the procession, they depicted the whole work of Redemption from Adam and Eve until the Last Day.

In addition there were plays in honor of individual saints dealing with their life or their martyrdom (among others Saints Dorothy, George, Catherine); plays based on the parables, such as that of the wise and foolish virgins; miracle plays dealing with miraculous events, such as the finding of the Holy Cross. Especially popular was the play on the anti-Christ.

These plays were not performed by professional actors; rather, the whole city, the whole village, cooperated in their production, as is still the case in Oberammergau. No efforts were spared, whether in the number of plays or in the time consumed. In Frankfurt-am-Main in 1498 a Passion play was presented in which 250 persons took part and which lasted four days. These plays were performed mostly in the afternoon.[36]

Every director who has anything to do with dramatics with school children or youth groups realizes that the players afterward retain the nicknames of the characters they have portrayed on the stage. This is an indication of how intimately the audience participates in the drama. The same held true of the actors in the mystery plays of the Middle Ages, and it is another proof of how much the spirit of the people was affected by the religious themes of these plays. Indeed, a significant number of our present family names originated in this manner. As examples we have in Germany family names like *Teufel* (devil) and *Neuenteufel* (new devil)—the old portrayer had died and a new one had been substituted for him—and also a name like *Herrgott* (the Lord God). There are others

[36] J. Janssen, *op. cit.*, p. 276.

like *Münch* (monk), *Bischof* (bishop), *Papst* (pope), as well as *Kaiser* (emperor) and *König* (king), names of characters practically all of which are taken from the play about the anti-Christ. And it seems that this practice was not restricted to Germany, for elsewhere we find the names King, Bishop, Leroy, Lhermite, Lemoine, Labbé, and many others like them whose origin could hardly have any other explanation psychologically.

The atmosphere of the last centuries of the Middle Ages was full of religious sentiments and forms. Christian instruction assumed a variety of patterns through its many institutions, its manners and customs, its forms of piety, its countless images and shrines. A child born into such a world as this had only to keep his eyes open, and he saw all around him representations of the next world. He learned about religion and its precepts and practices just as one learns one's mother tongue, spontaneously and without formal instruction, simply from contact with his environment.

Although in an advanced culture one does learn the mother tongue from one's mother, yet for its right mastery in speaking and writing there is still the need of school with its rules of grammar and clarification of more difficult forms. So also for young Christians as well as for the entire population of the late Middle Ages, a little more schooling and solid instruction would have been most useful. For what lay at the surface of those institutions, what the young person assimilated from his environment, was in no way the pure expression of revealed teaching. It was in many cases a remarkable conglomeration of truth and fiction, sacred history and legend, faith and superstition, usage and abuse. In all this, it is true, there was to be found a powerful expression of the belief that everything in life is oriented toward God and eternity; but how to reach this goal, how to attain salvation, was not so clearly shown. To make a pilgrimage or to found a pious institution seemed oftentimes more important than conversion of life and the sacrament of penance. Exaggerated notions were abroad on the value of indulgences. As the bearers of salvation, whether of this world or of the next, stood the saints, of whom an ever increasing number was venerated in a restless seeking after special needs. One cannot avoid the impression that, even though the thought of Him "who is the Mediator between God and men" was certainly in the background of consciousness, it nonetheless remained considerably obscured.

Along with this, the most incredible tales were circulated and passed on about the wondrous powers of certain saints who attracted to themselves a special veneration. What is more, there suddenly appeared on the scene relics of which nothing had been known earlier, the authenticity of which has since definitely been disproved. As an example we may cite "the head of St. Anne" over which two cities carried on a long strife, until finally the Pope was asked to intervene.

Even in the use of the Church's chief means of grace, the people's piety tended too much to the periphery of things. The era was truly "the waning of the Middle Ages" (Huizinga). It was true that the people valued Holy Mass, as is evident from the great number of Mass endowments established at that time and also from the number of priests whose support was assured on the one condition that they say Mass—*altarists* was the name given them. But the Mass was valued chiefly because of certain miraculous powers attributed to it in the popular mind. To gaze at the Host during the consecration would protect one that day from blindness or from a sudden death,[37] would remit the sin of carelessness in speech, and so on. In order to gain a special vantage point in church the better to see the elevated species, the faithful were willing to pay money and even engage in lawsuit.[38] Moreover they sought many opportunities to look upon the Host outside Mass. Receiving the sacrament in Holy Communion, however, was an infrequent occurrence limited mostly to the prescribed Easter Communion. The people were eager instead to receive a blessing with the Blessed Sacrament—or at least with the corporal—for their various interests and necessities. They were not content with having the Blessed

[37] A similar efficacy was ascribed to the practice of looking at the picture of St. Christopher depicted on the walls of many a church.

[38] E. Dumoutet, *Le désir de voir l'Hostie et les origines de la dévotion au Saint-Sacrement* (Paris: Beauchesne, 1926), pp. 67 f.

Sacrament carried through streets and fields in the procession of Corpus Christi but wanted it brought forth if a hailstorm threatened or a fire broke out somewhere.

Theologians were not lacking to condemn such practices and to emphasize that the Eucharist had been instituted as sacrifice and as nourishment for the soul, and not as a safeguard against the forces of nature. They found very few listeners.[39] Cardinal Nicholas of Cusa in his visit to Germany as papal legate in 1450 took action in various synods against the misguided Eucharistic piety, forbade exposition of the Blessed Sacrament outside the octave of Corpus Christi, and ordered that no new Corpus Christi confraternities were to be established.[40]

In other respects, too, piety was directed toward a one-sided emphasis on what could be taken in with the eyes. What the people wanted was a very realistic presentation of biblical happenings. At Christmastide it did not suffice simply to have the crib set before their eyes; they wanted to see a cradle set in rocking motion. On Palm Sunday they wanted to see a figure of our Lord riding a donkey—a *Palmesel*. On Pentecost the Holy Spirit had to be seen visibly in the form of a dove descending from the vault of the church and circling over the congregation.

Perhaps this was only an expression of the childlike and naïve spirit of the people, but it did reveal that their chief interest was in Christ *secundum carnem*, in His human aspect, a thing that St. Paul would not have acknowledged as the primary object of Christian piety. More serious was the danger of having religion become chiefly a matter of external practices. People willingly performed any number of external works, observed feast days and fast days, went on pilgrimages, joined many confraternities, gave money for pious causes, and so thought they had done all that could be demanded of Christians, no matter what their dispositions nor how they neglected the right ordering of their lives.

Even though no fault could be found with their morals, it re-

[39] Adolf Franz, *Die kirchlichen Benediktionen im Mittelalter*, II (Freiburg: Herder, 1909), 105 ff.

[40] Petrus Browe, *Die Verehrung der Eucharistie im Mittelalter* (München: 1932), pp. 170 ff.

mained a type of Christianity ruled far too much by outward conformity to an established order or to the pressure of environment. Exposure to a well-ordered milieu is good, just as learning by doing is good. So too a Christianity which is traditional to a land is good if it is infused with the proper spirit.

A milieu as such can have only a superficial influence on people. It needs as a complement spirit and enlightenment. It needs the enlightening word to explain its regulations and its institutions and to bring to consciousness the meaning behind them, so that the parts may be seen in their proper perspective and the essential distinguished from the accidental. It needs, moreover, the informing spirit which can comprehend in its essence the heritage bequeathed to it, which knows how to separate genuine substance from unhealthy accretions and then out of conviction make use of whatever corresponds to the authentic tradition of the Church.

This spirit of which we speak was to a great extent lacking toward the end of the Middle Ages. It became all the more necessary the more colorful, numerous and influential the outward forms became. What at last really happened can be readily understood. When the prophet of Wittenberg rose up and proclaimed a very simple Gospel: "Faith alone, the Bible alone! Away with all works! Only reliance on the merits of Christ brings us salvation!"—the mass of the faithful stood helpless and defenseless in the face of such tidings. Within a few years the whole picture was changed. Objects formerly venerated were put to the torch. Worst of all, sacrifice and priesthood, the very things that were at the heart of Catholic Christendom from the beginning, were eliminated.

We may rightly envy the Middle Ages for some of the rich forms of Christianity of the period as well as for its powers in molding a splendid community life. We must seek to revive so far as possible certain features of its life, at least in the smaller circles of family, school and church, or to rejuvenate them where they still exist. Yet we must not forget that for a sound, living Christianity sound teaching is also necessary, a proclaiming of the Gospel through catechetics and preaching in which the Glad Tidings are ever announced anew, in which Christ is acknowledged as the true Bearer of salvation desirous of drawing us closer and closer to Himself by means of the Church and the sacraments so as to lead us home to the Father; a proclaiming of the Gospel that will infuse spirit into the external forms. "For it is the Spirit who gives life" (Jn. 6, 63).

3.

Religious Education in England
in the Penal Days (1559–1778)
·
J. D. Crichton

A study of how the Faith was transmitted in England during the
Penal Days is of more than historical interest. It has a topical
relevance: for there are many parts of the Church which are suffering persecution now and, *mutatis mutandis,* the same efforts are
being made to keep the Faith alive where the usual means of instruction, and so on, cannot be expected to do so.

When Queen Elizabeth I, completing the work of her father,
established the Church of England as the only legal religious body
in 1559 by the Acts of Supremacy and Uniformity, all the ordinary
organization of the Catholic Church in England ceased. The religious situation, already very confused, became even more so. There
had been three changes of religion in just over twenty-five years.
The clergy were neither by training nor by experience capable of
giving any very effective instruction. From what we know of them
a little later such schoolmasters as there were were less shaken in
their Faith, though what part they took in religious instruction is
not clear. The best of the old priests, then, continued the traditional
instruction based on Creed, Our Father and the Sacraments, though
they would have been quite embarrassed to explain the last if they
paid any heed to the Book of Common Prayer which they were
obliged to possess and use by the feast of St. John the Baptist, 1559.
As we know, there were continual and habitual compromises up to
the coming of the Douai priests in 1574, and any definite teaching
in such an atmosphere was all but impossible. But it is in such circumstances that traditions are important, and from what we know
of the approach of the missionary priests to the converts they made,
much of the original substratum of Faith and practice remained.

It is impossible to rub out by a stroke of even a governmental pen a thousand years of religious faith and practice.

Yet the situation became increasingly perilous for the survival of the Faith. You likewise cannot go on year after year celebrating two sorts of religious service—the new ones of the Prayer Book, and the Mass—and living in the anomalous situation of bowing to Remmon on Naaman's terms and secretly acknowledging the Pope, without seriously compromising even the intellectual grasp of the Faith you hold. That is, in fact, largely how the majority lost the ancient Faith. There was, it is true, the steady propaganda of the government, though its ineffectiveness in parish churches is revealed by the lack of preachers which continued almost to the end of the reign; and there was the pressure of atmosphere that went increasingly (and to the point of violent persecution) against the Faith. Yet it remains true that England lost the Faith more through conforming to a religious situation than through positive teaching.

That this was so is shown by the work of the Missionary Priests as soon as they got back to England. Even the promulgation of the bull excommunicating Elizabeth in 1570 had not—as so many historians state—stiffened the morale of the Catholics. Large numbers of them were still attending the Prayer Book services when the priests from Douai came, and one of the immediate effects of their coming was that the incompatibility of those services with Catholic worship and belief was made plain. By the eighties and with the increased drive given to the movement by Fathers Persons and Campion, the religious situation and atmosphere had totally changed. There was a great religious movement which carried back thousands to an integral practice of the Faith so that we may say that there were probably more fervent Catholics in England in 1590 than there had been before the break with Rome in 1534.

What was the secret of this success? There was undoubtedly the renewed zeal of the clergy, a zeal that did not flinch before martyrdom, coupled with the gay brilliance and compelling eloquence of an Edmund Campion; there was too an anguished realization of what was at stake, which had hitherto been lacking; but above all there was the fact that the new priests, whether Jesuit or secular, had been prepared for their mission. First, there was the emphasis on Holy Scripture, so much the storm center of the conflict. "Once again (Dr.) Allen is an original. What first impresses one about the scheme of studies he devised (at Douai)—organised in a three-year course—is the immense importance given to the study of the text of Scripture." They are to have their Bible at their fingers' ends as the heretics do. "As to Scripture, there is a daily set lecture on the New Testament, twice a day a running commentary on the Old and New Testaments, chapter by chapter.[1] There are dictations of the texts around which the new controversies rage, with a note of the wrong interpretations, and of the arguments against these; there are weekly disputations on these texts, students set to defend the heretical position and, in turn, to criticise it; and twice every week a student gives an address on one or other of these texts, *as though speaking to persuade an audience of heretics*" (our italics). We are accordingly not surprised to learn that "at Douay there is to be much practice in preaching in English," and as "the main task of the missionary is to help the ordinary man," every possible care was taken "to make (him) *a good catechist* and a sound practical confessor. So he is formed on the catechism of Canisius, . . . and study of the so-called *Catechism of the Council of Trent* is urged upon him." Nor is formal theology neglected, and one of the features of the Douai school, in close association with Douai University—a stronghold of Thomism right up to the time of Challoner and Hornyold in the eighteenth century—is that theology was taught from St. Thomas: "We now teach scholastic theology chiefly from St. Thomas," Allen writes, thereby again declaring himself one of the new men, for Peter Lombard's reign as the inevitable introduction to the science was not yet ended. "There were two lectures daily, then, on the *Summa,* and once a week a disputation."[2]

All this may seem a little remote from the business of handing on the Faith to the people, but it serves to underline the fact that neither then nor now can we separate the preparation of the clergy

[1] They were fortunate not to be bothered by lengthy discussions of critical matters as we are, but Allen's method has much to commend it today.

[2] For all this, see Philip Hughes, *The Reformation in England*, III (New York: The Macmillan Company, 1954), 291 f.

from the practical matter of teaching the Faith to the people. What is more to our immediate purpose is that it was effective. The reaction of the government was immediate, and it was from the moment that they saw the Church was not to be allowed to die of inanition that an efficient system of persecution began to operate and rose to a dreadful crescendo of blood in the last decade of the century. Secondly, these priests laid the foundation of a faith that endured two centuries of persecution and began to form a type that we used to call "the old-fashioned Catholic," strong and reticent, solidly instructed, deeply pious, very manly.

Alongside the direct mission of the priests, and constantly supporting it, went the apostolate of the written word. No one who has not browsed among the shelves of one of our older Catholic libraries, such as those at Oscott, or St. Edmund's, Ware, or Ushaw, can have any idea of the volume of publication that took place from about 1565 onward, and it is not too much to say that the famous "Brag" of Edmund Campion (as fine a piece of prose as was written in the sixteenth century) and his equally famous *Decem Rationes* caused something like consternation in the ranks of the heretics who, be it noted, were the party in power with a stranglehold on the press. In the circumstances it may be wondered how the books were distributed; and we know that men, both priests and laymen, were imprisoned and martyred for carrying them. A contemporary letter gives a vivid picture. A priest writing to Father Agazzari in Rome in 1581 says:

There has been this year quite a battle of books, and the heretics have not been able to publish anything without its being immediately controverted. Charke and Hanmer, Calvinist ministers, first wrote against Campion, making a strange hash of the life of Ignatius Loyola in particular; but within ten days there appeared in print a short review by an unknown author [Persons' Censure] which convicted them of so many lies that both they and their followers were heartily ashamed of themselves: . . . So much for the books, which are as difficult and dangerous to publish as to print. The way is, all of them are taken to London before any is published, and then they are distributed by hundreds or fifties to the priests, so that they may be published all together in all parts of the realm. And the next day, when the pursuivants usually begin to search the Catholics' houses, it is too late; for during the night the young gentlemen have introduced copies into the houses, shops, and mansions of the heretics, and even into the court, and the stalls in the streets, so that Catholics alone cannot be accused of possessing them.[3]

The most dramatic publication of this sort was that of Campion's *Decem Rationes*, which the members of the University of Oxford found in their stalls at St. Mary's when they came there one fine summer morning for Commencement.

Naturally, most of this literature was of the controversial sort, but other needs were not neglected. The *Rheims* New Testament was issued in 1582, and it is interesting to find Father Persons asking Dr. Allen for "three or four thousand or more of the Testaments," even before they were published.[4] Obviously all these will not have been used merely for "dumping" on the heretics—although the appearance of the Rheims New Testament led to more controversy—but largely for distribution among the people. Most of the people the missionary priests won back to the Church were educated, both able and willing to read Catholic books. This is shown by the composition of many an old Catholic library (for example, that at Little Malvern Court, Worcestershire), where there was almost invariably a copy of the Rheims New Testament and later of the Douai Old Testament, as well as a large if miscellaneous collection of controversial literature and of spiritual books. The libraries of some of the greater landed gentry show a tendency to keep up with continental literature too in Latin, French and Italian. This habit continued until the end of the eighteenth century as can be seen from the library of the Throckmortons at Coughton Court and the fragments that remain at Harvington Hall, Worcestershire. The squire bought series of volumes of sermons, of a rather moralizing French sort, and possibly even breviaries, no doubt for the use of his chaplains. It was not until later that a tendency toward insularity set in.

It may be asked at this point, Was this bookish instruction,

[3] Richard Simpson, *Edmund Campion* (London: J. Hodges, 1896), pp. 287 f., 289 f.
[4] *Ibid.*, p. 294.

available after all only to the learned few, backed up by the living word? Although the evidence is scanty from the nature of the case, we can answer in the affirmative. Campion, whose eloquence rang through the country, was caught all but preaching his sermon on the Sunday gospel (Ninth after Pentecost, our Lord's lament over Jerusalem), and his capture the next day was due to the inordinate desire of the pious women in the Yate household to hear him yet again. Crowds flocked to hear him at great peril of their lives, and "people were so greedy of hearing that very many persons of quality spent whole nights in the neighbouring barns, so that they might be early at the place next day"; and Father Henry More, S.J., writing nearly a hundred years later (in his *Historia Provinciae Anglicanae Societatis Jesu*, St. Omers, 1660, p. 76), records that in the North, Campion's sermons on the *Hail Mary*, on the *Ten Lepers*, on the *King that Went on a Journey*, on the *Last Judgment* and others were remembered by the people. And again, Simpson quotes More to the effect that, "He (Campion) preached daily." [5]

Perhaps this was exceptional, and there is no doubt that a movement of spiritual revival swept through the country at the coming of the missionary priests, but until much later when the mood had settled down into one of just enduring, the same will have been done by all priests.

But if we are to understand how this and other instruction was given, we must look at the physical conditions that prevailed. For these were decisive to a large extent of the methods that could be pursued.

The one dominant feature of all post-Reformation history is that the Faith was maintained and saved in the large country houses of the landed gentry. Without their assistance the Faith would certainly have died. As we have said, after 1559 all parish organization came to an end. There were no churches, no bishops, no parish schools; no lay-catechist movement was possible. "Churches" became house-churches, as in the earliest days at Jerusalem and Rome, and the whole physical framework of church life was that of the country house. This was not quite so revolutionary as it would be

---

[5] *Ibid.,* p. 266.

today, for the gentry who were lords of the manor and who enjoyed an enormous prestige in their countrysides were the centers of life and leadership; their estates were largely self-contained; and the people, small farmers, laborers and the rest, naturally looked to the Big House for spiritual and material aid. To a great extent, what the master was, that was his man; and we know that when in the depressing years of the eighteenth century Catholic families died out or apostatized, as they occasionally did, the Faith died in those parts too. There were a few exceptions: the embassy chapels of the Catholic powers provided Mass at least for those in or near London who could get to them; and after the extreme danger was over, they formed centers that gave some faint semblance of parish life, though this did not take place until the eighteenth century. Two or three chapels survived, notably that at Stonor Park in Oxfordshire where Mass has been said since the fourteenth century, but they were family chapels supported by the lord of the manor. The priest was the private servant of the house and his status was that of a private chaplain. What pastoral work he did outside the house was conditioned by his zeal and the danger of the times and place, which after the death of Queen Elizabeth varied considerably. Private chaplains and tutors were of course quite common in the great houses during the whole of our period, and in Catholic houses the priest was retained as the tutor of the boys of the family. We have a moving picture of his activity in the person of Gother, the author of a very famous series of meditations, who instructed the young Challoner at Warkworth Castle near Banbury where he was chaplain, and received him and his widowed mother into the Church. Later he was instrumental in sending him to Douai and thus had some part in providing the Church in England with its most famous Vicar-Apostolic.

This throws light on another aspect of the instruction. The wife of Mr. Holman, the owner of the house, was the Lady Anastasia, daughter of the Viscount Stafford who had been martyred for the Faith in 1680, less than twenty-five years before. The atmosphere was thus redolent of the vital struggle for the Faith which had been going on since 1570. However formal and dry the schemes of instruction may seem on paper, they were humanized by the religious atmosphere in which they were given. The memories of the martyrs, the central importance of the Mass, celebrated in secret, the crucial importance of the Church which stood out as the rampart against a dominant heresy, all these things served to make the instruction actual and lively. In addition, the physical framework was domestic and not scholastic. The chaplain instructed the children of the house, giving special attention to the boys; but he would, too, take the children of the surrounding farms and cottages, as like as not with the children of the house, for in these days boys of the squire and of the local farmers often attended the same local grammar school and there was not quite the same distinction of classes that grew up when the great public schools of the nineteenth century were reformed or founded. But the instruction of the girls was not less important in the sense that what they received from their chaplain they passed on to the local children whom they visited in their own homes. Until the end of the nineteenth century, and in some places beyond, the lady of the Big House and her daughters were not only the chief "district nurses" and general helpers of the poor of the district; they were also the chief and sometimes the only catechists. They taught the little ones their catechism, and although a certain respect separated the children from them we know that the relationship was usually one of great kindness and warmth.

This is all very important in view of the rather arid mental food that the catechisms provided. The atmosphere was at any rate a human and natural one. That this system worked is shown by the strong Faith of these Penal-Days Catholics who were able to resist the overwhelmingly Protestant social pressure of the times. These old-fashioned Catholics were stanch in the Faith, strongly sacramental in practice, with a deep reverence for God and all that concerned Him. The best of them would spend three days in preparation for holy communion and three days afterward in thanksgiving. Some of them were by no means strangers to mental prayer. But this is to anticipate a little, for all this was characteristic of the "*Garden of the Soul* Catholics" formed by Challoner, though we may remark that he discovered the need already existing and his books sold well because it did.

We should not of course forget the colleges on the Continent from which almost all of our great schools of today, such as Stonyhurst, Downside, Ampleforth, English Douai, Ushaw, and to some extent St. Edmund's, Ware, derive. The English College at Douai, the first and the best known, founded by Dr. Allen, was not intended for a school at all; but it is interesting to observe in the college diary of the sixteenth century that young men, usually of good family, frequently visited the college for a sort of refresher course, often after they had been reconciled to the Church. As toward the end of the century it became apparent that chances of any rapid conversion of England were remote, the greater families sent over their sons in secret and at great peril (the penalties for so doing were severe), to be educated there. It meant years of separation for boys and parents, but they knew that it was only in this way that their boys could be educated at all and brought up in the Faith.

It was thus that was begun a tradition of English education that continues to this day: students for the priesthood were educated alongside lay boys to the great benefit of both. Poor boy and rich boy lived together for all their most formative years and learned respect and toleration. Some of the most illustrious names of England are to be found in the roll of the English College, Douai. The Benedictines had their college at Douai too, and the Jesuits their famous one at St. Omer's, the ancestor of Stonyhurst. The tradition in these schools was firmly, even enthusiastically, English. By present-day standards the discipline was rigorous and the curriculum narrow, but they produced fine types of men who for the most part weathered the storm of persecution and later stood up to the social ostracism of the eighteenth century very well.

Our period was above all the age of the catechism. Luther had won over thousands of people with his hymns and his catechisms. These called forth those of St. Peter Canisius, and Bellarmine had written his before the end of the century. The Anglican Catechism which is included in the Book of Common Prayer had been in circulation since 1549.[6] It is not surprising then that there was a certain amount of activity in catechism-making among the exiled Catholics. The first was compiled by Dr. Laurence Vaux, one of the first to resist the religious changes of Elizabeth, a learned man and a very congenial character.[7] It was called *A Catechisme of Christian Doctrine necessarie for Children and ignorante people, etc.*, and it first appeared in 1562, went into a second edition and a third in 1604.[8] He expressly says (p. 7) that he has taken something from Canisius.

The second of the three principal English Catechisms is the *Abridgement of Christian Doctrine* which came to be known as the *Doway Catechism.* It had a very long life and has much influenced our current catechism. Whether it was ever in use at Douai is uncertain (though we may assume that it was—it was certainly used at Standon Lordship in the eighteenth century), but it was written by a Douai priest, Henry Turberville, who came of a Staffordshire family, and was published "some time before 1649—the exact date of the first edition is not clear." The striking feature of this catechism was that it

seems to be an original one, that is, it was not a mere translation or adaptation of any previous catechism. True it is that he followed Bellarmine's order throughout and used him in several parts of his catechism especially in the early questions which are clearly based on Bellarmine, but on the whole his obligations to any previous catechism do not seem to have been great.[9]

Another catechism which appeared toward the end of the seventeenth century was an abridgement of the *Doway Catechism* and was probably compiled by Gother. It thus provides a link with the last catechism, composed by Challoner, *An Abridgement of Chris-*

---

[6] Though the section on the sacraments was not added until 1604. See Hastings' *Encyclopedia of Religion and Ethics,* III, 252.

[7] For details, see Hughes, *op. cit.,* pp. 248 ff., and the introduction to the edition of his catechism we are to quote.

[8] See Laurence Vaux, *A Catechisme of Christian Doctrine* (Manchester: Printed for the Chetham Society, New Series, 4, 1885), ed. by T. G. Law.

[9] These quotations are taken from a comprehensive article on the history of the English Catechism, by Dom J. S. Marron, O.S.B., in *The Sower,* 125 (Oct.–Dec., 1937).

tian Doctrine (1772). The whole period, then, was marked by a good deal of activity in the making of catechisms, and Dr. Allen's intention that the Douai priests should be good catechists was to that extent fulfilled. Further, it reveals a constant concern that such catechisms should be in accord with the changing needs of the times. These Douai priests who are sometimes regarded as ultra-conservative (as in many ways they were) had no notion that a catechism written in the sixteenth century was good enough for, say, the eighteenth. That outlook indeed inspired almost all Challoner's literary work.

Before passing on to consider some other literature of the sixteenth century and the work of Challoner, it will be of interest to examine briefly the content of Vaux's catechism. Catholic catechisms are usually regarded as mere counterblasts to the Protestant catechisms of the time, and those who write without knowledge of their contents usually say that they were filled with anti-Protestant controversy and conditioned by that outlook. Of neither Vaux's nor Challoner's catechisms is this entirely true. The first thing that strikes one about Vaux's is that it is more medieval in tone than anything else. His catechism rather looks back to the simple medieval catechisms or summaries of things to be believed and done than to the rigid statements of doctrine that became characteristic of a later age. He adopts, it is true, the Augustinian plan basing his material on faith, hope and charity, but his handling of it reveals another, that may be called the classical plan, of Creed, Our Father and sacraments. This, with its lists of virtues and sins (the addition of the later Middle Ages), takes us back to the earliest catechesis of the Church, to the liturgical pattern, when catechumens were instructed in church on the Creed and the Our Father, and after baptism on the sacraments. In his pattern, then, Vaux was thoroughly traditional.

He says (p. 10) that he bases his material on faith, hope and charity, the sacraments and "the offices of Christian righteousness." But faith deals with the things to be believed, so under that comes the Creed; hope, with what we are to look for, hence in this place the Our Father; and under charity he considers the ten commandments. Grace is given by the sacraments so they are dealt with together. By the Christian offices we are taught "to decline from evil and do good." Almost the only suggestion that there is a major theological conflict raging comes in an appendix (pp. 95 ff.) which is directed against the new heresies.

His section on the Creed consists rather of a commentary than of a series of abstract statements. The language is exact but remains human, and because it is the language of the sixteenth century it is vigorous and full of sap. As for example: "We must believe in God the Father almighty, the first person in the Trynitye, the Creator and maker of heaven and earth, and of all creatures therein, both visible and invisible." The answer on the Incarnation is a little more difficult but is closer to the great conciliar definitions than to the theological textbook. The author nowhere uses the word "supernatural" but expresses the concept perfectly in, for instance, his answer on hope: "Hope is a virtue *from God above*,[10] whereby we loke for the goodness of our salvation and everlasting lyfe with a sure trust." (I would submit that this is even *theologically* more accurate than most of the definitions of that virtue given in modern catechisms.)

A feature of his treatment of baptism and confirmation is that he gives a commentary on the ceremonies of those sacraments, quite in line with the best modern practice. We must remember that the use of ceremonies was one of the Catholic practices repudiated with scorn by the reformers, and so some account of them was necessary; but this was no mere anti-reform polemic. Vaux managed to use the occasion to fill out his doctrine.

His section on the Eucharist is remarkable for having virtually no reference to it as a sacrifice. Here he reflects the deep English devotion to the Real Presence and looks back rather to the Middle Ages than to his own time, although in all the anguished controversy that went on in the reign of Edward VI the concern of the Catholic party to establish the fact of the Real Presence is very striking. Rightly they saw that if this were not established there could be no

[10] Our italics.

question of sacrifice. But Dr. Vaux supplies the need in a long and interesting appendix, "Concerninge the Holy Ceremonies of God's Church" (pp. 78–94), in which his teaching on the sacrificial aspect of the Eucharist is conveyed in his treatment of the symbolism of the altar. In some ways we have not advanced much in that respect since his time. There are still to be found those who try to teach the Mass without reference to the liturgy.

This necessarily brief account of the Vaux catechism gives no notion of the charm of the little book. Its brevity, its sureness of doctrinal touch, its freedom from the polemical spirit in an age that was riddled with controversy, the living language in which his doctrine is dressed and the achievement of a robust simplicity without condescension give a strange satisfaction which we can be sure was felt by those children and "ignorante people" who first used it.

No doubt it was incomplete in some respects, and that will account for the issue of the *Doway Catechism* some fifty years later. This with its *Abstract* spanned the next hundred years or more until Challoner's catechism of 1772.

Before we go on to consider Challoner's great work, we shall look briefly at some other literature that was available to the oppressed Catholics of the sixteenth and seventeenth centuries.

No doubt someone will one day write an account of the spiritual literature of English recusant writers, Robert Persons, Benet of Canfield (though he has been largely explored), and of Dom Augustine Baker, to mention only the few well-known ones. It does not concern us directly here, though much of it *was* a means of instruction, for it kept before a number of people "the deeper things of God."

In spite of the pressing needs of controversy (which by the beginning of the seventeenth century had, unfortunately, become domestic controversy—the Archpriest affair), and in spite of the difficulties of printing and importing books—a criminal offense— the hard-pressed priests of the time managed to keep their people supplied with prayer books, books of devotion and spiritual literature. In all the old Catholic libraries of England there are pathetic little Missals that were printed for the missionary priests to carry with them on their journeys. Most of them contained but three or four Masses with the Ordinary and the Canon.[11]

Of the prayer books provided for the people it is less easy to speak, for these were of their nature "consumable." I have handled one such, still in private possession at Stone, Staffordshire. A tiny volume, it is traditional in pattern, deriving from the *Layfolks' Prymers* of the late Middle Ages. It contains four or five "little Offices," of Our Lady, of Corpus Christi, and of the Holy Cross. The hymns are translated into vigorous if rugged verse suggestive of the faith and character of those who used it. A similar book was the *Jesus Mattens*, "Certayne sweete prayers of the glorious name of Jesus, commonly called, Jesus Mattens, with the Howers [hours] thereto belonging." [12] There were many editions of the Jesus Psalter, and among others we find the following: *Certayne devout Meditations*, Douai, 1576, strongly Christocentric; in the same year, *A breefe Directory and playne way howe to say the Rosary of our blessed Lady;* finally we may mention the *Psalter of St. Hierome,* a sort of anthology of passages from the psalms.[13] It is clear that the orientation was Christocentric and that the books were redolent of Scripture, strongly traditional.

The book however that spanned the centuries was Father Persons' *Christian Directory*. This went into innumerable editions, and had as great a vogue with the Protestants as with Catholics. A certain Dr. Bunny bowdlerized it, removing from it all offensive "popery," and between the years 1584 and 1600 it ran into nine issues. This wanton handling of his work led Persons to issue his second edition in 1586 in which he added further matter. (It had first appeared in Rouen in 1582.) The book went on being re-edited at least as late as 1696, the date of the copy in my possession. At its

[11] There is one preserved at the presbytery at Harvington Hall, Worcestershire, that is a complete Missal, printed by Plantin in 1614, beautifully bound in vellum, and containing the proper collect of St. Ignatius before his feast was inserted in the universal calendar. This would show that it was used by the Jesuit missionaries who were numerous in the county.

[12] See A. C. Southern, *Elizabethan Recusant Prose, 1559–1582* (London: Sands, 1950), p. 226.

[13] *Ibid.*, pp. 207, 214, 223.

inception it was an original work and owed much to an Italian treatise called *The Exercise of a Christian Life*,[14] but by the time Persons had finished with it, it was a completely different thing. It is very long (792 pages in the 1696 edition, without the appendix), and contains much more than a consideration of the Four Last Things which it is its purpose to do. It is strongly exhortatory, as we should expect, but the author ranges over a wide field. Its instructional value is in parts great. There is constant quotation of and reference to Holy Scripture, the great story of salvation from the Old Testament to the New is ever before the eye of the reader, and surprisingly enough the whole of a long chapter (II) is devoted to proofs for the existence of God. This was added to the 1585 edition and may be a reflection of the growing infidelity of the Elizabethan court.

The general tone is stern, even gloomy, but this is partly redeemed by the liveliness of the observation and the concrete vigor of the English. As Dr. Southern remarks, it is "very much after the manner of the medieval sermon." [15] Its importance is that it was read for over a hundred years by a great number of people and so had a formative influence. It was of the Counter-Reform, if you like, but it was also strongly traditional and forms a link between medieval piety and the more flamboyant spirit of the seventeenth century. It may also be a link with the age of Challoner, for there are one or two indications in *Think Well On't* by the latter that he is providing an up-to-date *Christian Directory*. If so, this is characteristic of most of Challoner's work.

Before we go on to consider Challoner's contribution, we shall say a word about two other writers, one, Alban Butler, whose name is known throughout the English-speaking Catholic world, and the other a man who is largely forgotten. Right from the beginning, Allen and his circle had shown a concern for history, and Thomas Stapleton, an older contemporary of Allen's, a man of vast learning and one of the most considerable theologians of his time, had translated the Venerable Bede's *History of the English People*. A

[14] *Ibid.*, p. 183.
[15] *Ibid.*, p. 187.

sense of the past and its importance for the Catholic case was strong
with these men, and we can say that it was typical of the missionary
clergy. Combined with this was a veneration for the saints, especially of the old saints of England. Dr. Alban Butler sought to provide for this need by his very successful *Lives of the Saints* which
have been read by countless thousands of Catholics from that day
to this and have run into so many and so various editions that one
supposes they are uncountable. What Butler did to round out the
religious knowledge of his and subsequent generations it is impossible to say, but that that influence was very great is undeniable.
It is one of the wonders of the age that these priests, poor, without
prestige or position, with the very instruments of their trade as
writers hard to come by, should not only have supplied the needs of
their own countrymen but have fed a whole portion of the Church
with their learning and doctrine.

The other writer was John Hornyold, a younger contemporary of
Challoner's, and eventually Vicar Apostolic of the Midland District
(died 1778). He came of a very ancient family whose seat was at
Blackmore Park, near Worcester. There was something oaken about
Hornyold, very English, reticent, overdiffident, but his reserve cov-
ered a great zeal and warmth of piety. He was in some ways a
more typical Penal-Days bishop than Challoner, more withdrawn,
shunning the light of public life, and for all his ancient lineage,
very humble. He wrote two little books that are now all but forgotten and certainly never read. They are very much worth the
opening, for they are solid doctrine expressed in a straightforward,
manly sort of English, the whole lit with the glow of a genuine
piety. For our purpose their importance is that they are instructional
works. The first was *The Decalogue Explained* in which he exploits
all the traditional doctrine connected with the commandments, at
least since the sixteenth century. They are learned, and one is
surprised to find reference to St. Thomas and the Fathers. Under the
third commandment he deals with the Mass as sacrifice and the way
the people should assist at it. Many of the things he has to say would
more likely be found in a liturgical review nowadays than in a
study of the ten commandments. It is but one more indication of
the firm grasp these men and the people whom they instructed so

well had of the Mass and much that we call the liturgy nowadays.
For even if not many read these two little books of Hornyold's, they
remain significant as evidence of what the best priests of this time
preached.

The second book he wrote is called *The Sacraments Explained*,
(*In Twenty Discourses*), By J. . . . H. . . . (Dublin, 1770). The
choice of subject is again typical, something at once practical and
central. The pattern of each section is the same: first a theological
treatment and proof of the sacrament, in which liberal use is made
of the Fathers; then what might be called the moral theology of the
sacrament, and finally its effects and warm recommendations on
its use and value. It is in this last part that the piety of the man is
revealed. Moreover, his catechetical method is sure; he illustrates
his material with vivid, concrete examples as he goes along. There
is a liberal use of Holy Scripture not merely as "proofs" but as
illustrations and reinforcement of his observations and arguments
to such an extent that the book is a mosaic of Scripture texts. Nor
is he any stranger to what is called typology today. In developing
St. Paul's "We are buried with Christ . . ." (Rom. 6) he writes,
"We have, dear Christians, a Figure of this in *Naaman* the leprous
Prince of Syria, who washing himself in the Waters of Jordan, as
the Prophet had prescribed him to do, he came forth so clean, and
perfectly cured, that the Scripture says, *His Flesh was restored as
the Flesh of a little Child*" (p. 18). If this might seem but a fanciful
interpretation, in the next paragraph he immediately recurs to the
typology of Scripture itself and quotes I Pet. 3, 21, about the Ark's
being a figure of baptism, and the passage of the Israelites through
the Red Sea (I Cor. 10, 2) "as a Figure of our passing the waters
of Baptism to our desired Rest in Glory" (*ibid.*). In his treatment
of the Eucharist he makes full use of Old Testament types such as
the Paschal Lamb. As for liturgy, his instruction on the ceremonies
of baptism would do credit to some of the exponents of that difficult art today (pp. 12–15). Finally, here is an example of his style
as a catechist:

The Husbandman watereth his Trees, to the End they may bear fruit, but
the barren Trees he casts into the Fire; in like Manner God watereth
Man with the saving Waters of Baptism, to the End that he produce the

Fruit of good Works; but if he will not produce them, he delivers him up, being void of Fruit, to the Flames of Hell.

This may sound a little grim, but it is very close to the Scriptures.[16]

If ever the hope of Cardinal Allen that his priests should be good catechists was fulfilled, it was fulfilled in Richard Challoner. He was learned, holding the degree in divinity of Douai University; he was clear in exposition; his work was the fruit of a wide knowledge of people and of his priestly zeal to save their souls. He was more. He was a great bishop, tireless in his pastoral work, and farseeing. What he built, he built to last. The measure of his greatness is that the Church in England is still living off his heritage. For all this to have been achieved in the darkest time of the Penal Days when it seemed folly even to hope comes close to a miracle, and it is no wonder that many are now praying for his canonization.

Challoner was a catechist both on the practical level and as a writer. He taught his people tirelessly not as a bishop from the height of a throne but in the humblest of circumstances. As a teacher he went down to the people, and we must think of him in surroundings that few bishops at any time have taught in. The most famous picture is that of the venerable bishop in a hired room of an inn, The Ship (in Lincoln's Inn Fields), preaching to his congregation round a table with their pots of beer before them. Admission could only be obtained by a password. A burly Irishman kept the door, and the bolts were shot as soon as all the people had arrived. In an even more secret garret he would say Mass, but on Sundays only, of course. (He would say Mass during the week in his own lodgings.)

His other great contribution, not only to religious teaching but to Catholic education as a whole, was the foundation of two schools which still flourish and where his spirit is kept alive: Standon Lordship which became St. Edmund's, Ware, and Sedgeley Park which is now at Cotton in Staffordshire. Rightly foreseeing that the col-

[16] It should be remarked that some contemporaries said that Hornyold's chaplain, Mr. Richmond, had a good deal to do with the writing of the books. It may be so, at least to the extent that Richmond supplied many of the patristic and learned references, but the bishop was too honest a man to let a book go out over his name which he had not written.

leges on the Continent might one day have to be closed—as they were within twenty years of his death—and that in any case it was difficult for middle-class families to send their boys abroad, he made provision for the eventuality with these two schools which have nobly served his purpose.

Turning now to his writings, one is struck by the fact that for him catechetics had the widest connotation. He sought to provide for the entire religious needs of the people and he seems to sum up in his work all the great tradition that had gone before him. Scripture, doctrine, history, spiritual reading, meditation, liturgy (in however narrow a sense) and catechism, all were the subjects of his many books. In fact one of the patterns one can detect in his work is the desire to give his people up-to-date translations and editions of well-known and much used books. This was certainly the inspiration of his edition of the Bible, and the rest of his work corresponds almost book for book with what was written in the sixteenth and seventeenth centuries.

The scope of his work is so wide that one can only give some idea of his catechetical activity by setting out in a sort of *catalogue raisonné* some of his principal books. (The dates in the brackets are those of the first editions.)

As well as his revision (1750) of the whole Bible which was the sole Catholic version in use in England until that of Monsignor Knox's, there are two editions of the New Testament that we owe to him. Other little books on the Bible are his *Morality of the Bible* (1762) and two Abstracts of the Old and New Testaments (1767).

His theological output was mostly controversial, but we may note *A Profession of Catholic Faith* (a commentary on the Creed of Pius IV [1732]) and *The Catholick Christian instructed in the Sacraments, Sacrifice, Ceremonies and Observances of the Church* (1737), a compendious title that sufficiently describes the book.

Of his history we may mention *Britannia Sancta*, one of his few failures, which sought to revive devotion to the ancient saints of the British Isles—a book that was at once the expression of Challoner's piety and patriotism. There was a little book on early Church history, *The City of God of the New Testament* (1760); but his great work was a monument to his devotion to the English Martyrs and of his filial piety to his Alma Mater, Douai: *Memoirs of Missionary Priests* (1741–1742). This was genuine research work in which he had assistants. It is still a source book for the period in spite of the considerable quantity of research that has been done on the subject in modern times. The latest edition was that of 1924, edited by Father J. H. Pollen, S.J.

His writings on the spiritual life form the major part of his output and reveal where his heart lay. His first book was *Think Well On't* (1728), which went on being read all through the nineteenth century. It starts very similarly to Persons' *Christian Directory* (Of Consideration, etc.) and may have been intended as a shorter substitute for that rather cumbersome work. He made new translations of the *Following of Christ* (1737), still the one most commonly used by Catholics, and of *St. Augustine's Confessions* (1739) which was no doubt intended to supersede the now old translation of Tobie Mathew of the early seventeenth century. He compiled a Life of the Holy Mother, St. Teresa (1757), from her writings, and edited his spiritual father's writings, Gother's *Spiritual Works* (1746?), thus giving them currency for another century. The book by which he is best known is the famous *Meditations for Every Day in the Year* (1754). It ran into seventeen editions between that year and 1880 and was republished in more recent times. If anyone would know the soul of Challoner he should read this book, and if anyone would know the quality of the best Catholics who came after Challoner he will find the key to it here. The tone of the meditations is sane and balanced, the doctrinal content is marked, and if to the modern mood some of them might seem a little austere, they are redeemed by a glow of virile yet tender piety. Something of the *teaching* power of the book and its fundamentally liturgical character can be gleaned from the following excellent summary by Canon E. Burton:

The plan of the book is simplicity itself. After a brief preface explaining the nature of mental prayer, the author gives for each day in the year a meditation which consists of three points and a conclusion. He so arranges his subject matter that he blends a summary of Christian doc-

trine, both dogmatic and moral, with the cycle of mysteries commemo-
rated on the chief festivals. Thus for January and February he gives
preliminary meditations on the service of God and the evil of sin, introducing, as occasion serves, the Epiphany, the Baptism of Our Lord and
His first Miracle. From the 19th of February he ceases to observe the
day of the month, and inserts a series which follows the Calendar of the
Church from Ash Wednesday until the Octave of Corpus Christi is closed.
These meditations for Lent, Paschal Time and Whitsuntide treat of the
Passion, Death and Resurrection of Our Lord, the Descent of the Holy
Ghost and the mystery of the Blessed Sacrament. As a background to this
pageant of the Redemption, he chooses the subjects of fasting, works of
mercy, prayer, the three theological virtues of faith, hope and charity,
devoting special attention under the last heading to his favourite subject,
Divine Love. He also gives some meditations on the Lord's Prayer. Incidentally, he treats of Baptism during Low week and of confirmation
during the Octave of Pentecost. After the Octave of Corpus Christi, he
reverts once more to the days of the month, beginning with the 14th of
June, from which date until the end of the month he treats of the Holy
Eucharist as a sacrifice and of the Sacrament of Penance.[17]

These meditations were intended for the laity and though no doubt
the clergy used them a good deal, the present writer can remember
old Catholics who used them regularly, as their forefathers had.
That is why the book had so formative an influence.

Perhaps some apology might seem necessary for the use of the
word "liturgical" in connexion with Challoner's work. The public
celebration of the liturgy had ceased in 1559, and neither Challoner
nor any other missionary priest knew anything like full liturgical
practice once they had left Douai. Yet liturgy is much more than
ceremonial and High Masses, and the very fact that the Mass and
the sacraments were at the heart of the Reformation controversy
and that hundreds of priests had given their lives for them inspired
a deep reverence for these things in the recusant Catholics. Certainly Challoner was only typical in his devotion to the Mass and
the sacraments, but in his endeavors to keep alive a spirit of liturgical worship he was exceptional. We note two or three little books
first: *An Appendix to the Ritual,* containing Instructions and Ex-

[17] Edwin H. Burton, *The Life and Times of Bishop Challoner,* I (London:
Longmans, Green, 1909), 346 f.

hortations proper to be made by Priests in the Administration of the
Sacraments and other Ecclesiastical Offices: according to the Spirit
of the Church and the Prescriptions of her Canons (1759). This
was printed with the *Ordo Administrandi Sacramenta* edited by
Challoner and published in the same year. These instructions which
were evidently, from the wording of the subtitle, inspired by the
decree of the Council of Trent on the subject, figured in subsequent
editions of the *Ordo* throughout the nineteenth century. The modern
liturgical movement has but recently rediscovered the relevance of
that decree and put it into practice. Another work of re-editing was
the *Manual of Prayers* (1758) which in its essence went back to the
medieval primers of prayer and which still remains the basis of the
only official manual of vernacular prayers in England. With his
perhaps most famous book, *The Garden of the Soul* (1740), Challoner forged the instrument with which a whole people was formed
in the ways of Christian prayer and living. The phrase, "A *Garden
of the Soul* Catholic," meaning one who is solid in the Faith, steady
in devotion and regular in the practice of his religion, is still heard
today.

The *Garden of the Soul* was much more than a prayerbook. It
was a manual of instruction and a guide to the spiritual life for
those living in the world. At the beginning there is a synopsis of
Catholic belief. The body of the book is built up round the Mass,
the reception of holy communion and preparation for confession.
The rite of benediction—then very rare in England—is carefully
described, in the best manner of the modern liturgist. There is a
collection of prayers, mostly taken from the psalms, a short series of
meditations, and "sentences" taken from the gospels for the most
part, which were intended to be pondered on. The tone of the book
is one of sobriety and it is markedly scriptural. Psalms are suggested
both for holy communion and for confession and it is a great pity
that later editions reduced or omitted these elements. As to the
Mass, it was forbidden in those days to publish translations of the
Canon, and Challoner led his people to take part in it by a series of
Devotions" that keep remarkably close to the action of the Mass.
That Challoner met a need with this book is shown by the thirty-

three editions that appeared up to the year 1824. After that it is impossible to count them, though unfortunately as the century wore on, the successive editions bore little likeness to the original. A reprint of the original edition (with one or two additions) appeared some thirty years ago.[18]

The book that has a special interest for the purpose of this paper is *An Abridgement of Christian Doctrine,* Revised and Enlarged by R. C., St. Omer, 1772 (Oscott College, Pamphlet Section, *post* 1620. This is probably a unique copy. Canon Burton says that he has never seen a copy except at Oscott).[19] Challoner's authorship of the *Abridgement* is not quite certain, though, according to Burton, all his biographers except Barnard "mention the fact that he did bring out a revised catechism, but they pass it over as a matter of small moment, not even recording the date." [20] However, there have never been any other claimants and we propose to call it Challoner's catechism.

Why "Revised and Enlarged"? There were already several catechisms in circulation, and Father Marron lists them:

At the beginning of the eighteenth century the catechisms we find advertised in the printers' lists are the *Doway Catechism,* price one shilling, the *Doway Abstract,* price threepence, and Bellarmine's *Short Christian Doctrine* price twopence. These are evidently the standard catechisms of the time. . . .[21]

He goes on:

A Short Abridgement of the Christian Doctrine (1742) . . . is mentioned again later, about the year 1753, in the rules for Standon School. . . . There it is stated that after breakfast the boys went to school "to say their lesson in some catechism suitable to their age and capacity: at first the *Doway Abstract* with Mr. Gother's Instruction for Children: secondly Fleury's Historical Catechism, thirdly, Turberville's etc., with the chief Master's approbation." *The Short Abridgement of Christian Doctrine,* it adds, "is indeed the catechism in use for children very young." It was

---

[18] All the bibliographical information on the foregoing books will be found in the appendix to Vol. II of Burton's great work, 323–39.
[19] *Ibid.,* II, 159, n. 2.
[20] *Loc. cit.*
[21] Marron, *art. cit.,* p. 201.

"exceedingly abbreviated and simplified and contained only a hundred questions." [22]

It was in all probability this catechism that Challoner "revised and enlarged," and his new catechism "contained about two hundred and ninety questions," though since he added an entirely new chapter called the Christian's *Rule of Life* which was meant to assist Christian living, it cannot be said that he overburdened his catechism with theological matter. As we shall see from an examination of its contents, he did not.

That he owed a great deal to previous catechisms, to Canisius (whose order in one or two matters he restored), to Bellarmine, and to the Doway books, goes without saying, but there was enough of his own to warrant our regarding it as a new catechism. In any case its future was more important than its past, as it undoubtedly forms the basis of our present catechism which used to be called *The Penny Catechism.* Indeed, a comparison with that catechism, revised, enlarged and "theologized" in the nineteenth century is all in favor of Challoner's little book. If we omit the sections on the Christian's *Rule of Life* and his *Daily Exercise,* the catechism is reasonably brief and the answers are remarkably concise. One of the most pleasing characteristics of the book is the terseness of the language (at times laconic, as, for example: "Why did [Christ] suffer? For our sins"), and its avoidance of technical terms. The word "supernatural," for instance, never occurs in the book. Whereas in our present catechism we are told that Faith is a supernatural gift of God, and so on (and to bemuse the children all the theological virtues *and grace* begin in the same way), Challoner was content with this: "(Faith) is to believe, without doubting, all that God teaches, because he is the very Truth and cannot deceive, nor be deceived" (this last phrase coming, says Marron, from the Turberville Catechism). He immediately follows this up with the completely satisfying answer that we are to know what it is that God teaches, "From the testimony of the Catholic Church."

The pattern of the catechism is traditional: an introduction about

---

[22] *Loc. cit.* We may note here that the principle of graded catechisms was recognized in fact at this time and that whereas in modern times the tendency has been to lengthen catechisms, the constant tendency from the sixteenth century onward—the classical age of catechism-making—was toward brevity.

God and ourselves who are made as "to his own image and likeness," the Creed (prefaced with the above question on Faith), the Our Father (prayer), the ten commandments, the sacraments, and the "medieval" lists of virtues, vices, beatitudes, and so on. Finally come the Rule of Life and the Daily Exercise.

As an example of the avoidance of technical terms we take the answer to the question, What is God? "He is the Maker and Lord of Heaven and Earth." An early nineteenth century hand has over-written this, "God is a spirit, the Creator and Sovereign Lord of all things." The itch for theology had begun and was to end with this metaphysical answer which is no doubt the work of the nineteenth century revisers: "God is the supreme Spirit, who alone exists of himself, and is infinite in all perfections." Catechism reform has gone a long way to come back home to a reasonable and biblical simplicity. Challoner's answer finds its closest parallel in the new Dutch Catechism. (In one of his questions there seems to be a curious confusion of wording: "Is there but one God? *No;* there is but one God.")

The questions on the Incarnation are theologically exact and uncomplicated, looking back rather to Vaux's catechism than forward to the brain-teasers of our present one: "What do you believe of Jesus Christ? I believe he is the Son of God, the second Person of the blessed Trinity, true God and true Man." The nineteenth century revisers divided the matter of this answer into several answers and produced questions that have been notoriously catch-questions for generations. They elected to formulate two questions much the same in wording: "Why is Jesus Christ truly God?" (*Ans.* "Because he has one and the same nature with God the Father"); and "Why is Jesus Christ truly man?" (*Ans.* "Because he has the nature of man, having a body and soul like ours.") These are just sufficiently similar to lead children astray, and we observe the tidying-up process that was the product of adult minds. Challoner makes the matter much more concrete and avoids the jingle: Jesus Christ is God, "Because he is the true and only Son of God the Father" (thus all the difficult business about "nature" disappears) "born of him before all ages and perfectly equal to him" (and here we hear the echo of Scripture). Jesus Christ is truly man because "he is the true

Son of the Blessed Virgin Mary and has a body and soul like us."

The section on the Redemption is more realistic than we should like nowadays: Christ "suffered a bloody sweat, whipping at the Pillar, crowning with thorns and the Carriage of his Cross." It goes on, laconically: "What else?" and the answer comes that he was nailed to the cross and died between two thieves. Then comes the answer about why we make the sign of the cross, thus restored to the place where St. Peter Canisius had put it.

Challoner's treatment of the Church is full enough, though of course there is nothing about the infallibility of the Pope (nor does the *word* occur in connection with the Church, which is merely said not to err), and there is surprisingly little about St. Peter or the Pope. In fact a reading of these Penal-Days catechisms dispels one or two illusions: they were not so controversial in spirit nor so concerned to rebut heresy as they are usually said to have been. The nineteenth century revisers seem to have been more preoccupied with such subjects. In one place Challoner's answer is less good than the current one: "What is the Church?" *Answer* (simply), "All the faithful under one Head"; we now say, "The union of all those who, etc." On the other hand his answer on the Communion of Saints leaves the door wide open for a lesson on the Mystical Body and seems to demand it: "Have we any Communion with the Saints in Heaven? Yes; we communicate with them, as our Fellow-members under the same Head, Jesus Christ, and we are helped by their Prayers." The question of the apostolicity of the Church was a crucial one all through these centuries, and the answer shows a certain anxiety for theological completeness: "The Church is Apostolical because she comes down by a perpetual succession from the Apostles of Christ; and has her Doctrine, her Orders and her Mission from them."

Under the Lord's Prayer we surprisingly get a question on Faith ("Faith alone will not save us," but this is balanced by an answer against Pelagianism: "We cannot do any good towards our own salvation"). An answer that is retained for the most part in our catechism affords an enlightening contrast in the matter of language: We should say the Hail Mary frequently "to put us in mind of the Incarnation of the Son of God"; Challoner characteristically has the more concrete, "To put us in mind of the Son of God being made Man for us"—less elegant but more suitable to children. Indeed, in all the revisions we can detect a desire for rhetoric, often with a jingle, which more than anything gives our catechism a faded air and is in no way an improvement on Challoner's work.

What will surprise some modern catechists is that Challoner nowhere has a definition of grace. Like the new German Catechism he would seem to have preferred to let a notion of it emerge from other doctrines (though of course there was no chance of including the matter in the *Lehrstücke* as in the German book). In the question of good works we have just quoted he says we can only be saved by grace, and in a subsequent answer he states simply that we obtain grace by prayer. That is all. It is not quite adequate. All he has to add to this is an answer in the section on the sacraments: "Whence have the sacraments the Power of giving Grace? From Christ's precious Blood"; which at any rate has the merit of connecting the sacraments directly with our Lord's redemptive work.

His treatment on the Mass is brief and he defines it simply as "the unbloody Sacrifice of the Body and Blood of Christ." This, if laconic, is exact, and would have given a teacher the right *point de départ*. Whether teachers ever took it is another matter. In fact we do not know how or if at all these questions were expounded, though they give the impression over and over again that they were not much more than pointers to a lesson. In the treatment of the Eucharist as a sacrament, there are two answers of interest. The age of the use of reason is described as "generally supposed to be about the Age of seven Years," and children are considered capable of receiving holy communion "when they are sufficiently capable of being instructed in the Mysteries, and of discerning the Body of our Lord." These words remind one of the statement of St. Pius X, and one can only suppose, since holy communion was not received before about twelve, that the age of reason and the ability to distinguish ordinary bread from our Lord's Body were in fact interpreted more strictly.

Challoner was a learned man. But he was before all else a catechist and he expended all his considerable powers to see that the

oppressed Catholics of his generation had the means of instruction
in their hands. For all his learning he loved simple ordinary folk,
and we see that love reflected in his catechism. How, when and
where, and who instructed children at this time, we hardly know,
but if Challoner used his own catechism, as no doubt he did, we
know that it will have been filled out with illustrations from Holy
Scripture, the lives of the saints and lessons on the rites of the
Church and their meaning. But, like all education of the time,
the memory will have been the most exercised faculty and all we
can say is that Challoner saw to it that the memories of children
should not be overburdened with indifferent matters, and the
words they had to learn were honest words, for the most part
meaningful words, that of themselves gave a certain life to their
learning.

The systems of religious instruction in the three centuries
we have been considering had defects that we can now very well
see: the catechism was divorced from Scripture and history, and
there was an excessive belief in the magic of formulas and words
to teach and inculcate the Faith. There was a constant process of
desiccation. But we forget too often that life was much simpler,
more domestic, and that for the poor, at any rate, schools were few
or non-existent, and what instruction there was—elementary enough
as it was—was given in the circumstances of natural human group-
ings: the family, in domestic chapels by the priest, by the ladies
of the Big House. Moreover, in France, Italy, Spain, parts of Germany and other places where the Reformation had made no permanent headway, all instruction was given in an atmosphere of
living religion, supported by a strong tradition of religious practice,
and filled out by all that the eye could see: the village church in
the midst of the village life, statues at the street corners, pilgrimages
and the rest of it. England was deprived of all this; yet so far as
they could, the missionary priests supplied the essential instruments
of religious instruction which were in no way inferior to what was
provided in countries where the people could live an integral
Catholic life.

4.

The Catechetical Method
of Saint Sulpice
·
Joseph Colomb, P.S.S.

"There are not two good methods of teaching catechism effectively. All experience has shown that basically and but for a few indifferent matters of detail, there is actually but one: that of Saint Sulpice. This method has become renowned the world over and has produced admirable results everywhere it has been put into use."[1]

These lines of Bishop Dupanloup make one smile a little, so self-assured are they, but they show clearly the extraordinary influence of the method of Saint Sulpice on the teaching of religion.[2] Not only were more than one hundred and fifty local catechetical centers in France affiliated[3] with Saint Sulpice during the second half of the nineteenth century, but in a sense every parish was inspired by the famous method, for the claim was made that it was the only one which saw to it that "catechism was taught effectively."

Whence came this extraordinary success? It is easy to discern an extrinsic cause; namely, the link between the parish of Saint Sulpice and the seminary there. The method was put into practice by the young ecclesiastical students preparing for the priesthood. It profited by the fervor of their first steps in the apostolate. Sub-

[1] Mgr. Felix Dupanloup, *L'oeuvre par excellence*, 3ème édition (Paris: C. Douniol, 1898), p. 124. The first edition is dated 1868. In translation it is called *The Ministry of Catechising* (London: Griffith Farran, 1890), 640 pp.

[2] It is somewhat surprising that M. l'Abbé Diebold, in the rapid but extremely interesting survey which he gives of the history of the catechism and the catechumenate in *Catéchisme et mission ouvrière* (Paris: Ed. du Cerf, 1950), Collection "Rencontres," No. 31, does not even cite by name the method of Saint Sulpice.

[3] We shall explain later what is to be understood by this affiliation. One such is to be found at Algiers, another at Madrid.

sequently called to occupy important posts in various dioceses, they would bring, along with a spirit of religion, the memory of these generous years. A bishop who in his youth had been a top-flight catechist at Saint Sulpice could not but wish to have his clergy profit by this valued experience.[4] This was the case with Bishop Dupanloup among many others. It is from his book, *The Ministry of Catechising*, quoted above, that one can best learn the spirit of the method of Saint Sulpice.

It would scarcely be fair to omit an explanation of the distinguishing features of this method. Above all else it was a "*method*." For the *ancien régime*—perhaps the nineteenth century even more so—had a passion for regulations of the sort that ensure a fixed tradition.[5] When one engages in a careful research into the numerous handbooks (called "customaries"), describing the method, it is dismaying to see with what painstaking care every detail is provided for. They describe magnificent machinery which leaves absolutely nothing to chance! To study the method of Saint Sulpice is to contemplate the whole civilization which it reflects. It was admirably suited to a world that appears very far removed from us today and that was probably dealt a death blow by the war of 1939–1945.

This method relied on the extremely fruitful proposition, "To teach catechism one does not merely *instruct* youngsters in Christianity but tries to *rear* them in Christianity."[6] This principle necessarily tends toward some departure from the highest ideal, simply because it is a far easier matter to instruct than to educate. The method of Saint Sulpice must take its share of blame in contributing to this decline because of the great importance it attaches to

[4] From 1747 to 1920, it develops, twenty-eight who became bishops were in charge of catechetics there.

[5] The last request for affiliation (Notre-Dame, Alençon, Orne) is dated June 18, 1899; the last letter addressed to affiliates is dated Feb. 17, 1901; the ninth and last edition of the "Directory of the Associates in the 'Catéchisme de Persévérance' of Saint Sulpice" (Paris: Presbytery of Saint Sulpice) is 1901. The method surely did not die with the first years of the twentieth century. Cardinal Feltin, who was in charge of the advanced classes (*catéchismes de persévérance*) in 1907 and 1908, and Cardinal Gerlier, director in 1920, would protest were we to affirm the contrary, but their period of expansion seems to have ended around 1900. Is not this small fact of history of some significance?

[6] Dupanloup, *op. cit.*, p. 2.

mere intellectual assimilation, but at its best its whole intent was
that it should be a means to rear or educate.

One final cause of its success needs to be alleged here: the deep
piety which characterized children formed under this method. That
fervor, which did not rule out a certain religious exaltation, was
the best propaganda for the method of Saint Sulpice.

In reading those pages in the *Life of Father Olier,* written by
Father Faillon, concerned with religious formation in the Parish
of Saint Sulpice, one cannot but admire the breadth of view which
the pastor seems to have had.[7] Let us first cite certain lines from
his memoirs in which the distinctiveness of his program is apparent.

I am beginning to understand the design of God for the reform of this
parish. He wants me first to aid the young by sharing Christian principles
with them and inculcating the fundamental maxims of salvation, this by
means of the young clerics from the seminary who will go out to bring
instruction to the remoter neighborhoods.[8]

These two original characteristics are noteworthy: the combining of the work of the seminary with that of catechizing, and the
sending of catechists out on mission.[9] The project was vigorously
launched and it was just as vigorously promoted. At the church
proper after vespers every Sunday there were two catechetical
sessions, one for boys and the other for girls. Out in the various
sections of the parish there were twelve instruction classes, each
attended by two priests or seminarians, of whom one had the special
charge of assembling the children by going through the streets with
a bell.[10] Besides this, weekly catechetical series—one at Easter time
lasting two months and another of six weeks at Pentecost—prepared a number for first communion. A third weekly series took
place before confirmation. During Lent, Father Olier saw to it
that three times a week the court pages and footboys had an op-

[7] Faillon, *Vie de M. Olier,* II (Paris: Poussielgue-Rusand, 1873, 4th ed.), 1–54.
[8] Jean-Jacques Olier, *Mémoires,* I, 122, cited by Faillon, *op. cit.,* pp. 48 f.
[9] This sending out on mission had already been practiced by St. Francis of
Sales, but something of Father Olier's great personal experience in the Auvergne
region and the west can be recognized here.
[10] This assembling process was not accomplished without a certain pressure,
against which a hand-written customary warns. We shall refer to it later.

portunity to make ready for their Paschal communion. There were still other catechism classes held in the burial crypts of the church "in which he was careful to grade the programming in accord with the age and instruction of the children, from the littlest and most ignorant to the farthest advanced." [11] The number of children who were receiving religious instruction at the one time in this parish, which happened to be the largest in Paris, is estimated at 4,000.

Father Olier's solicitude did not limit itself to children. Even beggars were prepared for their Easter communion by a thrice-weekly Lenten instruction. The old men used to have an instruction class every Friday throughout the year.[12] There was a class held in church for adults, more advanced in form than the children's but within the reach of simpler souls. Workingmen as well had a sermon of their own. In summer it took place every morning at four so that persons employed as laborers could be present at it. Lastly, so as to reach those who would not put themselves out, Father Olier sent out among families clerics armed with printed leaflets with illustrations meant to catch the eye. These sheets were to be affixed to the wall to help in the saying of prayers and the sanctification of all the day's actions.

The schools located in the parish deserve consideration too—there were ten of them at least. Father Olier saw to it that they were visited by inspectors twice a month. Every week one of the priests from the seminary went to them to give an instruction. Father Olier would bring the schoolteachers together, men and women, to keep them posted on their obligations. Furthermore, he used to see diligently to the formation of young women of the best type. These had to be very well instructed, for theirs was a truly missionary role with shut-ins.

Father Olier had a little "Catechism for the Use of Children in the Parish of Saint Sulpice" printed which was approved in 1652. One of his first disciples, Father de Lantages, produced at the

---

[11] Charles Hamel, *Histoire de l'Eglise Saint-Sulpice*, 2ième éd. (Paris: Gabalda, 1909), p. 81, citing Doncourt, *Rém. historiques*, Part 4, 616. Many of the details given here are drawn from Hamel's book.

[12] Following the custom of the time, material gifts rewarded faithful attendance.

direction of Bishop de Veny d'Arbouze of Clermont a "catechism of faith and Christian behavior" which went to no less than two volumes, 12° (1674 and 1679), of 444 and 972 pages. This work was still being brought out in 1887.

It is principally to Father Baüyn (1641–1696)—often referred to as Bauhin—that the rules and customs which make up the method of Saint Sulpice are attributable.

He conferred with Father Tronson and the oldest faculty members of the seminary over them. He established or perfected several practices of the catechism classes of Saint Sulpice, such as recitation from cards, merits and demerits, rewards, debates among the pupils, sitting in the front row, excuses for absence, monthly communions, sung vespers, hymns.[13]

The library of Saint Sulpice owns several books of customs in manuscript. The two oldest appear to be the following:

"Record of the Conferences Given Weekly to those Gentlemen Employed at Catechetics," in 12°, 377 pages. This volume has no date. On the flyleaf is written: "This book of customs incorporates the latest practice." It includes first some forty-three lectures on ways to teach catechism (pp. 1–264), then an "Examination of Conscience to Be Made with Children before their Confession" (pp. 265–76), "Directions for Catechizing for Confirmation" (pp. 277–320), "For First Communion" (pp. 321–68), and finally a note "On the Instructions to Be Given to Footboys during Lent" (pp. 369–77).

Whose work is this volume? It is hard to say, but it seems very old; it is much more direct and familiar than our other books of customs, and it is priceless for the study of the manners of those times. Let us cite two passages:

For pupils who are more difficult, as is ordinarily the case with boys, one can at need threaten them, take and lift them by force out of their

[13] This citation is taken from a manuscript life of Father Baüyn which Faillon gives in his anonymous *Histoires des catéchismes de Saint-Sulpice* (Paris, 1831), p. 24. One may also consult the account of Baüyn in L. Bertrand, *Bibliothèque Sulpicienne*, I, 105–08, or a handbook in manuscript of the catechists of Saint Sulpice which dates to the Restoration, and which is to be found at the presbytery of Saint-Sulpice, 50 rue de Vaugirard. The information on Fr. Baüyn is found there on p. 5.

benches so as to put them on their knees and chastise them; but rarely should one give them blows on the head with the roll book, punches, boxes on the ears, switchings or stripes, for such is not our custom, and the least measure of it will not be tolerated long, for good reasons. Not long ago one of our men struck a child severely, and as the teacher resumed his place the child said, "You mean thing! I'd make you pay for that if it wasn't for the respect I've got to give you in your job." [pp. 154 f.]

The other passage is found in the preparation for first communion (pp. 333 f.). It is the beginning of a paragraph entitled, "Of Children Who Merit Disapproval: Those Who Are Always Sleeping":

When a child sleeps all the time no reference should ever be made to it, but two classes before communion time children such as these should be told to bring their parents along, no reason being given, or else they will not make their communion. . . . When the parents come it is up to the catechism instructor to speak with them without letting on that sleepiness is the thing he is concerned over. He should ask the parents if they are pleased with their child's progress, and in the midst of many other questions, he should try to learn if the youngster sleeps alone, provided that he is sleeping apart from them by now, and whether he has a bed which is consistently his own, etc.

One senses a rather grim existence lurking behind these prescriptions, considerably more realistic as they are than the idyllic pictures which encumber the nineteenth century customaries.

The second manuscript work is dated 1720 and is entitled "Catéchisme de Saint-Sulpice." It is in square octavo and has 614 pages. It is dedicated particularly to giving model catechism classes, but the first pages are devoted to a description of "the order of catechism lessons and the rules to be observed in them." Notably, one finds a "method for rendering pupils intelligent and painstaking in the study of catechism" (pp. 7–18). Those lucky eighteenth century teachers!

During the Revolution catechetical instructions continued as regularly as possible. They were really interrupted only between September, 1712, and March, 1715, then for another two years starting with September 5, 1797. Religious life was organized anew after the Concordat of 1801, but the parish of Saint Sulpice had been dismembered: "losing some of its territory and much of its former splendor, it saw the number of its catechism classes diminish, which were now fixed at four. Two large groups were set up, one for children who had made their first communion and another for those preparing to make it soon. There were also two small classes for very young children." On November 18, 1804, Father Frayssinous solemnly reestablished the advanced classes (*l'association de la persévérance*).[14]

These first years of the nineteenth century were marked by an intense activity in the re-editing of catechetical manuals. The intention was to tie them in strongly with previous tradition. The texts preserved from the former period were reworked, altered and brought up to a single standard by the tireless Father Faillon (1800–1870). Still on hand in manuscript form are a customary of the Saint Sulpice catechists in quarto and a collection of parables and illustrations for the use of this same group, two volumes in quarto.[15]

Primarily it is Father Faillon to whom we are indebted for the basic efforts in the matter that interests us most. The form his labors took was an anonymous work which he published in 1832 under the title "Method of Saint Sulpice in Conducting Catechetical Classes."[16] From that point on the method was fixed; it

[14] *Histoire des catéchismes de Saint-Sulpice*, p. 146.

[15] L. Bertrand, *op. cit.*, II, 334. We have not been able to put our hand on these manuscripts. However, we have discovered at the parish a handbook of weekly catechizing which carries this note: "Paris, copied from the original manuscript by Père Charles, 1852"; and a similar customary from morning classes (first communion, girls) and a girls' advanced catechism, copied from the original in 1859. These texts are the perfection of the genre.

[16] *Méthode de Saint-Sulpice dans la direction des catéchismes*, 1ère édition (Paris: Meyer; Lyon: Perisse, 1832), in 12°, pp. xviii + 420. We also cite a second edition put out by H. I. Icard in 1856, in 12°, pp. xii + 417, published by Lecoffre. There was to appear still a third published by the same house in 1874 of 404 pages. A translation done anonymously under the auspices of the Church of England is entitled *The Method of S. Sulpice for the Organising of Catechisms* (London: Griffith Farran Browne, 1896), 370 pp.

Fr. Faillon set himself the task of publishing ten volumes on the subject of catechism teaching. His plan is to be found outlined in the introduction to *Histoire des catéchismes de Saint-Sulpice* (Paris: Gaume, 1831, in 16°, pp. xxxvi + 333. This little work, likewise anonymous, is filled with reminiscences of edifying lives. It was Fr. Faillon who compiled the *Directoire des Associées*

would remain so for a hundred years without serious modification.

It was impossible, however, for the removal of the seminary which went from Paris to Issy at the time of the law of separation (December, 1906) not to have its repercussions in the catechetical classes of Saint Sulpice. The close link between seminary and parish was a very important element in the catechetical picture. To be sure the seminarians from Issy continued to come to Saint Sulpice, but this would no longer be their sole field of apostolic action. Besides, one may say that this magnificent method had arrived at a point where it was too strained by adaptation to be able to survive any profound change of milieu. Since 1940 it no longer appears to have had any role save that of an admirable model ready-made for a completely new era.

If, before studying the method of Saint Sulpice in detail, one wished to determine in a general way the religious assumptions underlying it, he might at first be led astray by Faillon's book. After an historical note there is an immediate point-blank launching into Chapter One (page 4): "Concerning the Most Suitable Place for Catechetical Instruction." In the interest of complete honesty, mention should be made of the book's first two pages, which explain to us the success of the method. It is the result of painstaking preparation of the smallest details: the distribution of holy cards, of cards with the acts of faith, hope, and so on, and the precise arrangement of the benches. Our curiosity remains unsatisfied, it is true. But this method of approaching the subject is most significant. In this method exact preparation of the tiniest elements is of capital importance. The whole thing is presented like a scenario which must not encounter the smallest slip-up. It relies on the same principle as do rules of etiquette in the court of the great king. To be sure, it is a matter of holding the children's attention, but also of inculcating in them a sense of the solemnity and order which prevail in the things that pertain to God. There is a liturgy in this

du catéchisme de persévérance de Saint-Sulpice (Paris: Adrien Le Clere, 1830), in 18°, pp. 160, of which there is mention above in note 5.

method. One adverts to the preface of the *Book of Ceremonies* of Constantine Porphyrogenitus: "Imperial power exercised with order and measure should be capable of reproducing that harmonious movement which the Creator gives to all this universe. . . ." [17]

If it is true that Father Faillon is entirely at ease in describing means and accepted procedures, it would be unjust to say that he does not have in view the end to be achieved. Nonetheless, it ought to be admitted that Bishop Dupanloup knew better than he how to isolate the principles essential to the method.

Father Faillon attributes a double purpose to catechetics: the instruction of children, and their sanctification. [18] We have already observed that the Bishop of Orléans affirmed, from the very first, that catechetics had not only *instruction* in view but also *an introduction into Christian life.* [19] The catechists of Saint Sulpice understood vividly the need to go beyond the mere recitation stage.

This seems to have been accomplished either by the orientation toward the sacramental life or else the careful specification among the catechists of the place of conversion in the formation of the young. Their thoughts on the method to be employed with children is a distillation of experience gleaned from their various missions. The catechist has fulfilled his task if in his own person the child lives in accord with the spirit of the sacrament of penance. Here are a few significant lines from the first organizer of the method, Father Baüyn:

> In our catechism classes we must make an effort to instill in children an extreme horror for sin, a high esteem for the sacraments, and a spirit of great awe so that they will approach them rightly disposed. There should not be any satisfaction taken in instructing them in the things absolutely necessary for salvation. One should do all that one can to

[17] Constantinus VII Porphyrogenitus, *Le Livre des cérémonies,* ed. A. Vogt (Paris: Les Belles Lettres, 1935), p. 2.

[18] The very place accorded to the development of these themes is characteristic, the instruction of children forming Chapter 4 and their sanctification Chapter 5 of the method. It is with reference to the two activities of any catechism class, the instruction and the homily, that the matter of these essentials arises. On the fundamentals of instruction, Fr. Faillon is very brief (pp. 58–60). He is rather more expansive on the question of sanctification (pp. 101–31), but the relation of the one to the other is not clearly set in relief.

[19] Cf. in *L'œuvre par excellence* (note 1, *supra*), the entire first discourse.

touch their hearts, make them achieve a thorough change, uproot their bad habits, and help them make good confessions.[20]

Teaching the heart is indisputably the essential purpose. The customaries revert to it constantly:

In a word, it is necessary to begin by winning hearts, and then all is won. That is what St. Francis of Sales and after him, Fénelon, developed with such care, and put into practice with so much success. "Set fire to the house, first," the Bishop of Geneva used to say, "and before long all sorts of things will be thrown out the windows." [21]

This warmth of heart which animates the catechetical effort of Saint Sulpice must never escape from view. Devices are multiplied and detailed prescriptions grow more minute, but what matters above all else is the opening wide of hearts, and that joy which children must experience in their personal discovery of Christianity. It is not a mere matter of a sentimentality that does not go below the skin. Sulpician directness is entirely contrary to showy display. Regarding the retreat for first communion, Father Faillon writes:

Some catechists attach great importance to bringing children to tears. They believe that these strong impressions, by stirring them deeply, assure their conversion better. We do not share this view. The customaries of Saint-Sulpice say on this point: "Do not aim at producing in children those emotions which get them all upset, and make them cry out so that one can not be heard. Major efforts such as those exhaust children and are of almost no value to them. Something gentler and calmer is needed which will go to the depths of the heart." [22]

It is by the radiation of the charity in the heart of the catechist that charity will take fire in the hearts of children. When the method

[20] Cited by Faillon, *Méthode de Saint-Sulpice*, p. xi. Confession is to be an integral part of the program of catechetical classes. It will be required every month at the higher age level and every two months at the lower. The oldest handbooks of customs contain detailed formularies for the examination of conscience. Every class before the Revolution closed with this examen exercise, preached during a quarter-hour's time. It comprised five things: proposing the matter, invoking the Holy Spirit, going into some detail, attempting to arouse contrition, and seeking purpose of amendment.

[21] Manuscript customary of the Restoration, "Manuel des Catéchistes de Saint-Sulpice," pp. 10, 11.

[22] Faillon, *op. cit.*, p. 308.

speaks of the "virtues of the cathechist," it lingers over gentleness and love for children. Gerson is cited abundantly; the tone becomes lyrical. It would be rewarding to be able to cite lengthy pages of the ancient customaries on that sovereign esteem for the child which comprises the soul of the method. Unquestionably Bishop Dupanloup has spoken best of this "osmosis" of charity. Was he not the affectionate catechist that he was because, buffeted as a poor youngster, he had found the whole joy of his youth in those blessed instruction classes? [23]

The instruction will always be devoid of attraction if the one who gives it does not love those who receive it. Here then, gentlemen, is the great secret which will ensure that catechism classes are to be the education of souls; there is no other. Teachers must love God in their children and must make them realize that they do. Then the children will love both their instructors and God in these catechists, and marvels will be wrought in their young souls. You may ask me how they can be made to experience this. Gentlemen, here we face what can not be defined. What I can tell you simply is that when I was a catechist, I succeeded in making it felt. How? I cannot say. But were we to feel it ourselves, we would then love these young souls for God's sake and we would try to love God in them; and God would deign to bless this devotedness of our hearts.[24]

Don Bosco would have treasured those lines.

One point is established that cannot fail to surprise us, and that is that a method which places emphasis on a "high esteem for the sacraments" does not utilize in any way whatever assistance at Mass as a means of initiation into the sacraments. Participation in the Holy Sacrifice does not hold the attention of the books of customs for a moment. We spoke a while ago of "liturgy" with reference to the method. Sadly, this fact must be understood, that the central act of all liturgy is absent from it. In passing we are told that during the retreat for first communion the order of exercises is as follows: in the morning, prayer, a brief meditation,

[23] F. Lagrange, *Vie de Mgr. Dupanloup* (Paris, 1883), tr. by Lady Herbert as *Life of Monseigneur Dupanloup* (London: Chapman and Hall, 1885); and particularly *L'œuvre par excellence*, pp. 566–639, where the Bishop of Orléans takes up with emotion all the memories of childhood relative to the classes at Saint Sulpice.

[24] Dupanloup, *op. cit.*, p. 11.

Holy Mass, instruction and discourse. With reference to the ceremony itself, a necessary word is said about the Mass, that it should
especially be seen to that children not grow bored with it. In the
interests of perseverance, monthly communion shall be provided
for, but about the Mass itself there is no development.[25] It was
vespers that was the great liturgical function of the catechetical
classes. There was a time when they could not be conceived of
without vespers. Here is the order of the sessions given by an
undated customary anterior to the Revolution: "We do six things
in catechism class: the first interrogation; the presence of God;
the second interrogation; catechism teaching; vespers; and examen"
(p. 28). The motives given in justification of this sung exercise
(p. 229) are these:

Vespers should be sung at all instruction classes, whether for the older
or the younger children, for boys or girls. It may be done more or less
completely, but everywhere some part should be sung, and for these
reasons: first, because it pleases the children; second, so as to teach
them early to sing God's praises (this sees to it that they sing them around
their homes rather than bad songs); third, so that they will think of
themselves at the catechism classes as if they were at their parish church,
and be able to say to those who do not come to classes in order to be at
vespers that vespers are sung at the classes.

From the time of Father Faillon, vespers were no longer sung
except on feast days and days of a little more solemnity.[26]

The method of Saint Sulpice anticipated, one might say, the
practice of reading the gospel publicly. Was this in some small way
a liturgical proclamation of the sacred text? It would not seem
so. What it resembled was a feat of memory more than anything
else. The catechist made each child recite certain lines from the
gospel, requiring the next one in turn to take up from where the
one behind him left off.[27] Only before the preaching of the homily

---

[25] *Méthode,* pp. 307, 315, 358.
[26] *Ibid.,* p. 173.
[27] *Ibid.,* p. 49. Is it out of place to suggest that these catechetical sessions
resemble Protestant services very much? Later on, the fundamental importance
of hymn singing will be seen, the very important role of exposition, an
atmosphere of warm, felt intimacy, and the putting to the fore of certain children called "dignitaries." Religious sensibility has its laws in any given era.
The revolutionary tribunes will speak as bishops.

was the gospel read solemnly by the catechist himself, so as to be understood by all.

We should not ask of this method what it was not able to give. The Restoration customary quite successfully expressed the "nature and fundamental principles of the spirit of the catechetical instructions at Saint Sulpice" (p. 9) in this way:

> The spirit of the catechism classes of S. Sulpice is none other than that interior spirit of simplicity, wisdom and kindliness, of humility and prayer which should always animate the Company and the seminaries of S. Sulpice. It need only be modified in such a way that it may be applied to the religious education of children, but in going to a higher level it does not become anything different from that spirit of love which characterizes the New Law, animates Jesus Christ the Prince of Shepherds, and must be the soul of the pastoral ministry.

This primacy of charity is the catechist's constant concern, but his activity is exercised in the realm of instruction particularly. *Fides ex auditu.* The missionaries who inaugurated the catechetical ministry had a very lively awareness of the bad effects of ignorance of religious truths. They wished to nourish faith. But they were carefully on guard against confusing memory and faith. The following statement of the question by Father Faillon will not be denied by any modern catechist:

> However clear, however simple a catechetical instruction may be, the expressions and turns of phrase are entirely different from the language spoken by children. They find there almost none of the terms familiar to them, or if they find them they do not assign them the same meaning. What medium is there to aid their understanding, therefore, if they are not provided with clear explanations proportioned to their limited capabilities? And what will knowing the catechism from memory profit them if their understanding is not enlightened beyond that point? A child who knows his catechism by heart but is unable to understand the things he has learned if they are proposed to him in other terms should not be viewed as one who knows his religion.[28]

Lastly, a very obvious characteristic of the method of Saint Sulpice must be pointed out, and that is the considerable importance

[28] *Ibid.,* pp. 58 f.

attached to rivalry. It is a trait deriving from the customs of those times which disconcerts us somewhat. We might even say that Father Faillon foresaw our raised eyebrows. A paragraph from his book which takes refuge behind St. Francis of Sales, Fénelon and St. Jerome is headed, "There is no need to fear exposing children occasionally to the danger of vanity" (p. 177). Despite these august authorities, we have some difficulty in swallowing the following injunction:

The highest dignity attaches to the office of monitor, whether boy or girl. It is an extremely honorable post. The child who occupies it must be put in a place of distinction on a slightly elevated bench so that he may be exposed to the view of the whole class. As the boy and girl who are monitors must be models for the others they should only be chosen from among the brighter and better instructed. If the teacher speaks of good example, they should be there to be singled out. . . .[29]

We shall satisfy ourselves here with a brief summarization of the arrangement of the catechism lesson as it is presented in Father Faillon's method. We saw in passing what the older order was, and that it included particularly an examination of conscience delivered orally at the session's close. The method varied slightly, therefore, in the unfolding of its phases, but once fixed by Father Faillon, it was kept intact for more than a century. Bishop Dupanloup no more envisaged a modification of its elements than a tampering with the rites of the Mass; his book is an eloquent reproduction of Faillon's.

There were, to be sure, some adaptations for the weekly classes which the children immediately preparing for first communion attended by way of supplement twice weekly, during the three months preceding this ceremony. The chief modification was the suppression of the homily. The lower-level classes for children six to ten provided for the same elements as the upper level, called the "first communion" classes. As to the fourth kind of catechetical instruc-

[29] *Ibid.*, p. 180. It will be recalled that in *Les Petites Filles Modèles* by the Countess de Ségur, Camille de Fleurville is given a streamer as a sign of her designation as the best-behaved child in the village. Democracy has made us more modest, at least exteriorly.

tion, the continuation class, here is what Fr. Faillon has to say of it:

The activities of the continuation class are no different from those of ordinary classes. . . . As the children are older and in no way obliged to attend, they are treated with a considerable respect. All the deference that Christian charity demands is employed toward them, but there is no softness in the matter of keeping the regulations.[30]

What happened during a session of the older group, or of the first communion class?

It was a plan of attack made in ten stages: (1) entrance; (2) questioning; (3) point-scoring game; (4) recitation of the gospel; (5) report on homework; (6) instruction; (7) announcements; (8) homily; (9) point awards; (10) dismissal.

Other supplementary exercises might be added which did not find a place each time: vespers, recitation from cards, discussions, talks.

Lastly, certain days were marked by a special character. Catechism Days five or six times a year were observed with the distribution of pictures, the visitation of classes every year made by the catechetical director of Saint Sulpice, and the important distribution of awards. Each of these days had its ceremonial carefully outlined.

Hymns played a capital role in all of the classes. Before speaking briefly of the different elements in this important arsenal, the extreme care devoted to the physical arrangement of the locale should be pointed out. This was customarily a chapel, not the nave of the church. The benches were parallel and divided into several groups of rows described as "sections." The children were arranged there according to certain principles which diplomatically set the poor apart from the rich. There was no particular desire on anyone's part to engage in favoritism, but it was not thought charitable to offend the sensibilities of the weathy. The first student in order had to mark absences on charts divided with ledger lines; those who sat on the first benches were "honor students." Over them was

[30] *Op. cit.*, p. 330.

placed an assistant monitor to deal with one quarter of the class, and at the very top the monitor of whom we have spoken. Great care was taken to have the roll books ready to hand (those famous objects with which the children should not be hit too often). Priests were informed of absences.[31]

Coming in had to be in silence and with religious decorum; the genuflection was made together by all. When all were in their places the opening prayer was said and three or four verses of the first hymn were sung. (There were to be five of them during the lesson!)

The catechist did the interrogating from the pulpit; the child arose, made the sign of the cross and answered. Here is an example of the minuteness and refinement of the prescriptions:

> If a child has a ridiculous name, calling it out publicly should be avoided. Rather the one next to him should be purposely called on, or the child in front who is his immediate neighbor, and then after the two just mentioned have given their answers, the catechist can simply say: "Next."

The game for points was nothing but a prolongation of the questioning during which the catechist posed questions of his choice to those pupils who had made the best grades, thereby setting up a sort of tournament. Whoever answered best got one point. Three points entitled one to a picture when the class celebration day came along.

The gospel recitation which followed was an optional exercise. The children who had learned a Sunday gospel passed a sheet of paper with their signatures forward to the first child who gave it to the catechist. The latter made the children recite in the way we have indicated. If a child recited in French, he got one merit, in Latin two merits, in Greek three.[32] Copies of the gospel were awarded as prizes at the end of the year.

This whole first stage of control was accomplished by the reports

---

[31] The children were divided into several classes. Girls and boys were separated. A number of classes were likewise set up according to age. The specifications on this point are not too clear.

[32] One can only admire those twelve-year-olds who were able to learn the gospel in Greek. The study of this language was begun early.

called *diligences*. The digest by the child of the previous instruction was so termed, with his notes taken during it to help him and of course the aid given by parents. It was a commonplace, actually, for parents to attend the classes so as to guide their children subsequently in the work of review. Not all of the children were capable of making these résumés. An account was kept by listing in columns those who had received the best commendation. This was indicated by a whole hierarchy of seals (large black, green, blue and red ones). In the continuation class the papers bearing seals were copied by the child onto special paper and then bound. The archives of Saint Sulpice are rich with a whole series of volumes bound in red morocco: *Diligences*.

The second part of the class was devoted to the Instruction. This was preceded by the singing of the second hymn. The Instruction was an explanation of a lesson in the diocesan catechism. It lasted half an hour. It should be noted here that it bore on the lesson which the children *had learned by heart*. "This is the principal and fundamental function of the catechism class," and the hardest. The attention of the children had to be kept by main force, by familiar questioning especially. The Instruction had to conclude with a practical resolution. Following this a third hymn was sung to help the children relax.

The third part of the session had nothing further to do with the children's instruction but with their sanctification. It began with the announcements. The catechetical head spoke of life in the little community: of progress made, approaching feast days, the sick. That was the time during which family spirit was formed. Then came a fourth hymn to get the children ready for the homily. The latter was a very brief exhortation to fervor, its duration being fixed at half a quarter-hour. A solemn-enough ceremonial preceded it. The catechist who was to give the homily knelt on the altar steps. He then mounted the pulpit with the book of gospels. The children rose. The gospel of the day was read, followed by his remarks on the text selected.

After the homily points on good behavior were given, followed by the intoning of the last hymn. Dismissal was accomplished procession-style.

What most struck the young Dupanloup in this arrangement were the hymns and the *diligences*. He paid special attention to "those two things which we ourselves might do, in which we would not be wholly passive but be made to take an active part." With reference to hymns: "To be honest about it, this was the life of the catechism class. Without the hymns, despite all the zeal and ability of our catechists it would have been a pretty chilly performance." [33]

Recitation from cards was another procedure borrowed from mission technique.[34] Short reflections on a feast were printed on these cards. These the children used to learn by heart, and the catechist would then explain them so as to draw moral conclusions. "Children," we are told, "are interested in this approach and give it much greater attention than they do the discourses of their catechists." A further example of the benefits of personal activity is evident here.

"Dialogues" are little arranged sessions in which children exchange views acquired beforehand on some aspect of devotion, dogma, or morality. Rehearsal is required for this—and a prompter.

The conference or debate consists of treating some topic in dogma or "moral" in the form of objections and responses among several catechists.

The principle of pedagogy animating these sessions can be summarized thus: all the various activities must be linked together without a moment's loss of time. Continuity is essential. That is why the preparation must be so extensive. On the other hand, periods of relaxation need to be provided for by singing.

It is evident that this age witnessed the reign of recitation by heart, but it was accompanied by a serious effort (which unfortunately came too late) to see that what had previously been learned was understood.

These sessions required a rather large personnel, but in proportion as groups of children were not fragmentized the number of catechists demanded was not excessive. The Restoration customary

[33] Dupanloup, *op. cit.*, p. 578.
[34] Faillon specifies that the custom seems to have been borrowed from Père Romillon (p. 1650).

is specific: "After various changes the catechism classes were irrevocably fixed on Sept. 1, 1814, at the number of six, accommodating twelve or fifteen hundred children and directed by about twenty-four catechists." Father Faillon writes: "At Saint-Sulpice, five catechists are ordinarily assigned to from two to four hundred children." One of them is the director of catechetics, who never leaves the sanctuary (p. 26).

One can only admire this magnificent plan, but it supposes for its full realization that the least detail be followed. A well-prepared staff is likewise required for it.

Here we put our finger on a very important point. As we said at the beginning, this method has exercised a considerable influence. Imitation was attempted everywhere. What was the result? Modest parishes could not succeed in staging the whole scenario. Instead of considering a setting compatible with local needs and possibilities, the full method of Saint Sulpice was whittled down. Too often it was forcibly introduced on terms of half-strength and thus it lost the best part of its value. All creative originality was interfered with. This devaluation almost inevitably calls for comparison with that of the High Mass in the Lyonnaise rite, so imposing when it is celebrated by the archbishop surrounded by his thirty-seven ministers and so pitifully curtailed when one tries to adapt it to a small parish.

To complete the description of the method, a word must be said about two institutions to which allusion has already been made: the association and the affiliations.

The associations were established to maintain zeal and fervor among the children of the continuation classes. There was one for girls and one for boys; they had almost the same organization.

The number of participants was fixed for the girls' association: thus forty or at most fifty associates, thirty aspirants, and some affiliates. One had to be an aspirant for at least two years to be presented for election to associate status. Marriage, withdrawal or death were the causes which terminated association.

It would be surprising indeed if there were no "*dignitaries.*" They number eight—the president, the overseer of the sick, the zelatrix, the secretary, the treasurer, the librarian and two sacristans. Associates, without incurring any obligation in conscience whatever, were consecrated to the adoration of the Blessed Sacrament. They were bound strictly together, dedicating themselves to every work of charity. Lastly, they devoted themselves to the instruction of children in the catechism classes at Saint Sulpice. There were monthly meetings and Masses in common. We have several texts of the statutes, handsomely bound. One among them reports on a "secret precept," which is to abstain from dances and shows.

Every year the reception of aspirants and associates was the most solemn celebration of the continuation classes. We have the manuscript account and the signatures of candidates admitted since 1804. The ceremony concluded in 1944 with the 224th admission.

Along with this association there existed a sort of common bond in the classes which was carefully maintained by recounting the edifying lives of children in the classes who had died prematurely. We have before us a little book published in 1886 by Lecoffre, entitled, "Elementary Class of Saint-Sulpice—Model Children (1809–85)." In the preface we are told that many other edifying accounts are carefully kept in the archives of the catechism classes of Saint Sulpice, which may also be given to the public one day.

Finally, there exist at the parish of Saint Sulpice two manuscript volumes in quarto which contain the list of affiliated catechetical centers. A large folded sheet situates them on the map of France. The formation of this catalogue was begun in 1863. The first affiliations go back to 1822, and they continued up until 1899. Each center had to send annual letters to Paris. All of the correspondence exchanged with each affiliated catechetical center is noted on the catalogue, whether of Paris or some province or even in foreign parts. The annual letter was answered, and occasional circular letters were sent out. There were notable gaps; between 1889 and 1897 especially, it would seem, the secretary was not very active.

It would be to little or no purpose for us to maintain that we wished we could preserve the scattered fragments of this method. We hope we have shown, though, what a magnificent apostolic effort it represented. If only the primacy of love in the catechetical venture could be held onto, the need of a family spirit met, and the care demanded in preparation be given! Those are the great requirements. The fact that a thing so important as the transmission of the faith is in question gives us the right to demand as much.

5.

General Tendencies
in Contemporary Catechetics
·
Pierre Ranwez, S.J.

Shortly after the First World War, a good number of Catholics became aware of a crisis in religious instruction. They saw that there was a spirit of discontent among pupils in catechism classes which took the form of a general boredom and lack of interest. They also observed that too great a number of former pupils of catechetical programs or of Catholic schools were losing their faith or giving up practicing their religion, especially when family or professional surroundings were not particularly Christian. Even among those who had seemed to profit from religious instruction there were many, they noted, who were keeping up an external fidelity, more perhaps out of habit than conviction, who never seemed to achieve any genuine spiritual life.

Close examination of religious instruction led these persons to perceive the mediocre quality of the spiritual and pedagogical means employed to teach Christian doctrine. It became clear to them that Catholic leaders were bound not only to improve whatever could be improved in existing methods, but also to make certain radical innovations. Attention was concentrated first of all on improving the methods used in catechetical classes. The realization came early that catechism lessons often sinned in three ways in particular: (1) They were deductive and abstract. Only the concrete, it was seen, interests a child. The learner can be introduced to general concepts in a gradual way only by starting with tangible realities and having experiences out of which concepts may grow. (2) They were chiefly expository, and the participation of the pupil was limited. (3) They took little account of the diversity among groups of learners, and of the temperaments and intellectual or emotional capacities of individual pupils. In short, they were characterized by a lack of adaptability.

112

A diligent search for means to remedy these weaknesses was therefore begun. Leading theorists tried to make the teaching more inductive and concrete, to catch the student's attention through those immediate perceptions which interest him and to go step by step with him from there. A pastoral letter written in 1922 by Monseigneur Landrieux, Bishop of Dijon, became a kind of manifesto of the catechetical revival. "Instead of going in directly by the open doors of the child's imagination and sense perception, we waste our time knocking on the still bolted doors of his understanding and his judgment," wrote the Bishop. So he proposed to catechism teachers that they begin by leading the pupil into the marvelous realm of the Gospel and personal contact with our Lord before giving him an outline of Christian doctrine.

In a book published in Belgium some years later (1929), Chanoine Dupont set forth what the method of a catechism lesson ought to be.[1] The point of departure should be a picture shown to the children or a story told to them. They should then be asked to express themselves freely and let their hearts speak up. Little by little, with delicacy and tact, they should be guided toward the discovery of the catechism formula or the prayer text which the picture shown to them at the beginning suggested in the concrete.

Certain catechists were soon anxious to make religious instruction more active—something in which students could become "engaged." Around 1920–1925 a great deal was said about the new pedagogic methods of the "activity-school." According to the methods of this school, the child should participate more and more personally and freely in his own education. Purely cerebral approaches were judged insufficient; activities theretofore unheard of were given a place in the curriculum. Would it not be a good thing, it was asked, to follow these new trends in the teaching of catechism?

A book by Madame Fargues which appeared in 1934 took up this question.[2] The author encouraged group work, singing or recitation of verse in rhythm, and occasionally games or projects. She

[1] H. Dupont, *Pour apprendre la religion aux petits* (Tamines: Duculot, 1929).
[2] Marie Fargues, *Les méthodes actives dans l'enseignement religieux* (Paris: Ed. du Cerf, 1934).

believed that the time spent by the children in preparing the equipment needed for the lesson is not wasted. Madame Fargues is convinced that a truth can be understood only in so far as it is personally experienced, that an idea, to be really got hold of, requires
first a personal reaction of some sort. Another catechist, Mademoi-
selle Derkenne, made some interesting experiments while catechizing the children of a parish. These she set down in a book
published in 1935.[3] She took pains to fit the development of the
teaching into the liturgical cycle and to get the children to enter
into the spirit of the liturgical season in various ways, for example
by working together on the staging of a show based on the mysteries
of Christmas or Easter.

Madame Lubienska de Lenval, concerned for a Christian formation based on the Bible and on the liturgy, became the advocate
of a system of teaching in which gestures and attitudes inspired
by both Bible and liturgy are designed to foster the awakening
of a balanced religious sense. Meanwhile Madame Damez, the
foundress of a catechetical course for small children, brought out
very strongly the need to arouse first of all in children the essential
religious activity: prayer. She reminded us that the baptized child
bears within him the sanctifying grace which enables him to sense
divine realities and put him in contact with God. She argued that
catechism teachers ought to guide their four- or five-year-old pupils
toward a meeting with God. By praying in their presence and with
them, by creating an atmosphere of silence and by preserving an
attitude of reverence teachers can, she asserted, set free the flight
of the Christian child toward God his Father.

As is evident, all the catechists mentioned were endeavoring to
make the teaching of religion more active, especially in these three
ways: (1) by introducing various activities so as to sustain interest
in the lessons—drawing, singing, acted-out scenes, and so on; (2)
by introducing the child to the liturgical life; and (3) finally and
most especially, by awakening that supreme religious activity:
prayer.

[3] Françoise Derkenne, *La vie et la joie au catéchisme* (Paris: de Gigord, 1935;
also Lyon, Ed. de l'Abeille, 1943).

Meanwhile expression was being given to an additional concern, namely, that of individualizing teaching while at the same time making it more *communal*. In large catechism classes children were often lost in the crowd. In spite of their numbers they became terribly isolated. No account was being taken of different aptitudes and temperaments, or, above all, of the intellectual backwardness which completely thwarts some children. It was necessary, there-fore, during at least a part of the time devoted to the lesson, to break up the large classes and to sort the children into groups of six, seven or eight under the supervision of a catechist. Care was required to put children of like temperament together; these would be set to work at various projects—drawings, writing. A long-term experi-ment in one of the large parishes of Paris was described in a book entitled *Individualized Work in Catechism.*[4] In it the authors favor the use of a system of "cards" which outline a definite program. This program was to vary according to stages of emotional and in-tellectual development, underdevelopment, and so on. On these cards the child finds the outline of the studies to be done either by himself or with a group, questions he will be expected to answer, drawings to make, and so on.

During the Second World War, and after it, several important surveys were made in the field of religious sociology. Men of vision could see how much attention had to be given to these problems in relation to the care of souls. In this connection a great debt is owed to Abbé Godin,[5] Chanoine Boulard,[6] and Abbé Michonneau.[7] Many priests and laymen had their eyes opened by reading the

[4] Equipe Saint-Germain de Charonne, *Le Travail individualisé au catéchisme* (Paris: Presses d'Ile de France, 1950).

[5] Abbé Godin's book (with Yvan Daniel), *France, pays du mission?* (Lyon: Ed. de l'Abeille, 1943; later Paris: Ed. du Cerf) was the starting point of a magnificent renewal in the apostolate. It is available in English as translated and adapted by Maisie Ward: *France Pagan? The Mission of Abbé Godin* (New York: Sheed and Ward, 1948).

[6] F. Boulard, *Problèmes missionnaires de la France rurale* (Paris: Ed. du Cerf, 1945), 2 vols.

[7] G. Michonneau and H. Chéry, O.P., *Le Paroisse, communauté missionnaire* (Paris: Ed. du Cerf, 1946), translated as *Revolution in a City Parish* (West-minster, Md.: Newman, 1950).

studies of these men; they saw how great could be the influence of surroundings on the behavior of the Christian. They realized that at the catechism stage the lessons, however well they might be taught, would more often than not be without durable effect unless they formed part of a whole education inspired by the same spirit. Abbé Rétif, Abbé Michonneau's successor in the Sacré-Cœur parish in Colombes, tried to find out how the different background elements could be brought to collaborate in the religious education of the child, even in a spiritually indifferent and sometimes hostile area. He wanted to make the catechism classes into a "cate-chumenate."

A catechumenate is a sort of novitiate for the Christian life. In it doctrine is studied, and those who are members learn to conform themselves to the precepts of Christ. In such an atmosphere children should be encouraged to help one another, and the whole parish community should be invited to assist in the effort to educate the young. Children of the same age group are divided into bands or patrols of six, seven or eight (*cordées,* for the boys, *chainettes* for the girls). They are brought together not only at the catechetical classes but in their games, in school and on the street; they are made to feel a fellowship among themselves. The whole parish community is enlisted in this joint effort. Catechism instruction given in private homes (as it should be at least occasionally), provides an opportunity for parents to meet, or neighbors who have an interest in religious training. In this way mothers of families take on the responsibility of giving catechism lessons to the children in their neighborhoods. Adults are selected to give a helping hand to young people in the environment of work and recreation. Last but far from least, the members of the parish are helped in establishing their human brotherhood and comradeship on a supernatural basis by a liturgical life in which adults and children alike participate. This relates in particular to the Sunday Mass which is carefully prepared and explained in elaborate detail.

The example of the catechism classes at Colombes and other parishes has given rise to much thought and experiment.

More and more the awareness has grown that solid religious

education presupposes joint effort and agreement among the various types of educators: parents, parish priests, catechists, schoolteachers, and those in charge of outside activities. For this reason the catechist must not think that he has completed his job once he has conscientiously prepared his lesson. The greatest part of his work, perhaps, consists in making certain that a unified spirit characterizes all who have a hand in educating the child. He must see to it that the parents are visited or assembled so as to be made interested in the religious development of their children. He must see that care is taken to coordinate the liturgical effort of the parish and the religious instruction in the school—in a word, that all the educators are reminded of their responsibility and their efforts unified.

After considerable thought had been given to the method of teaching and to the need for coordinating the various educative agencies, religious educators began to attend to the content of the lessons themselves. The catechism had, of course, been taught to children from their earliest years. Often enough this catechism had become a summary of theology rather than an introduction to the Christian message. But a summary, educators began to see, is normally understood only by those who have first assimilated that which is summarized. More than that, the abstract notions of theology are only within the reach of those who have been in direct contact with the Story of Salvation. The way that God has made Himself known to men is through His providential interventions from the time of Adam's sin up to the return of Christ to the Father in glory. Such is the message entrusted to the Church. Philosophical systematization will come afterward to form the science of theology. But to children it is primarily the Story of Salvation that must be presented. Before learning definitions of the Holy Trinity or of the two natures in Jesus Christ or of grace, the child must first have learned that God is Someone, a Father all-powerful and all-kind who led and protected the children of Israel as a father watches over his family, who sent His Son Jesus to redeem us, and who continues, in His Church and through His Spirit, to be present among us.

It was in the light of this outlook that the textbooks used in religious education began to be transformed. Sacred or biblical history, formerly cast in the role of an optional supplement to catechism lessons, became the base and the very fabric of the whole presentation.

A mere recital of past events, however, does not suffice. The reason for this is that God keeps intervening anew at this very moment in the Mass and in the sacraments. By taking part in the life of the liturgy and by following the cycle of the Church year, the Christian enters into the vast stream of grace set in motion by God since the foundation of the world. Thus an historical catechesis is made complete only by a liturgical catechesis. Let us indicate what the distinctive features of this catechesis will be.

1. Because it depends intimately on the interior and sacrificial life of the Church, this catechesis should be built on a framework identical with the succession of seasons in the liturgical year; the heart of the development should be the explanation of the Easter solemnity.

In the course of the yearly cycle the Church does in fact summarize the Story of Salvation and relates again the account of mankind's upward climb toward God across the centuries. The itinerary of this journey becomes the model for our own spiritual ascent. By it we are invited to share in the same series of gifts as those which were offered to our fathers. The message of the liturgy does not bring us mere concepts. It speaks to us of Jesus Christ in those who prefigured Him, in His person and His life, in His teaching, His miracles, His death and His resurrection; it speaks to us of Jesus Christ still living in His saints and increasing within ourselves.

2. The language in which liturgical teaching is conveyed is a living, "prophetic" word, the very word of the Church inspired by the Holy Spirit. The texts read or sung during the celebration of divine worship are mostly drawn from the Bible, but they have been meditated by the Church. Their meaning is made more specific by the context in which they are set, for the Holy Spirit gives a new life to the inspired word when He places it on the lips of the Spouse.

In addition to the reading of these unchanging texts, liturgical religious education requires a commentary offered by a priest in the name of the Church. Like the text itself this commentary too can be moved by a breath of life and take on the aspect of a message inspired by God. The catechist or the preacher who proclaims the mystery on which he has been nourished continues the action of the "prophets" in the *agapes* of the first century, and of the "deacons for extempore prayer" of the fourth century. Through them the living thought of the Church is expressed, at least in so far as they let themselves be guided by the texts and by the Spirit in union with the teaching Church. Instruction joined in this way to a liturgical act of worship is vivified by it. It becomes as it were a translation into personal life of the Mystery that is being enacted.

3. A third characteristic distinguishes the liturgical method of teaching. It is prepared for through a sensed experience, and carried on by means of a participation. The rites with their verbal and gestural forms, colors, poetry and music proclaim the message and give some advance idea of what needs to be rendered clearer. But above all, the knowledge imparted by liturgical teaching is brought to full bloom by prayer and sacrifice. Here it is not merely or chiefly man's sacrifice but Christ's. The Lord grants His disciple this privilege: to be divinely transformed in accord with the message that is proclaimed to him.

We have described the preceding changes from the standpoint of the *catechetical instruction*. Catechists were trying to find out how to make the lesson more effective by presenting it in accordance with a better method, by giving it the benefit of a like-mindedness among teachers and educative agencies. They were attempting to construct it after the scheme of God's manifestations of Himself to mankind, and to take the feasts of the liturgy into account in assigning matter for study.

As these improvements were made, the best catechists came to realize the need for a change in the perspective of religious education. Primary concern for the *religion lesson* had to be replaced, in

accord with the solidest traditions of the Church, by primary concern for *religious initiation.*[8]

What we call religious initiation, or introduction into the Christian mystery, is not only the teaching process itself but the whole
of religious formation, that is to say, the employment in Christ's
name by representatives of the Church of the combined apparatus
of supernatural and natural means at their disposal to arouse the
divine life in a child or an adult. Their aim is to help him accept it
and comply with it. In the perspective of Christian initiation thus
defined, religious instruction is one element. Its place and the
means by which it is presented form part of a whole greater than
itself.

In reading the Bible we observe that throughout sacred history
God revealed Himself by giving Himself. In each instance He made
Himself known to Adam, Noah, Abraham, Moses, and later to the
contemporaries of Christ, through "breaking in" on them prov-
identially and redemptively. In each of these encounters God Himself or the prophets sent by Him give an explanation of the divine
course of action, and bring men a little further along in a knowledge
of the secrets of God. For example, it is in the setting of the divine
missions that the mystery of the Holy Trinity is revealed by Jesus.
Later on, theology was to take hold of these revealed truths so as
to present them in a systematic manner. God has kept up this
course of instruction for the sanctification of Christian generations
by means of the sacramental system entrusted to His Church. What
are the sacraments, after all, but divine movements toward an encounter with men? In them a saving act once performed in historic
time is symbolically recalled and put into operation in the present.
By means of the sacramental rites God gives Himself and shows
Himself. The basic function of religious instruction, therefore, is to
prepare souls for the divine gift, to show its mysterious grandeur
and to make known Him by whom salvation comes to us. It was in
this manner that the catechesis presented to catechumens and
neophytes was developed in the early Christian centuries.

[8] It is precisely with such an outlook that priests like Abbé Rétif and most
of the catechists cited in the preceding pages have labored.

In the following pages we should like to describe the chief characteristics of a catechetical attempt recently conceived in this spirit. To do this our method will be to take up again in inverse order the three points we have been considering, and to examine: (1) the tie between catechetical instruction and the sacramental life, and the biblical structure of the former; (2) the need for co-operation by different educative agencies; (3) the nature of a pedagogy which meets the demands both of human nature and of grace.

We shall see that in this perspective religious formation takes on an extraordinary coherence: instruction and Christian life are welded to each other. The part played by the Christian community assumes its true meaning, and Christian education is seen as that which befits a son of God, not as some optional "extra" attached to a human training already complete in itself.

CATECHETICS AND THE SACRAMENTAL LIFE

The growth of the Christian is set to the rhythm of the sacraments of "initiation." Baptism gives a new adopted son to the Father, confirmation a new disciple to the Holy Spirit, while the Eucharist brings the Christian into intimate association with Christ the Redeemer in His death and resurrection. The first aim of catechetics should be to enlighten the young Christian about the Father, the Son and the Holy Spirit, and about the gifts which they lavish upon him. This catechetical instruction should be given to accompany, to precede and to follow the reception of the sacraments.

Those responsible for religious education should take care first of all to give to the sacramental life of the children in a concrete way the importance it deserves. Nothing should be neglected which will bring out the significance of baptism, confirmation, and first communion. The solemnized religious ceremony should be followed by a family party from which every trace of worldliness is excluded. Care should likewise be taken to present a clear and thorough explanation of things at the time.

We recalled above how in the course of history God has revealed Himself at the very center of His providential dealings with men.

There was a perfect harmony between the revelation and the particular redemptive measure taken. It should be the same even now. The catechetical instruction on baptism (which normally follows the sacrament) should teach the child that he is a son of the Father; the one on penance should aim at giving him a sense of sin, and so forth. At the outset the need is not to define concepts precisely, but to introduce the child to some awareness, as yet indistinct, of the mystery. We might say that the first concern should be to communicate a "sense of God," a "sense of sin," a "sense of faith-inspired response to the call of the Spirit." Catechetical instruction like this should include preparation before the reception of the sacraments and explanation afterwards, but, perhaps most important of all, an explanation during the liturgical ceremonies themselves.

This catechetical instruction should be marked by two features: it should be concrete and it should be historical. It should be *concrete* in the following three ways particularly: (1) by being connected with an action which the pupil is taking or preparing to take, as the reception of a sacrament or some other religious function; (2) by revealing the Living God and not just the idea of Him; (3) by adopting the very concrete language which the liturgy borrows from the Bible: for example, rather than saying: "Without actual grace we are incapable of doing good," the words of Christ should be repeated: "Without me you can do nothing," and so forth. And the catechetical instruction should be *historical* because the framework or plan of this instruction should be that of the providential design of salvation.

Thus the early catechetical instruction should be more an education in faith than a learned study; it should be religious rather than academic, historical rather than speculative; it should bring the pupil into the presence of the mystery of God more than attempt to shower him with facile expositions which so often are fruitless as far as the child is concerned. Rooted in the redemptive mediation that each sacrament represents, it will join forces with the illumining and vivifying action of the Holy Spirit in souls.

Teaching which deals with concepts, even theological teaching, is possible only after this first stage of Christian formation has been reached. Then it can be developed on the solid foundation of an enlightened faith. Moreover, we must underline the importance of serious, systematic and thorough doctrinal instruction illumined by theology which should begin in the adolescence of the pupil and extend to maturity. As a matter of fact, our insistence in pointing out the danger of premature teaching of abstract ideas is based not on any lack of regard for such teaching (on the contrary, it seems indispensable to us), but solely on the fear that, if given too soon, it will produce only illusory results. In addition, far from intensifying the light of faith, it will only create confusion.

COLLECTIVE RESPONSIBILITY
OF THE DIFFERENT EDUCATIVE AGENCIES

Mere observation of the conditions for success in religion courses highlighted the desirability of collaboration among the different educative agencies. The harmonization of diversities in the backgrounds of pupils was seen as equally desirable. If we take a broad view of the sacramental life and of religious education as a whole, we are forced to hope for the same two objectives. In order to understand this hope, we must remind ourselves that the initiator of the coming of God into souls and their knowledge of Him is God Himself who gives and reveals Himself in Jesus Christ. He goes on doing this in the Church, the Body of Christ. The Church performs her task as living organisms always do by calling the various members of the body into action, each according to its function. Thus it is by no means the place of any one educator to claim the exclusive right to educate and to teach. Neither priest nor parents nor religion teacher can get on without the assistance of the others. All have the joint responsibility of insuring an effective mutual collaboration. The guidance of this collective effort is in the hands of the Holy Spirit. He makes its general pattern known through the authority of the Church, but he entrusts to the enlightened perspicacity of the educators the task of discerning the special vocation of each child.

In the concrete, what form should the collaboration we look for take?

The ministrations given by the priest should be prepared for and continued afterward by the parents. Catechists, schoolteachers, those in charge of outside activities should all contribute their assistance, each in accord with his sphere of action. Even then, real ties need to be established among them through meetings and various other contacts, in the interests of a coherent effort. This working together of the various agents of formation should apply particularly to liturgical activity, devotions within the family, and to the teaching of religion in the parish or school. Let us illustrate each of these three points by an example.

Under the heading of *liturgical activity*, let us take the question of the first communion Mass. If the little first communicants can see nothing but the uninteresting movements of a priest who turns his back on them and if all they hear is his murmuring of Latin words, we can be sure that the Eucharistic rites into which all this is to be their initiation will be stripped of any meaning for them. Will music or the singing of hymns be enough to arouse their interest and their emotional response? Must they recall all that had been told them in the preparation period, without the event itself having any instructive significance? The whole problem resolves itself into seeing to it that singing, attitudes, explanations, responses, all lead the child into the spirit of the Eucharistic Mystery and help him to have a part in the rites. Normally this result can be achieved only through an intelligent cooperation between priests, religious, and lay people. Together they must look for ways in which certain leading ideas of the Mass can be made understandable. A processional entrance into the Church would create an atmosphere of confidence and joy and lead to an offertory procession, then to a solemn approach to the reception of holy communion. A layman if not a priest might read extracts from the proper of the Mass. This could be followed by a well-chosen commentary. Another person would take charge of helping the children make the brief Latin responses to the celebrant (*Amen, Et cum spiritu tuo,* and so on). In this way priest, sisters and laymen would work together in leading the children into the Eucharistic Mystery.

Let us take an example relating to *devotion within the family.*

A new baby is going to be baptized. At this point it is not the baby who must be instructed about the meaning of this sacrament but his parents who henceforth are to have the responsibility of bringing him to the knowledge of God. Will the brief ceremony of administering the sacrament in the church be enough to imprint convictions and resolutions in the hearts of the parents? It will help if the liturgical ceremony is preceded by a family gathering at the home of the baby's parents.

The immediate family and if possible some neighbors should join the priest at this gathering. Commentaries, Bible or other devout reading, responses and singing should be alternated so as to reveal to an attentive audience the grandeur of the privileges with which the baptized child is to be endowed and the seriousness of the duties incumbent on his parents and all his friends.[9]

In the domain of *parish or schoolroom teaching*, examples are easy to find. In rural districts where the people live far apart from one another and where it is difficult to bring the children together frequently to be with the priest, certain pastors call the children together once a week at the rectory. On other days the mothers take charge of explaining the lessons and supervising the children's work. To prepare them for this task, the pastor assembles the mothers once a month and gives them the instructions they need.

SUPERNATURAL PEDAGOGY

The child transfigured by baptism is a son of God. His nature and his faculties have been ennobled and are now capable of a new activity. A special pedagogy must be adapted to this situation.

We noted earlier how catechists had improved their methods: (1) by starting with concrete facts; (2) by stimulating an active participation; (3) by making the teaching individualized; (4) by encouraging a spirit of work in groups.

When we consider what is required for a supernatural pedagogy, we observe that these same general directives are needed, but that the process of applying them alters their appearance.

(*a*) The requirement that teaching be founded on concrete experience is set clearly in relief in the sacramental life. There indeed

---

[9] For an example of such a ceremony, cf. Marie-Louise and Jacques Defossa, "Ceremony of Preparation for Baptism," *Lumen Vitae*, IX (Jan.–March, 1954), 9–16.

God reveals Himself through sacred sign. One of the most characteristic features of Christian pedagogy should be its efforts to accustom the child to ritual gestures and attitudes. Their symbolism will evoke at once past providential happenings and the divine gift of the precise moment.

Preparation for meditation or silent prayer should bring about a feeling of the immensity of God and create an atmosphere of attention and docility in listening to His Word. As a matter of course, a gathering of Christians who come together around the priest to take part in the Mass should be a living image of the Church and a conscious remembrance of the Last Supper.

Moreover, the formula used by so many catechists, "We must proceed from the concrete to the abstract," needs to be reconsidered and taken a step farther. In Christian education we must rather proceed from the concrete to the concrete; starting with a ritual, a gesture, an attitude, a specific thing which has the power to evoke the mystery of the presence of the Lord, we must then let ourselves be brought by God up to Himself. The abstractions will come afterward and are not always indispensable in any case.

(b) The need for active participation in the teaching process (so that what is taught may be assimilated) poses certain requirements in the domain which concerns us here. It is scarcely a question of absorbing the child's energies with "busy work" but of giving him consistent training for a truly religious behavior. Two classes of experiences are particularly interesting in this connection. *First,* there is participation in liturgical life which has as it were two aspects, the one invisible and supernatural, the other perceptible to the senses and standing in relation to the first as a sign. Thus, the child should be given the habit of seeking the company of God and familiarizing himself with His mysteries by taking part in liturgical celebration, serving Mass, helping in the preparation of ceremonies, and so on. But this first kind of activity is effective only if it is associated with the *second* which is more interior, the activity of prayer itself in the midst of which the meeting with God takes place.

(c) The process of making teaching an individualized affair: this normally presupposes a study of character, temperament and the manifold individual intellectual traits. In the supernatural setting it takes on an entirely new significance. Over and above particular qualities imposed by the heredity, social background or acquired habits in the child, the action of the Holy Spirit issues him a call and leads him toward his destiny. Thus it is that a regard for the particular vocation of each child and diligent watchfulness for the work of the Spirit must above all else guide the efforts of the Christian educator.

(*d*) We have stressed the need for working in teams or work groups in which the children help one another. This should provide the framework for a more interior communion, a profound mutual sharing in prayer and sacrifice. The children will not necessarily be aware of this aspect of the matter. But a healthy community will be the normal expression of a deeper unity of souls in Jesus Christ.

To sum up, the Christian educator must put into play not only the tangible data which experience provides, but also those realities the existence of which is revealed by faith. Faith and hope should guide his action; not human forces alone should be taken into account. He must not be frightened off from objectives which appear humanly impossible, for God Himself is working with him.

CONCLUSION

The catechetical instruction we have been seeking to describe is without doubt the most solidly traditional one in the Church. Its normal effect should be to give a strong unity to the whole of Christian formation:

(1) unity between *education* taken broadly and the actual *teaching,* as well as among the various aspects of the teaching;

(2) unity among the *agents of education* who should be aware that together they are bringing the same work to perfection;

(3) unity, lastly, brought about progressively within the *child* himself through the enlightening action of the Holy Spirit.

PART II

RELIGIOUS EDUCATION
Some Theological and Scientific Considerations

6.

Introduction to
a Pedagogy of Faith
•
François Coudreau, P.S.S.

Current debate about the objectives of catechists reveals the existence of two quite different schools of thought on this matter. One
of these schools emphasizes actual *instruction,* that is, the transmission of the content of revelation. It therefore seems to defend a
pedagogy of object. The other school insists on the education or
vital formation of the pupil, that is, his initiation into a way of life.
It thus appears to be in favor of a pedagogy of subject.

The controversy between those who defend a pedagogy of object
and those who defend a pedagogy of subject is not confined to the
lecture halls, to formalized treatises on religious training, or to
learned journals of catechetical instruction. It is found to be very
generally though not altogether consciously held by priests, brothers
and sisters dedicated to the active ministry of the word, as well as by
lay instructors who generously give themselves to the catechetical
apostolate. Indeed, wherever one looks in the field of religious
education today, one encounters one or the other tendency.

And yet, it must be admitted, each tendency is wrongfully one-
sided and harmful to a really fruitful implantation of the Christian
message or to the formation of the authentic Christian spirit, for
each tendency encompasses certain errors in regard to fundamentals
of true religious education.

The basic error, of course, is that we should be obliged to choose
between *instruction* and *formation.* It ought to be entirely evident
that both pedagogical approaches contain much that is true, and
that a person ought not to limit himself solely to one or the other
point of view.

That we are obliged to *instruct,* that is, to transmit the content
of the Faith, is a truism beyond any need for discussion. Christ has

given us the explicit command, "Go, teach." Faith is impossible without an object, for to believe is to believe in something or in someone. Knowledge of course is not faith, but one does not believe without knowing what one believes.

It goes without saying that the importance of actual instruction in catechesis needs to be frequently repeated. Certain present-day methods of religious education, though oriented toward bearing witness to the faith and toward dedicated Christian living, sometimes tend to minimize the indispensable role of this positive presentation of doctrine. It seems that insistence on this necessity is not out of place at this very hour, and that those responsible for the pedagogy of faith should honor, defend and clarify the role of informative teaching in religious education.

But we must not overlook the fact that a well-grounded catechesis will also *form* pupils by initiating them into the ways of Christian life. For, even though belief presupposes knowledge, knowledge is not belief. Instruction can all too easily terminate in mere religious knowledge and not in a living faith. Perhaps it is because the efforts of catechists are always menaced by this danger that there is a very pronounced reaction nowadays against *mere* didacticism in catechesis. It is recognized that there can never be any real instruction except where a person is religiously awakened and already possessed of some genuine religious life. Though didactic instruction gives content and articulation to a living faith, it is still necessary that this faith be aroused, grow and expand. The considerable role that religious formation must have in the pedagogy of faith should be evident.

In brief, to choose the view of one or the other school is wrong. To think of catechetics as religious didacticism to the exclusion of formation, or as formation to the exclusion of instruction, would not respect the requirements of a true pedagogy of faith. It must be admitted that there is a serious temptation along this line, but that as soon as one adopts a partisan position in the matter he is no longer in touch with truth. Christian educators, catechists and pastors need to examine their consciences. It is so easy to become an exclusivist, and it almost always happens unconsciously.

If one ought not to choose between instruction and formation in catechesis, the solution would seem to be a combination of the two. Does this mean that catechizing would be simultaneously instruction and formation? Such would be much too simple and easy a solution: the truth is more complex. For, if one must refuse the choice, teach *or* educate, one must also reject the juxtaposition, teach *and* educate, instruct *and* initiate into Christian life. For to juxtapose is to dissociate the real, whose true richness can only be expressed in a total context. To understand the nature of a real pedagogy of faith, therefore, one must first deepen the analysis, then reunite teaching and formation, the two terms that define it, let them overlap one another, and seek the law that governs their fusion. In the pedagogy of faith there is an internal dynamism springing from the mysterious link that unites teaching and formation. Like a river, which is not simply the running side by side of two streams, but a basic mixing of the waters of the one and the other, a true catechesis unites both teaching and formation in order to form something more than the two of them.

The experience of every shepherd of souls confirms this conclusion. Is not the divorce of religious knowledge from Christian life the very thing from which so many adult Christians suffer today? Many know and practice their religion, but they do not live by the Gospel; their doctrinal existences do not transform their day-to-day living. They lack a real grasp of what supernatural life is. We know that being a Christian is not simply a question of accepting the truths of Christianity and of receiving the sacraments. It is regarding all human realities—love, wealth, suffering, life, death, peace, war—with the eyes of Christ, and utilizing them as would Christ Himself. The tragedy is, how many Christians are so logical in their faith? How many say, "I have my faith," but do not truly believe, do not live by faith?

Unquestionably, there are many causes—sociological and other —for this dissociation. It is not our task to analyze these causes here, but one is tempted to wonder if one of the profoundest of causes is not a view of religious instruction which first juxtaposes and then separates, even during the earliest days of catechesis, instruction and formation, doctrine and life. Religious knowledge and habits of Christian life are often divorced from each other, whereas it is Christian doctrine itself that ought to bud and flower in Christian living in its very presentation of Jesus Christ. For is not Christ truth and life?

But if we must not choose and must not juxtapose, what is left? There remains the possibility of searching for that link in catechetical instruction which will unite teaching with formation. To discover it and define it is assuredly to give to the pedagogy of religious instruction its true stature as a pedagogy of faith.

There is a lead given us in the words of our Lord which are often quoted by those who reduce catechetics to mere instruction. This lead is found in Christ's command to the Apostles: "Go, teach." But far from confirming a partisan position, these words lead us to a more fruitful consideration. There are two Greek words for "teach," *didáskein* and *mathēteúein*. *Didáskein* means "to teach a doctrine" and *mathēteúein* means "to make disciples."

We all know professors who engage in one or the other type of teaching. There are those who give their course in an impersonal fashion and transmit a body of knowledge. And there are others who, through the medium of their message, communicate themselves and attract a following among their hearers. The first-named are the professors who teach students; the second are masters who win disciples.

The word used by our Lord in the Gospel is *mathēteúein:* "Go, teach," that is, "make disciples." Teaching in Christ's name is only of this second type. We must be faithful to the precise nature of His charge. We are not professors of religion; we are masters of Christian life. We must make disciples, teach—teach sincerely and well—but with the objective of introducing the catechized into a new life which is the following of Christ. We need a teaching which, once received by the child, will transform him. It must "renew" him first interiorly and then in his entirety until it works in him a "conversion"; such is the condition of all Christian life.

We are now on the way to discovering the link which in catechesis unites at their depths instruction and formation. To catechize is neither to instruct *or* form, nor instruct *and* form, but instruct *while* forming; or better, it is transmitting a doctrine *for* living. The catechist should teach in such a way—and this is the definition of his pedagogy—that doctrine is received in the one catechized at the level of faith, awakens in him a living faith, provokes in him an act of faith, arouses in him the life of faith. It should address itself to his supernatural being in such a way as to activate, develop and expand the supernatural life. The final goal, the ultimate objective is to establish "a believer."

But the problem is that a certain pedagogy of religious instruction can convey religious information—what might even be called "religious beliefs"—without developing "believers." It can transmit Christian truths without making a person live by faith. All catechists must beware of this temptation or illusion. It is so easy to remain on the level of knowledge or beliefs. It is ever so much more difficult to pass to the level of conversion and faith. All of us need always fear that we are only producing "knowers" when we should really be producing "believers."

The thing that specifies Christian catechesis, from the point of view of its proper objective, is the uniqueness of the doctrine. Transmitted at one and the same time by the words of the catechist and the evidence of his life, it is received by the person taught not through intellect alone as in the case in profane learning but by his whole being, by his flesh and blood and by his grace-illumined self. In the same act, Christian doctrine is at once the object of knowledge and the nourishment of faith. That is why in the single act we instruct and we form. This act is an awakening, a development, an expansion of a living faith—the goal of all catechesis. Only this act exemplifies, most exactly, true religious education.

Some relate the word *"credo"* to the expression *"cor-do"*: "I give my heart." I become a disciple. I adhere not only with my intelligence but with my heart, with a heart that expresses the adherence of my whole being. A profound conversion is at issue here: the dedication of my life. This is what gives the pedagogy of faith its originality and its complexity, but also its grandeur. For what is it that we are seeking in catechetics if not this attitude which "renews" the whole being? Our catechesis thus becomes a true school of faith: "*et renovabis faciem terrae.*"

The fact that religious education is described in these lofty terms does not permit us to overlook the demands of the teaching process. Faith is life, and the catechesis is the food of this life. But faith is first of all a type of knowledge. The faculty of knowing even in the study of Christian doctrine retains all its rights and obligations. It operates according to its nature.

The catechist must teach. Classroom, schedule, manuals, method, discipline will all be necessary to him even at the risk of betraying his role and of causing him to be unfaithful to his mission. At the same time, because of the goal envisioned the pedagogy proper to this teaching will take on a thoroughly specialized form. It will see to it that all needful Christian truth (and truth is ever the object of knowledge) becomes the object of faith in the very act of its acceptance by the one catechized. It will ensure that by means of the doctrine that is transmitted, explained, memorized and retained, there wells up a life of faith which is both an interior attitude and an exterior conformity. This life should be awakened and promoted, enriched, stimulated, expanded by the doctrine taught. In no way does this deny or minimize the demands of instruction, but rather it puts them all in the service of faith.

Allow me to illustrate here what these demands will be for the average catechist. Every catechist is, to some extent, a theologian. Theology is of course essential to his task of transmitting Christian truths as the Church has given them to us. But it is one thing to study Christian doctrine in order to know it and an entirely different one to present Christian truths in such a way that they are understood by the pupil. The problem is particularly acute because the procedure of the theologian as such is the exact opposite of that of the catechist who, having finished his study of theology, wishes to transmit the content of faith.

Theology is the application of intellectual categories to the data of revelation. In theology one advances from faith in these data to reflective knowledge: "*Fides quaerens intellectum.*" In catechesis on the other hand the approach is the opposite: one proceeds to faith from knowledge of the revealed data. The person catechized is not primarily in search of a better knowledge of revelation, but in search of an object for his faith, truth from God in which to believe, nourishment for life. In his regard one might say that catechesis is *"Intellectus quaerens fidem."*

Any radical opposition of theology and catechesis should, of course, be avoided, because a true theology serves a living faith and a good catechesis aids religious knowledge. But we must note —and from a pedagogical point of view this is of key importance— that theology since it is the science of revealed data tends to make the theologian a knower, whereas catechesis being a school of faith tends to make the one catechized a believer. The object studied is the same, but the perspectives are different. The road to be traveled is the one road; it is simply traversed in opposite directions.

We will have to specify the nature of the catechetical approach and define the dialectic proper to this discipline. But first we must have an acute sense of the distinction between the two points of view. The realization that catechetical work has a unique function with respect to the initiation and development of faith is fraught with consequences. It could be that we who are theologians by profession often work under a delusion, walking in the wrong direction with the children, with our backs turned on the objective to be attained. We are too exclusively devoted to transmitting knowledge when we should be devoted to educating in the service of faith.

Enclosed as we are in the dialectic of theology alone, we tend to have as our sole view of the data of revelation that of the theologian. The pedagogical and pastoral viewpoints dictated by the need for education-unto-faith should lead us to discover another dialectic; namely, that of a catechesis which will lead those under instruction along the road to faith.

The catechist is not only a theologian; he is also an adult. As such he has an adult frame of mind. He is at home with concepts and ideas, judgments and reasoning processes, abstraction, deduction and logic. But a child does not have the same system of thought; on the contrary the things familiar to him are the sensible, the concrete, the image. His realm is induction and association. This, then, is the first difficulty that faces the adult catechist: he will have to free himself of his habitual way of thought in order to enter into the world of the child.

But the difficulty goes further. Because of our adult psychology which gives the primacy to the "mental," we have a tendency to consider the data of revelation primarily as a system of logically organized truths. For us revelation is considered chiefly as an object of scientific and deliberate thought.

The child cannot—and in catechesis should not—have this as his first reaction. His psychology gives primacy to the all-embracing and to what is applicable to life. In an entirely natural fashion the data of revelation appear to him globally. They are seen in their entirety as the object of faith and the source of life. If the adult is not careful he will misunderstand the psychology of the child. An actual purification is required in the adult to rid himself of the tendency to be intellectual, analytic, scholarly, scientific, and to respect the tendency toward the all-inclusive and the vital which the child manifests. This tendency conditions the efficacy of a true catechesis as a school of faith. If catechists allow themselves to be victims of an adult perspective, they will discourage the good will of children from the very start and discover that their teaching is ineffective, even sterile.

But there are other difficulties that originate with the child. These may be summarized in the colloquial expression the "daily grind" of school. The normal child has all the habitual dispositions associated with this term. He goes to school to listen passively (even if the school is an "activity" school) to learn, to retain, to recite or to forget. How can he avoid carrying this same attitude over into his catechism work? Everything encourages just that—classroom, schedule, homework, textbooks, tests, marks, and so on. Under these conditions catechism rapidly becomes for him a question of knowing religious facts. In catechism class just as in the rest of the school day it becomes simply a matter of knowing. It is impossible for the child to transcend the school-day level, or to realize that catechetics deals with something beyond knowledge.

The catechist must seek a pedagogy that will lift the child out of this "school-day rut." Otherwise he will miss his goal. What is most important in such a setting is the advance toward faith of the child who is being catechized—a faith that is the action of both man and God involving the whole man in a personal response to the spoken word of God.

Would not the beginnings of a solution for the painfully real problem of the perseverance in the Faith of our young people be found in a catechetical program which attempted to form them in faith during the whole period of their religious education? This could be the case even though it preserved its didactic form, particularly during the ages nine to twelve. A mother, for example, is not content simply to nurse her child. She helps him when he tries to walk. She watches, follows and supports the child's efforts. She guides his first steps. All catechesis because it is the food of faith should likewise be a launching into supernatural existence, an education toward a personal Christian life. In other words it is an apprenticeship in the life of believing.

This, actually, is the necessary condition for Christian perseverance. One does not persevere in something taught. Of a teaching we say merely that it is known or it is not known. To believe there must first be knowledge, of course; and catechesis is certainly a form of conveying knowledge. But what one perseveres in is a life, an interior and exterior attitude, a rectitude of thought and action. One is faithful to the gift of self to someone. He commits himself to a greater love. It is to the fullness of this Christian life that all catechesis is linked.

We know what the normal steps of entry into the Church in the early centuries were. First one had to be "converted," then tested over a probationary period and duly certified by a sponsor who presented the catechumen to the bishop. Conversion, even prior to all catechesis, was from the first moment a personal and basic act making choice of Christ and the Church. For this reason the bishop was sometimes severe; aspirants had to wait as long as two and three years. After their inscription on the day of *"electi"*—and only then—came the instruction of the candidates for baptism. The elementary instruction was relatively short because the time of probation had been long and because a post-baptismal catechesis would continue it. Finally, baptism was given at the Paschal Vigil which was followed by the mystagogical catechesis during the week "*in albis*."

This articulated process of entry into the Church respected the absolute primacy of a supernatural life which embraced religious instruction, the latter providing nourishment for the nascent faith of the convert.

The present-day practice of the Church, for reasons which we need neither analyze nor evaluate here, has reversed the order of this triple approach. The infant is first baptized, then he is instructed and thereafter "converted." The chief preoccupation of the catechist in instructing the child at each of the steps during the period of religious education must be to obtain this third step, "conversion." All this underlines the urgent need to create a pedagogy that will be not simply the pedagogy of religious teaching in the narrow sense (with an object similar to that of secular teaching), but a special pedagogy that corresponds to the objective of catechesis. This proportion to its proper object and to the needs of the child will make of it a pedagogy that is truly a pedagogy of faith.

It can be objected to this presentation of catechesis as a school of faith that baptism is the sacrament of faith, and that as an efficacious sign of grace it brings about what it signifies. It is of course clear that a person baptized, even an infant, has achieved perfect justification and is in full possession of the supernatural configuration that makes one a Christian. But it must also be admitted that the baptized infant, though he possesses all the structures of the supernatural life, can not yet perform the corresponding functions. Grace does not destroy nature. It is only gradually that first the child and then the adolescent enters upon a personal life of faith.

Faith is virtue, act and life. Baptism gives to its recipient the virtue of faith. But, as we know, this virtue is a mere disposition, an aptitude. As we say in theology, it is a potency, a *habitus*. What is necessary is that this virtue of faith, given and received in baptism, should become *act*. Religious instruction, by presenting an object to the faith of the baptized, allows this faith of the baptized to pass from virtue and potency to act and life. According to sound philosophy, the passage from potency to act constitutes movement, and life consists of movement: *"vita est in motu."* Catechetics, by making it possible for an act of faith to flow from the virtue of faith, sets in motion the life of faith.

The realization of the bond between catechesis and faith places faith in a baptismal context that it is important for us to note. Baptism is the sacrament of faith, in the first place because it is administered in the Faith of the Church. This is expressed by the exactly specified sign, the intention of the minister, and the witness of the godparents. Moreover, baptism tends toward the development of a total faith: virtue, act and life. It usually remains unfulfilled or unrealized in part, however. The shadow of the catechist falls upon the minister of baptism, who in turn seems to have his eyes fixed upon the catechist. The latter will "fulfill," give the plenitude to that which the dispenser of the sacrament begins.

It is an immediate indication of the lofty dignity of the vocation of catechist to say that it finds its correct niche in the ministry of baptism. To some extent it is a participation by way of prolongation or transition unto act of this royal sacrament.

A comparison with the steps from natural birth to the fullness of natural life should clarify still further the role of catechesis with regard to faith. The entry of an infant into the world takes place in three steps: conception, that is the act of generation which gives to each being all that it needs both to be and to exist; the moment when the child really comes to life in the womb of the mother, in the sense that she has the physical certainty that the infant she bears is indeed alive; and finally birth, which gives autonomy to the life of the infant. It is an initial and relative autonomy, to be sure, but one that will continue to increase until the point is reached when the being takes complete charge of its own existence.

Of these three steps, each having its own importance, the most thrilling from a mother's point of view is the marvelous instant when in her womb the infant suddenly takes life. Now if baptism is the act of generation that gives supernatural life, it is surely catechizing that is the womb of Holy Mother Church in which the children of God take life. By it, a believing people comes to birth. Over the months and years of catechetical instruction in the Church, a community living by faith nourishes, warms and animates the incipient life of baptism. Those who have been begotten by water and the Spirit must be fed with the milk of the doctrine and the power of the Word. This instruction helps the baptized to fill out the contour of the life of faith they have been given, until the day comes when they can feed themselves and live on their own as spiritual adults.

Is there, then, any place more sacred or time more marvelous than the catechism classroom and its class hour? Truly this is a sanctuary because in it the awakening of a living and personal faith takes place. This is where the children of God are slowly but surely brought to life, where the Church is upbuilt into the assembly of a nation of believers.

There is no ministry more lofty than that of catechizing, for it is a participation in the sacrament of baptism itself; we have seen its great *dignity*. But some mention should be made of its grave *responsibilities* as a participation in the spiritual maternity of the Church. For this all-important generative function the Church appeals to catechists. To them she gives her own powers, and the catechists lend their hands to the Church for the task of molding the souls of these children. They carve the living statues who will be the Church's believers.

A look, a word, a gesture have great importance in this domain. We know that some infants otherwise normally conceived never come forth to life from their mother's womb. We call them "stillborn." Are there not many children conceived normally in baptism and instructed catechetically who never really come to life? For them catechism is not the womb of their mother Holy Church; doubtless what it lacks is the dimension of consecration and prayer, the dimension of a liturgical community that gives the primary role to the formation of faith.

The hands of the catechist must become one with the hands of the Church. They must be as maternal as her own. It is a matter of awakening a faith that slumbers. We know that it is only a mother who knows how to wake her infant—slowly, tenderly, without harshness; the father's hands have neither the same delicacy nor the same success. In catechesis we need a mother's hands to awaken because it is for the whole of life that the eyes of faith are opened in those years. The need for the greatest caution in this task is obvious. We do not have the right to fail.

The catechist has a dangerous ministry therefore. But it is also a fruitful one. It is through catechesis that baptism achieves its fullness, through it that men come to faith. The action of catechists is situated at the very heart of apostolic activity. Is there in the Church any more truly missionary work than that of developing believers?

At times we have depreciated the vocation of the catechist by not according it the respect and admiration it deserves. The reason is that until now the meaning of the true role of catechetics has escaped us. If catechism teaching is nothing more than the painful and wearisome memorizing of formulas beyond the child's grasp in order to pass an examination that checks on nothing more than knowledge, then catechists become drillmasters or at most professors. But catechists are not meant to be that.

Catechetical instruction is the school of faith in the complex sense in which we have just defined it. Catechists are awakeners, educators of faith, spiritual fathers and mothers of the supernatural life, builders of the Church.

There has been a great deal of talk of the collaboration of the laity with the hierarchy in Catholic action. The collaboration of the laity with the hierarchy in religion teaching deserves equal attention. If one grants catechists their true "dignity" their number will increase, their mission will bear fruit and the Church will grow.

We must now try to see, in greater detail, how religious teaching brings about an awakening of faith; or more exactly, in what it consists, and what are the major preoccupations of a catechist who educates unto faith. An analysis of faith, not in its entirety but in its process of expression, should provide the necessary preliminary distinctions. What is belief? In our perspective of religious teaching aimed at developing a believer, what does faith suppose?

Faith, in order to be truly personal and living, supposes an acceptance, a conversion and a consecration. To reflect upon these three steps is to give the bases of a pedagogy of faith.

ACCEPTANCE

To believe is first of all to accept, because faith, while it is adherence to truths, is at the same time and primarily an encounter with a person. Christ, the fullness of the utterance of God, is truth and life. Our Lord is the object of our faith and He is not something but someone.

In all his teaching, the catechist must be careful to permit this reception of Christ by the one catechized, and to ensure constantly the passage from the level of ideas to the level of persons. This is not easy. Children live in a world of the concrete, the sensible, the visible. They must be led to the spiritual, the invisible, the divine. How true is this of children in today's neo-pagan world where the sole values reckoned important are material and carnal, where mathematics and technology are the only standards for measuring men and things. Only that is true which is proved, which is subjected to experiment, which is manufactured. Life is a constant matter of going higher or farther or faster. The world seems to be made to the measure of the man who dominates it. What have we to do with "mystery," with "utter gratuity," with "the beyond"? Our contemporaries are no longer capable of appreciating the world of symbol and sign; they are walled up in a universe where God no longer has a place.

This indicates the new dimension of a pedagogy that hopes to lead and introduce to faith. In order to present the mystery, the gratuity, the "beyond," all of which are strange and ill-suited to our contemporaries, there is need of preparation. The catechist will first have to make possible the transit from the profane to the sacred, from the sacred to the religious, from the religious to the divine: so many indispensable steps in forming a sort of pre-catechism. This process is never finished and must go on beneath the surface, because the evil is so deeply rooted. In the same way, the entry into the world of signs—signs that reveal the "presence" of the Lord, and effect His "passing"—demands an invitation without which a child can perhaps know the world of religion superficially, but can never enter into it. This world remains for him a closed and forbidden world or, even worse, a world that is worthless and dangerous. Modern civilization encases the children of today like a covering of lead that closes them off from the divine.

But we must admit that our pedagogy of religious teaching ignores far too much a twofold, fundamental truth concerning a catechesis that educates faith: (1) faith is an encounter, and demands an acceptance of Christ; (2) a child is doubly shut off from the mystery of God, by his psychology and even more by the world in which he lives.

What good does it do to teach a doctrine if Christ is not welcomed and accepted? We must guard against sowing without having first thoroughly worked the ground. Until then the soil is not open to our planting, the earth is dry; nothing can enter it; nothing can grow. Reflection on this matter reveals major obstacles for the catechist. If he does not guard against them, he will teach but he will not educate unto faith. The pedagogy of faith is a pedagogy of clearing the ground and of plowing, of acceptance and of encounter.

The difficulty is greater still if we wish to give this encounter its true depth. Actually, there are several ways of receiving someone. We can either greet him by shaking his hand or else take him in our arms as a mother embraces her child, with an affection that gives voice to our whole being. A believer receives his Lord as a mother receives her child. Here it is a question of mobilizing strength or of setting in motion one's whole being. The catechist will have to react against the all too frequent tendency—natural enough in a matter of teaching only—to move the intelligence of the child and no more. The child in his entirety, body and soul, with his intellectual, volitional, emotional and sensory-motor powers all under the influence of grace, should be put in a state of expectancy and eager receptiveness for the Lord.

This means that in catechism teaching education unto faith will require an all-embracing pedagogy, necessarily complex.

CONVERSION

Faith is not only a contemplation; it is a transforming union, a communion. The spoken word of God transforms all that it touches. Our Lord, once He is received by us, demands still more. Faith is a change of heart, a conversion. The word "faith," in Latin *"fides,"* in Greek *"pistis,"* in Hebrew *"emunah,"* signifies finding stability in someone or something. "It is sure, it is solid; I believe in it." The Bible tells us that the Lord is the Rock, that He is solid, that He is "amen." To believe is to renounce the attempt to find solidity and stability in oneself in order to find it in God: it is to turn oneself about, to change axis, to give up looking at and loving oneself in order to contemplate and love God. Claudel says somewhere that to believe is to quit the world of the immediate, of self-security, for the world of the beyond, of security in God. There is a sacrifice, a renunciation, an asceticism in faith. Claudel says again, in speaking of his conversion at Notre-Dame de Paris, "It was as if I had changed my skin."

The pedagogy of catechism should allow for all this interior effort. Here, again, there is a new dimension unknown to a simple pedagogy of teaching but indispensable to a pedagogy of faith. As faith is gradually awakened and fed by religious teaching, it becomes a matter of effecting little by little this turning or conversion that is indispensable to faith. Assuredly this is the work of the Holy Spirit and of human freedom. But it is the task of pedagogy to foresee the atmosphere, the activities, and the techniques that will respect this fundamental need, and that will place the child in the conditions most favorable to a successful development of his faith.

PLEDGE OF SELF

Faith ought to result in expression and in further manifestation. The life of the believer is entirely transformed by the life of faith. To believe is to become involved in a new life. How could it be otherwise, for the object of faith is the utterance of God. If every word addressed to a man demands an answer, how much more so must the divine message, which the Scriptures tell us is able to attack and transform everything upon the earth? To believe is to reply to the word spoken by God, and this reply is manifested in a "divinized" mode of living: the mentality of Christ, the views, the gestures, the words of Our Lord. Faith is both reply and dedication.

To catechize is to arouse through the medium of teaching this interior activity which is entirely supernatural in its germ and entirely incarnated in its term. Catechesis, the acceptance of the Lord and conversion of heart, must provide for this "supernatural realism" of the divine life.

Such is the act of faith. All religious instruction that respects its proper goal has this act as its objective. Such is the believer "born" of a catechesis that educates unto faith. One cannot overemphasize the need of meditating upon these views, in order to break with the routine and the sclerosis that too often reduce religious teaching and catechesis to sterility.

If we were to set before the eyes of catechists a model believer capable of acting as an inspiration to their pedagogy, there is no better example than Abraham, the "father of believers." It is quite easy, in reading the Scripture, to grasp the three vital moments of Abraham's all-important act of faith:

"Abraham, Abraham"—"Here I am, Lord." Here is his acceptance.

"Depart, leave Chaldea and go into Canaan, the promised land." And Abraham departs, renounces his immediate world, his family, his lands, his riches, his native heath. He turns, he chooses God, he no longer relies upon himself. This is true conversion of the heart.

Abraham dedicates himself to an entirely new life. This is what constitutes the richness of Abraham's faith and makes him in the eyes of God and in our eyes the "father of believers." It is not the content of the message he received, for his religious knowledge was indeed quite limited. It is rather the spontaneity and the generosity, the depth and the fidelity of his giving. His acceptance, his conversion, his answer and his self-dedication were all of that stamp. What light this casts on the pedagogy of expounding the divine utterance, the pedagogy of a religious instruction in the service of faith!

Like an echo of Abraham, at the other extreme of the Bible, is the story of St. Paul.

"Saul, Saul, why do you persecute me?"—"Who are you, Lord?"

"I am Jesus of Nazareth whom you persecute." Paul, recognizing Christ, accepts and adores Him.

Then comes the combat of conversion, the inner battle. Without a word, Paul struggles with himself while the call of the Lord presses upon him. He chooses: he burns what he had adored and adores what he had burned. He renounces his Pharisaism, and in turning from it he alters the direction of his love so as to give himself to the God of the Christians.

Faith, for Paul, is both reply and dedication. "Lord, what do you wish me to do?"—"Go to Damascus." Paul, though he is blind, departs. The eyes of his body are closed to this world below, "of the immediate" as Claudel says; but the eyes of his soul, the eyes of his faith, are open to the world beyond, the invisible world of faith.

What a picture and what a lesson. Would that all catechesis could bring forth believers so wonderfully dedicated and inspired, and that all religious instruction could awaken such genuine faith! Such a sublime ideal ought to be the constant preoccupation of all catechists in the Church. For the true catechist there can be no more terrible anguish than to see revelation become mere matter for schoolroom teaching, and cease to be a nourishment for faith.

Let us hope that in the light of the objectives outlined above for a true catechesis, careful attention will be given, in the concrete, to the following three matters:

(1) the *atmosphere* of a catechism class: its sacred and religious character, its atmosphere of silence, of joy, of loyalty, of freedom; its biblical and liturgical flavor; its sense of the person and the community.

(2) the *activities* of catechetical instruction which give due place to the three preoccupations of all pedagogy: impression, assimilation, expression—with insistence on techniques of expression, so important in a pedagogy of faith in order to make

possible the act of faith (acceptance, conversion, response) and the life of faith (awakening, development, expansion).

(3) the *dialectic* of catechism, allowing us to specify correctly the necessary but limited roles of concrete and abstract knowledge, sensible and rational knowledge; and to clarify all that is peculiar to the knowledge of faith.

7.

Primary Religious Education
and Primary Teaching
·
Chanoine André Boyer

For a long time the education of the child rested on the a priori assumption that he was a man in miniature, that he was a being endowed with all the faculties of an adult on a reduced scale. The educators of the past—a past which in some cases still lives on— undoubtedly acknowledged very great differences between the adult and the child. But these differences were of the quantitative and not the qualitative order.

Biology, experimental psychology, psychoanalysis and sociology have shown that this was a superficial view. They have quite clearly established that the child is not a man in miniature but a very different thing: man's offspring, a being in process of evolving. The child lives a life which, although it should lead to fulfillment in adulthood, differs from adulthood at every stage through which it must pass to reach it: in its needs, it possibilities, its interests, its manner of being and of acting and of reacting.

Moreover, experimental psychology tells us that it is not merely a question of the child and the adult. There is the child, the adolescent, the youth and the adult. There can be designated first, second and third phases of childhood. Within each of these phases various substages can be distinguished: the stage of the newborn infant, the stage of the baby, the stage of the older baby; the age of resistance at two or three years, the age of animism and of transferences of identity, the age of grace; then the age of reason, the age of syncretistic thinking, and, around ten, the age of arrival at formal thinking. A little later come the awakening of the personality, prepuberty, at thirteen or fourteen puberty, and so on.

In each of these phases the educator who is anxious to do his work conscientiously and effectively is confronted with new problems. He needs to consult not only the psychologist but also the biologist. The biologist can show him something of the organic development which accompanies progressive myelinization of the brain and marrow and underlies the psychological development. He can help him see in the life of the newborn child not a completely new departure but a continuity, since myelinization begins five or six months before birth. He needs to consult the psychoanalyst, who can show him the repercussions of the mother's condition on the child and who calls his attention to the importance of the prenatal period, of the subconscious, even of the unconscious. He must hear the sociologist, who helps him put his finger on the influence of environment, for indeed before birth the child is already marked by it whether the environment be rich or deficient. So much is this the case that it can be said that environment is actually within the child.

The educator ought likewise to hear the theologian's view, for it is all these other aspects of the child's life that are to be baptized. Grace does not overpower nature but elevates it, so that the educator has to make a synthesis of all that concerns nature. That is why he must know exactly in what this elevation consists, and why he must not separate natural life from supernatural life as he is too inclined to do.

If the way of life of many practicing believers does not show a greater difference from that of many who do not practice, it is often because these Christians have been brought up as if they had two lives—a worldly life on the one hand and a religious life on the other—and not just one life which derives its form from the grace and the charity of Christ. If the vital synthesis of nature and the supernatural has not been effected in them it is largely the fault of their education—an insufficiently enlightened and stilted form of education.

In saying this we are not expressing personal views. Not long ago Pope Pius XII took up a similar subject before the members of the Fifth International Congress on Psychotherapy and Clinical Psychology. In a speech of uncommon scientific and theological precision delivered on April 13, 1953, the Pope vigorously brought out this vital unity. He asked his audience of Christian specialists to consider man first as a psychic unit and whole, all of whose dynamic forces are dependent upon a spiritual soul; second as a unit structured in itself, that is, as man concrete and real and not as man in the abstract; third as a social unit, that is, as a man at once personal and social; and fourth as a "transcending" unit, that is, one tending toward God.

First of all, what is meant by "man as psychic unit" and "whole"? We have seen that psychologists, biologists, sociologists and psychoanalysts have all had a word to say about the development of the human offspring. A danger is latent in the possibility that each might try to steal the show and, by virtue of the undeniable parallelism existing between psychological evolution and organic evolution, or the influence of environment, might lose sight of the originality proper to man, and bestow (here we quote from the Pope's text),

the decisive function in the whole upon a single factor, for instance upon one of the elementary psychic dynamisms, and thus install a secondary power at the helm. These dynamic forces may be *in* the soul, or *in* man; they are not, however, the soul nor the man. They are energies of considerable intensity perhaps, but nature has entrusted their direction to the center-post, to the spiritual soul, endowed with intelligence and will and normally capable of governing these energies. That these dynamic forces exert pressure on a given activity does not necessarily mean that they compel it. To deprive the soul of its central position would be to deny ontological and psychic reality.[1]

Man who is a psychological unit, the Pope tells us, is also a structured unit,

an ordered whole, a microcosm, a kind of sovereign state of which the charter, determined by the purpose of the whole, subordinates to this purpose the action of the parts according to the rank of their value and function. In the last analysis, this charter is of ontological and metaphysical, and not of psychological and personal origin.[2]

---

[1] Pope Pius XII, *"Discours aux membres du Congrès international de Psychothérapie et de Psychologie clinique,"* *L'Osservatore Romano,* April 16, 1953. Cf. *The Catholic Mind,* LI (July, 1953), 429; *On Psychotherapy and Religion* (Washington: National Catholic Welfare Conference), p. 5. The above translation follows neither exactly.

[2] *The Catholic Mind,* p. 430; NCWC ed., *loc. cit.*

In other words, we can undoubtedly establish a certain parallelism between the organic evolution of man and that of beasts, between biological evolution and psychological and social evolution. But parallelism does not mean identity. The general laws of a child's development in all domains do not prevent a specific character in that principle which governs his evolution, the presence of which is affirmed at every moment. The most earnest partisans of the biological and psychological parallelism have to recognize that the correlation between the two seems to loosen in proportion as this parallelism becomes more complicated and as the complexity of the external background increases. Doubtless they attribute this loosening, which they consider obvious, to our insufficient knowledge of the functioning of the nervous system. But this interpretation is not required by the facts, all the less so in that certain of these facts, on the contrary, oblige the same authors to acknowledge an active principle by nature superior to all that we meet with in animal life. One such psychologist writes:

A child's apprenticeship in language does not belong to the same class of training as that training which consists in strengthening in him conditioned reflexes like the salivary reflex. The child's action anticipates the efforts an adult makes to help him to acquire the use of language. His imitation is not at all like a mechanical operation and is never slavish; it is of the same quality as the intelligence.[3]

What is this free intelligent action, then, if not a manifestation of a principle which is ontological and metaphysical and on which the structure of the whole man depends: his spiritual soul?

In addition to being a psychological unit and a structured unit, the Pope goes on to say, man is a social unit. The child as well as the man is profoundly influenced by environment and in turn exercises an influence upon it. But the tendency of the sociologizing interpretation is to exaggerate the importance of society in relation to the human person. Soviet pedagogy, for example, does not hesitate, as we know, on the one hand to proclaim the incomparable effectiveness of the social factor upon moral education and, on the other, to assign "the general advancement of society" as the end in

[3] Youssef Mourad, *L'Eveil de l'Intelligence* (Paris: Félix Alcan, 1939), p. 375.

view for both the family and the individual. In this view the authority of parents "can be justified only by their duty toward society." [4]

The child should know, Makarenko tells the parents, "that you answer not only for yourselves but for him as well before the whole of Soviet society." Good, therefore, is whatever serves that society, and evil whatever might harm it.

There is no question of denying either the influence of environment upon the individual or the responsibilities of the individual toward society. But man's moral criterion as a social unit is something different.

There exist (Pius XII says) a self-defense, a self-esteem, a love and service of self which are not only justified but demanded by psychology and morality. This is both evident from nature and is a lesson of Christian faith. (Cf. *Sum. Theol.* 2a, 2ae, q. 26, art. 4, *in capite*.) Our Lord taught: "Thou shalt love thy neighbour as thyself." (Mk. 12, 31) The measure of love for neighbor proposed by Christ is charity towards oneself, not the other way around. Applied psychology would be scorning this reality if it were to characterize every thought of self as a psychic inhibition, a mistake, a relapse to a prior stage of development, on the ground that it is opposed to the natural altruism of the psychic being.[5]

Here again there is a balance to be maintained, a hierarchy to observe.

Finally, the Sovereign Pontiff teaches, man who is psychic unit, structured unit and social unit, is a transcendent unit whose tendency is toward God. But in what sense? What precisely is this "mysterious dynamism"?

It is the province of the methods of your science (the Pope told the psychotherapists), to throw light on the question of the existence and the structure and manner of action of this dynamic tendency. If a positive result were reached, this should not be declared irreconcilable with reason or faith. It would go to show that the *esse ab alio* (being from another) is likewise, down to its deepest roots, an *esse ad alium* (being for another), and that Saint Augustine's words, *Fecisti nos ad te Deus et inquietum est cor nostrum donec requiescat in te* (*Confessiones*, Bk. 1,

---

[4] Irène Lezine, A. S. *Makarenko: Pédagogue soviétique* (Paris: Presses Universitaires de France, 1954), p. 126.

[5] Pope Pius XII, *The Catholic Mind*, p. 432; NCWC ed., p. 9.

ch. 1, n. 1), are confirmed anew down to the very depths of man's psychic being. Should it be a question of a dynamism affecting all men, all peoples, all epochs and all cultures, what a help and how invaluable in the search for God and the affirmation of His existence! [6]

This, however, does not alter the fact that,

religions, the natural and supernatural knowledge of God and worship of Him, do not proceed from the unconscious or the subconscious, nor from any affective impulse, but from a clear and certain knowledge of God by means of His natural and supernatural revelation. This has been the doctrine and the faith of the Church beginning with the word of God in the *Book of Wisdom* and the *Epistle to the Romans,* down to the encyclical *Pascendi Dominici Gregis.*[7]

In other words, the tendency of man the "transcending unit" toward God must not be confused with a doctrine of immanency. It cannot be said that nature requires the supernatural.

Baptism is a "second birth," but above all a grace. The death and resurrection of Christ were needed to merit the life we receive at this birth. But, in order to develop fully, this new life must complete, little by little, the conquest of our nature, for we are and never cease to be psychic, structured, and social units.

To put it another way: while becoming children of God we remain the offspring of man and thus wounded by original sin. The life of the baptized person

is altogether paradoxical. On the one hand it is, as we must never forget, a life which has already been raised from the dead because it is wholly new, because it is the life of the risen Christ, because it is brought about by the Spirit who is the force of glory and resurrection. . . . But on the other hand, this life is an incompletely resurrected life and one that is doubly so because our body has not yet been seized by the force of the Risen One, because it is not immortal, because it remains a perishable carnal body, and because the soul is not wholly sanctified; it has not been wrested in one snatch and forever from evil and the Evil One, and it can fall back into evil and perish. *Spe salvi facti sumus.* It is only in the realm of hope that we are saved.[8]

[6] *Ibid.*, pp. 433 f.; p. 11.
[7] *Loc. cit.;* p. 10.
[8] Jean Mouroux, *Du Baptême a l'acte de foi* (Paris: Ed. de l'Ecole, 1953), p. 19.

It will be understood by now why it is urgent that the educator know all about the growth of this body to which the soul is united, about the various forces of the soul itself at the different stages of its development; that he know all the depths of this "structured, individual and social unit" to be able to cooperate with the sanctifying action of the Spirit and move in the direction of the vocation of each one. And, on the other hand, how necessary it is if he is a Christian educator that in all of these delicate questions in which he constantly skirts the coasts of error, he should be illumined by the light of the Church's teaching.

Fortunately there is beyond all this the maternal instinct, an art of education in itself, which the Holy Spirit will not leave without direct enlightenment. Everyone knows that a good and deeply Christian mother leaves an indelible mark on the souls of her children. These mothers seem relatively rare nowadays. How many mothers of baptized children there are who have no concern for education and who know not the price of a soul. They appear to have no inkling of its complexity and to be almost powerless to "bring up" children.

To tell the truth, those who bear the weight of responsibility are often not aware of the difficulty of their task. They believe that they can trust entirely to rule-of-thumb empiricism. Often enough, those responsible for preparing them for the task do not believe it at all important. Is it not the fact that many are still convinced that no serious educational activity can begin before the age of reason? They should understand that just as one cannot expect normal growth in a plant which has been left to fade away without any cultivation, a moral life and all the more a Christian life cannot be brought to full flowering when for six or seven years it has been given no care.

It can be said however that for some time now unanimous agreement has been reached by the widest variety of minds on the major importance of the early years of life. The sciences, practical and concrete human experience and religious faith are represented in this agreement. It could not be merely a chance meeting of minds when biologists, psychologists, students of character, philosophers, pedagogues, theologians and the popes themselves conclude identically.

Some people believe that serious education should be begun only around the age of twelve, or at least they think that before the age of seven it is not important. According to the analysts, it is, on the contrary, after that age that the child's affective nature ceases to be malleable; it is before the age of six, before the age of four, that the decisive impacts are experienced. So the child must not be turned over at that age, as is so often done, to those influences which are the least carefully chosen.[9]

Emmanuel Mounier judges that it would be very useful for religious formation and a knowledge of the religious attitudes of adults to "ascertain the age divisions of religious awareness between birth and puberty." This is because "the adult's religion is rarely quite freed from the weaknesses and survivals in his affective life which carry over from childhood." [10]

Dr. Stocker brings out clearly what is in a way final about a bad education given in early childhood:

However intelligent the child may prove later on, at the tenderest age in his life he is unable to make a fully conscious judgment and to reject error. . . . Set in the direction of error from his earliest steps, error is what the child will love, since it is the only thing he knows.[11]

Madame Herbinière-Lebert, inspectress of French nursery schools, gives an excellent explanation of this influence of the unconscious by which events, impressions received, sensations experienced, emotions felt are recorded at so deep a level up to the ages of two, four or five years that only exceptionally will it be possible for the psychoanalyst to bring them to light should they become malignant later on.

All the more powerful because unsuspected, they will move in the dark, adding new elements to the hereditary legacy of instincts and tendencies

[9] Charles Beaudoin, *Visage de l'enfance* (Paris: Horizons de France, 1937), p. 206.
[10] Emmanuel Mounier, *Traité du caractère* (Paris: Ed. du Seuil, 1946), p. 756.
[11] A. Stocker, *Psychologie du sens moral* (Geneva: Ed. Suzerenne, 1949), p. 245.

which form the basis of that affective life from which stem the motives of most of our actions.[12]

Another factor—the importance of which at this period of life must not be overlooked—is time. It is different for the child from what it is for the adult, months having for the child the value of years for the mature man.

If we admit the existence of those impressionable periods which Mme. Montessori speaks of, moments of mental development in which the mind shows a sudden aptitude for certain forms of activity, for certain kinds of training; privileged moments of rather brief duration which must be watched for and taken advantage of because before they came nothing was yet possible and after they are gone everything will be difficult and perhaps impossible; if we are aware of all this how careful we should be of minutes which are ill spent. We can make up for a failure in an examination, but who could ever make up for time wasted in early childhood? [13]

What makes the *école maternelle* important in the eyes of Mme. Herbinière-Lebert is that it is "the educator of the unconscious."

Even in relation to this nursery school, however, the influence of the parents comes first. A philosopher explains why:

The younger the child, the easier it is to obtain a result. The rules [with which parents have had the wisdom to acquaint the child before his instinctive reaction to the limited universe he faces] will impress themselves indelibly, and all other influences resulting from his contact with his environment will never be anything but *superimpressions,* which will never efface the first impression. On the contrary, if the more complex rules of true morality, which will follow as soon as the child begins to speak, are imposed *after* he has himself already reacted, it is they which will act as superimpressions, and will be incapable of completely eradicating the imprint of the first.[14]

The theologian is even more affirmative. In the eyes of Canon Michael Pfliegler it is during his early years that "man acquires his essential moral pattern." If no religious direction has been given

[12] S. Herbinière-Lebert, *Leçons de pedagogie* (Paris: Presses Universitaires de France, 1950), p. 182.

[13] *Ibid.,* p. 206.

[14] Pierre Lecomte du Noüy, *Human Destiny* (New York: Longmans, Green, 1947), pp. 211 f.

then, "it will be as useless later on to try to exercise a religious influence over the individual as it would be to insist upon filling up a basket without any bottom." [15]

The Church for its part has been trying for a long time to make educators aware of the decisive character of early religious influences. St. Pius X was so insistent on the right of children to receive communion as soon as they were able to distinguish the Eucharistic bread from ordinary bread because he knew to what an extent prior training is a sensitive period for religious education as for any education. He was likewise anxious to give little children the sustaining force they need when they need it. Pius XI underlined explicitly what a child's faith is at that age, and how desirable it is to give him the nourishment which suits him:

Children go to the Lord if they are not prevented from doing so . . . they go to the Lord, to Jesus, and the Savior's expression is terribly severe . . . when He threatens with the most awful punishments him who scandalizes one of these little ones who, as he said, "believe in me." We must measure the deep meaning of this saying. The little ones do not go to the Lord only in an instinctive way, in a material, bodily sense; it is first of all their souls which go to Him because these little ones *believe in the Lord.*[16]

Monseigneur Chollet, Archbishop of Cambrai, has observed in this connection that Christ did not say, "Bring the little children to me," but, "Let them come." His divine purity is like a magnet which draws them.

Regarding Christian formation at an early age, no one has spoken with greater understanding and authority than Pius XII. In order that "a man's education may begin in the cradle" as he puts it, it is indispensable that parents be prepared for their task. He forcefully reminds young married couples that education is a primary end of marriage on the same footing with procreation,[17] that for their children they are "as it were spiritual precursors," priests of the cradle and childhood. Competency for so important a "ministry"

[15] Michel Pfliegler, *Le bon moment* (Paris: Casterman, 1939), p. 52.
[16] Pope Pius XI to chaplains of Italian students, *L'Osservatore Romano*, Sept. 15, 1933; *La Vie Spirituelle*, 37 (Nov. 1, 1933), 198.
[17] *Allocution to Young Married Couples*, March 18, 1942.

can hardly be improvised without thought of the consequences. And yet,

> while it would never occur to anyone to turn himself suddenly, on the spot, without any apprenticeship or preparation into a mechanic or an engineer, a doctor or lawyer, every day great numbers of young men and women get married and come together without for a single instant having thought of the arduous duties which await them in the education of their children.[18]

How few of them take thought of the extent to which a well ordered love, implying mutual respect, can have a profound influence on a child! "O fathers and mothers in whom the faith of Christ sanctifies your mutual love, prepare even before the birth of the baby the purity of the family atmosphere in which his eyes and his soul will be opened up." [19]

Fathers and mothers ought indeed to receive the child as a gift from God.

> As soon as the child is born (Pius XII tells the midwives), hasten like the ancient Romans to carry him to the arms of his father, but in a spirit which is incomparably more lofty. With them it signified a claim to paternity and the authority which proceeds from it; now it is the homage of a commitment to the Creator to fulfill with affectionate devotion the mission which God has given to him. . . . As for the mother, doubtless the voice of nature speaks in her and puts into her heart the desire, the joy, the courage, the love, the will to care for her child, but to overcome the suggestions of faintheartedness in all of its forms, this voice needs to be strengthened and assume a supernatural tone, so to speak. It is you who, more by your whole manner of being and acting than by words, must help the young mother appreciate the greatness, the beauty, the nobility of that awakening life. . . . In her heart and eyes you must see that there is a reflection of the great gift of God's love for her and her child.[20]

---

[18] *Allocution to Mothers of Families (Davanti a questa)*, Oct. 26, 1941, AAS 33, p. 451; (London: Catholic Truth Society, 1951), p. 7.

[19] *Ibid.* (AAS, p. 452).

[20] *The Apostolate of the Midwife (Vegliare con sollecitudine)*, Oct. 29, 1951, AAS 43, pp. 839 f.; (New York: Paulist Press, 1951), p. 9, par. 16. See translation in *Moral Questions Affecting Married Life* (Washington: NCWC, 1951), pp. 7 f., pars. 15 f. The above follows neither English version exactly.

A reception of the child like this, religious and thankful, will not be without its effects. For who can take the measure of the mysterious influences the mother exerts over the growth of her child?

Many of the moral characteristics which you see in the youth or the man owe their origin to the manner and circumstances of his first upbringing in infancy: purely organic habits contracted at that time may later prove a serious obstacle to the spiritual life of the soul.[21]

The reason is all the stronger why it is important to arrange for the child's baptism as soon as possible. The fact is that there is no other way to impart supernatural life to the child. "For an adult an act of love can be enough to acquire sanctifying grace and to make up for the absence of baptism. For the unborn or the newly born this way is not open."[22] We see into what detail Pius XII thought it wise to go and with what care and precision his directives are given, bearing witness to a rare knowledge of the subject. His writings on the topic are sprinkled with aphorisms which psychology and pedagogy sustain, for example, that man's education begins in the cradle, that Christian education must be a continuous, permanent, progressive undertaking. How accurate they are we can easily see in the study of the development of man in the earliest ages of life.

THE NEWBORN CHILD

In the terms used by psychology the child is newborn for a period from three to six weeks. Is he from nature's standpoint simply a "digestive tube" as some biologists say? If this were the case, how does it happen that he is sensitive in regard to the welcome he receives to the point where, if it is cold, it can affect his very vitality?[23] How does it come about that no amount of care, be it the most intelligent and devoted, is enough for him; that he misses his mother's love so much that he does not develop normally with-

[21] *Allocution to Mothers of Families,* Oct. 26, 1941, AAS 33, p. 453; CTS, p. 9.
[22] *The Apostolate of the Midwife,* p. 10, par. 19; NCWC, p. 9, par. 19.
[23] Etienne de Greeff, *Nos Enfants et nous* (Tournai: Casterman, 1948), ch. II, "L'enfant et le milieu," pp. 42–55.

out it; that nothing nor any person taking her place can give him the feeling of security needed for his full blooming?

Doubtless his soul remains mired in biological reflexes. For a time after the "shock" of birth the newborn child seems to go on with its fetal sleep. But it is not just a small animal; it is a soul, perhaps a baptized soul in which the Holy Spirit dwells and which He has sanctified. It is likewise the soul of a "sinner," a soul for which concupiscence lies in wait. Belief in this twofold aspect of her newborn child ought to guide the mother's attitude toward him.

While his infant stare is taking in his surroundings, let her take thought that *her* child is likewise a child of God and that she should give thanks to Him for the child's redemption. Let her remember that it is her prayers which open for him the road to heaven. Let her consider that by overcoming the fits of sentimentality which lead so many mothers to pamper the baby's existence, by refusing to be impressed by crying which has no cause, by quietly imposing her will under all circumstances, she is being in truth God's envoy at the side of her child. In the joy that he feels in basking in her presence with their faces close together, her little child of God may experience a meeting with the Lord, for is there not a single presence in mother and child? If it is true that we act more "through what we are than through what we say," we must, when we are unable to say anything, recognize the summons to be, in order that we may finally act. A Christian mother more than any other ought to feel the need to be sanctified in order to be able to raise her child.

THE BABY

After the first weeks the child becomes a baby, a nursling. He begins to emerge from his drowsiness. He opens his eyes wide, utters some guttural sounds. He stirs about with his whole body. At last the smile so long awaited is shyly outlined, and is the hallmark of his intelligence. Little by little his tiny clenched fists open up, he begins taking hold of things, then the faculty of grasping improves: the one who looks is about to become one who takes, then one who manipulates. He moves from the horizontal to the vertical.

He begins to vocalize, then to prattle. At nine months he can say: Dadda, Mamma. Soon he will be putting one foot in front of the other. At eleven or twelve months he will leave the cradle stage. In this stage affectivity plays a leading part, but it is a period of acquisitive affection.

During this period the mother has the advantage of a "concentration of influence" which will never again recur. She is not only the educator in all that she does; she is the child's emotional horizon and his life environment, since he has not yet acquired the possibility of wider exploration. She has to be especially careful of all her gestures and attitudes.

Over and above the joy she gives her baby in return for his smiles, beyond the material objects which busy the little being who wants to look at them and play with them, she will accustom him to living in a world in which things invisible have their place. She will acquaint him with a world where God lives if she brings him a picture of Jesus, of the Blessed Virgin, of his guardian angel to fill up his heaven; if she teaches the little babbler to pronounce along with the names of Daddy and Mommy those of Jesus and Mary; and if from time to time she shows him the example of her meditation and prayer in the midst of devout silence.

THE OLDER BABY

Baby is about to begin walking, which will broaden his horizons. He will be able to undergo new experiences and to run new risks. His means of expression will increase. Through contact with people and things his intelligence will develop. It is of the highest importance that God too be present in this enlarged world which the baby will legitimately be exploring now, personally and systematically. It is important that he should be able to find Him in the routines of the household where crucifix, holy water font, statue or picture of our Lady are in their places, in the family atmosphere of the meals, the prayers of his brothers and sisters, prayers recited together, in Sundays and holy days. What a lesson Christmas can be! The mother should be anxious too to lead him into the silent atmosphere of God's house, to incline his heart toward the real presence of Jesus. At this age her child is not influenced by words; he can understand only his own kind of speech. But he is impressed by his surroundings, and everything that he experiences enters his unconscious and contributes to the shaping of life tendencies.

THE LITTLE ONE

In the course of his first year baby has completed the exploration of his own person, distinguishing it from its surroundings, and then, thanks to the facilities of investigation which walking and talking give him, the exploration of the family home. Now he is on the point of becoming aware of his ego. He begins to feel that he (by way of contrast to others) is. By the age of two and a half or three, he has become the child who says No. He says No to everyone and everything, sometimes fiercely or sullenly. Merely suggesting something to him is enough to make him refuse it. At first his mother is surprised at this obstinacy which she takes for inadmissible disobedience. Then sometimes Father will take a hand in things and grow angry. They declare the child insufferable, but nothing will make him change.

His case needs to be understood. He has just made the discovery that separately from all the things of which he has already taken stock he himself exists, and he refuses to deny what is evident to him. He wants everyone to acknowledge this. Naturally, by force or by crushing him with authority one can finally subdue him. But should this inglorious kind of victory be sought? It runs the risk of breaking the mainspring of his will, of impeding his development, of giving him an inferiority complex and turning him into a shapeless being.

It is better to let him find out through experience the limitations set on his own will rather than to meet the problem head on. For this nothing is more useful than that he should learn through his contacts with the world that others exist just as much as he does. This means that the ideal family in which to bring up a child is a large family. When he is an only child it is well to find associations for him with his equals. Indirect action is much better from the standpoint of education than direct action. In any case this stage lasts only a short time.

Careful treatment is all the more needed in that at this age awareness of the ego is fragile. The child is entering upon the phase of a distorting subjective outlook in which he manufactures a universe for himself: a world which has nothing to do with that of adults. In the midst of this universe he assigns himself fanciful roles made up by his imagination out of the bits and pieces of life which he has grasped. He becomes lost in transferences of identity and naturally assigns the most flattering role to himself. "I am Madame Beauchesne," Françoise, aged three years and eight months, tells me. "I have two small children, Annie and Christian. Annie is sick and I must telephone to the doctor." And she grasps the instrument to give herself the illusion of reality.

At this age a child sometimes goes through an affective crisis which fastens, according to whether it happens to be a girl or boy, upon the father or the mother. For the child this causes an intense temporary confusion. He will show curiosity about the most surprising subjects.

For the small child there is life in all sorts of things, especially the things with which he plays. He holds conversations with his soldiers who, unlike other people, will do anything he wants them to do. He confides solemnly in the ear of his Teddy bear. This is the period of his animism.

In the midst of this world he has built to his own specifications, however, he gradually loses the awkward clumsiness which marks the older baby. We wonder, seeing him suddenly leave his game to stand observing the grownups as if to penetrate their secrets, if he still believes in the fanciful inventions with which he amuses himself. Soon he will be moving into the age of grace with its charming freshness.

Here again we must try to understand this life which is so remote in our own past. It behooves parents to act very prudently with their child to help him through the affective crisis he may undergo. They must not imagine that the distorting subjectivism which forms the child's outlook is to be considered lying. They have more constructive things than that to do. The mother in particular should help her child to emerge from the world of unreality in which he is lost by showing him things exactly as they are and by calling them by their right names. She must listen to his questions and evade none of the answers. At times of course, some of these will be embarrassing. By taking advantage of all the opportunities which the child himself brings up she can get on with the training of his moral sense.

She can proceed with his religious education in much the same way. In the midst of a family environment governed by Christian practices, a small child will be curious to know their meaning, just as he is to know the meaning of everything else. He will ask his questions: "What is it?" "Why?" "How?" about the crucifix, the holy water font, the book of holy pictures, morning and evening prayers, Sundays and holy days, a christening, a wedding, a visit to the Christmas crib or to the church, Mass, communion, just as he does about his games or things seen during his walks. In her answers to these questions of her child the thoughtful mother can give him the earliest instruction concerning God, Christ, the Blessed Virgin, prayer, and an introduction to the Faith and divine life. All of her answers will have a bearing on the life of her baptized child, for it is life itself which puts these questions to her. In this way the primary Christian thoughts, gestures, attitudes will be carried down to a level of the child's unconsciousness so deep that nothing will be able to efface the recollection of them.

At this age a small child is not ready to receive any systematic teaching. But on the other hand, his soul does open up to the lesson calculated to corrrespond to his interests of the moment. This is by no means easy to do. On the occasion of visits to the repository on Holy Thursday, a mother had explained to her little child that Jesus died on Good Friday but rose from the dead on Easter, that He had been placed in the tomb and had come back to life. The child took it all in and said nothing. But waking up on Easter morning he glanced at the crucifix in his room and when his mother came to his beside, he said to her: "You see, He didn't rise from the dead." These words upset his father when they were repeated to him, and yet there was nothing skeptical about this child. He was merely like all children of his age: an "animist" closed up in his own subjective world. The Lord they had been talking to him about who was supposed to rise from the dead could of course be none other than the One in his room.

THE CHILD OF SIX AND SEVEN

We have not yet reached the age of reason but it is at hand. Every now and then a sudden gleam of inner light makes it seem as though the child had reached the knowledge of good and evil with regard to the will of God, as though the faculty of judgment were being exercised; but the night of ignorance settles down again. Nevertheless the child is intelligent; his mother says that "he understands everything." A Christian mother and a Christian school are then able to give more systematic instruction. It must be borne in mind moreover that soon, in six months or a year, it will be time for confirmation, first confession, first holy communion. To direct the child's steps toward these decisive acts in a Christian life, even before the immediate course of preparation begins, a long-range preparation is needed to develop the love of God and the desire to receive Jesus in His sacrament in the soul of the baptized child.

For him who is God? He is the One before whom everyone gets down on their knees. He is the One from whom we can ask things we can ask from no one else, not even Daddy or Mommy: that our little brother or sister should get better, or grandfather or grandmother. He is the One we cannot see but who knows everything . . . in short a mysterious, all-powerful Someone.

Who is Jesus? He too is someone before whom we go on our knees and keep silence, who was born in a manger and who died on the cross. He is nearer to us because He made Himself into a little child. He had a mother as we have. He lived on the earth. He died on the cross. We have seen His picture. And He especially loved little children.

This is the modest beginning of knowledge which must now be completed. With Jesus it is easy, provided a beautiful, simple and true picture of Him is given and not the sugary, weakling one. If someone like St. Teresa had need of the Incarnation in order to help her reach up to God, what wonder is it that it should be necessary for a child?

In our opinion this knowledge of Christ is what is most apt to lead to a more precise knowledge of the Father who is in heaven and of the Holy Spirit whom He sent.

The line of causal reasoning can lead only to a *Deus ex machina*, the God of the Philosophers, and we all know that at this age the line of causal reasoning is not yet open. When the child asks questions, he is not looking for answers that will satisfy reason because at that time reason is making no demands upon him. What he is looking for is merely an affirmation of faith.

Since he is open to contemplation, he is able to go directly up to God from what is good and what is beautiful. But to help him know what good is, who is there better than Jesus; what is there more beautiful to contemplate than His actions? Is not Christ the direct and providential way that leads to the Father? For us it seems preferable to take this way rather than fall back on that rudimentary and inexact philosophy which zigzags from the egg to the chicken and from the chicken to the egg, from the tree to the seed and from the seed to the tree, to bring us finally to the Creator.

This kind of teaching obviously remains unpretentious. It is essential to it that it should unerringly direct the child toward knowledge of the few truths he will need when, around seven, he is introduced to the sacraments. Essential too is the idea that in the child's soul love of Jesus and confidence in Him should continue to be fostered, and, through Him, love of the Father and of the Holy Spirit from whom Christ cannot be separated.

SPIRITUAL GROWTH

So it is that our method of religious education in early childhood should follow in the footsteps of nature, using every opportunity which she provides for it. In truth the Spirit breathes where He will and is not subject to our laws. Those who train early childhood will often find themselves outdistanced by Him and will sometimes marvel at the precociousness of progress wrought by divine guidance.

For their own part, however, such educators should move forward with all humility in their dealings with the child, bearing in mind that his bio-socio-psychic development can be slow and complex. The effectiveness of their influence depends largely on the extent of their concern for this development. They cannot hope to move faster than the developmental process. But in their concern for it they can count on the help from within which God grants to all who do His will.

8.

The Meaning of Sacred Doctrine
in the College

•

Gustave Weigel, S.J.

During the last three decades, those who have been formulating the syllabuses for college courses in religion have been plagued with the complaints of numerous parties. There seemed to be a great deal of dissatisfaction and disappointment with the existing texts and methods as well as with the results of the teaching of religion in college.

The older "religion" texts, such as Wilhelm Wilmers' theological handbook and Joseph Deharbe's *Catechism* were proving unsatisfactory. Many students found the courses lacking in content and in impact. The religion course often seemed to them to be an arid memory exercise, concerned with material irrelevant to the problems of their day, and unmindful of the interests of the heart. Certain modifications in the program soon began to appear. We all recall such attempts as manifested in the books of Fathers Herzog, Doyle, and Chetwood.[1] These efforts consisted in simplifying the treatises taught contemporaneously in the seminaries. For example, Father Doyle's book *The Defense of the Catholic Church* closely followed the apologetic developed in the latter part of the nineteenth century. College students did not therefore personally experience the difficulties against which this apologetic was oriented. They found this, too, inadequate, and their dissatisfaction eventually returned.

At this time there was a world-wide reconsideration of the essence and the conception of theology. The problem was more than a

---

[1] F. X. Doyle, S.J., *The Defense of the Catholic Church* (New York: Benziger Bros., 1927); Thomas B. Chetwood, S.J., *God and Creation* (New York: Benziger Bros., 1928); Charles Herzog, S.J., *God the Redeemer* (New York: Benziger Bros., 1929); *idem, Channels of Redemption* (New York: Benziger Bros., 1931).

concern of American colleges: it was world-wide. An initial solution was the "living theology" proposed in Germany. Its proponents insisted on sacrificing scholastic categories in favor of contemporary modes of presentation, and in constructing the course from elements relevant to modern preoccupations. "Living theology's" influence extended to France. But its development was impeded by various factors.

Kerygmatic theology was another answer. The University of Innsbruck fostered this approach. Father Joseph Jungmann, S.J., and Father Hugo Rahner, S.J., made significant contributions. Father Rahner's book expresses the whole theory guiding their efforts.[2] After much investigation and discussion, kerygmatic theology is still for many a suspect enigma. Unlike "living theology" it sought to retain the traditional theology of the schools. It appeared to be a parallel but distinct theology, with two advantages: it would respond to a need; and it could be taught for lay Catholics who were not professional theologians. The dominant concern of this theology is to find salvation rather than to search for disinterested truth. "Finding salvation" epitomized their outlook.

In 1944 Father John Courtney Murray published two essays in *Theological Studies.*[3] These essays contained his conception of theology for the layman. Essentially he conceived the layman as occupying an ecclesiastical position in the Church, and precisely at the point where the Church joined itself to the temporal order. Hence the layman should in this priest's view be equipped for his role by an understanding of the gospel of salvation and its permeation of the work he is to do.

Father Yves Congar, O.P., shares this point of view, and his book *Lay People in the Church* contains a definite program for it.[4] He proposes the expansion of ecclesiology in order to show the layman his function within the Mystical Body, since the Mystical Body is organized according to functions. By understanding his function,

---

[2] Karl Rahner, S.J., *Hörer des Wörtes* (München: Kösel-Pustet, 1942).

[3] John Courtney Murray, S.J., "Towards a Theology for the Layman: The Problem of Its Finality," *Theological Studies*, 5 (1944), 43–75 and 340–76.

[4] Yves M. J. Congar, O.P., *Lay People in the Church*. Trans. by Donald Attwater (Westminster, Md.: Newman Press, 1957).

the layman would be able, according to Father Congar, to understand the truth and the goodness of the gospel. Thus, by using the doctrine of the Mystical Body as the basis of ecclesiology, all of theology-for-the-layman can be viewed from the standpoint of the life of the Church.

In the last few years in this country certain concrete problems have engaged our interest: what rationale shall we follow in our college religion (or theology) courses, and what textbooks shall we use? These problems are most practical, for they concern different notions of what constitutes college theology, and show that there is no unanimous agreement on the question of what college theology ought to be.

If we use the general term St. Thomas applied to the content of his *Summa Theologica,* "sacra doctrina," as the generic name for theology, perhaps we can approach wisely the precise task we encounter. Sacred doctrine is a disciplined formulation of the message of the Catholic Church. It is nothing else. This, I think, is for all Catholics a basic tenet. We believe what we do believe because it is presented for faith by the Catholic Church. Through the Church we possess our dogma. Our faith, of course, is divine, but the Church is the medium through which we attain to God, so that what she teaches is the basis of sacred doctrine.

We need not be reminded that the Church teaches in various ways. Not only does she use many media, but she also employs different teaching methods for diverse types of people to whom she wishes to speak. All of us know (probably the sisters know better than anybody else) that the catechism is certainly a form of sacred doctrine, a form that is primarily designed in our day for instructing children.

All are aware of a great evolution taking place in catechetics. Today grammar-school catechetics is very different from the catechetics in the classroom of my boyhood. We elders recall the question-and-answer method. Both the question and the answer were memorized, and they were rattled off with the glibness of a parrot. That particular method is no longer in common use, although I know it has not disappeared entirely. It represents one method.

I term the total enterprise of catechetics as strictly positive instruction. Using some central pattern—for example, the creed, sacraments, and commandments—the instructor communicates basic teaching. The teaching is given in the form of statements. No proof is attempted, and if something like a proof is suggested it is not expected that the children will understand it as proof. It is a sheer statement of the Church's message. The statement is simple, but not simplified. It is simple so that children with their particular, limited grasp on doctrine can assimilate just a little more than they actually understand. It is presumed that with the passage of time these formulas which they have learned will take on deeper meaning.

However, we teach catechism not only to children, but also to adults. There are catechetical sessions held in parish halls and in the parish pulpits. Two different groups are contemplated.

There is the Catholic adult group, desiring to know more about sacred doctrine than what they have retained from their childhood catechism. Again the same method is used as was done with children; but the different words and concepts are analyzed so that the adult will find more in the formula than he did as a child. Experience has filled his life; he has met problems of which the child could not dream. In the light of the problems of his own life and work, he receives the statements of a preacher or lecturer. He does not verify the affirmations. He does not know what source work is.

The second adult catechetical group is composed of catechumens, those joining the Church. Their instruction will not be, shall we say, as expansive as catechetics for Catholic adults, but nevertheless it will be a little fuller than the catechetics prepared for children. In fact, a child's catechism is often used in preparing converts for baptism. But the catechism will be explained so as to meet the demands and the interests of a mature person.

In a similar fashion we teach more than grammar-school catechism to secondary-school students. The method here is not strictly the question-and-answer technique. Answers learned in grammar school are reviewed in the light of the development made by the pupil. The adolescent has new problems, with new appreciations of the reality of life in the world. In the perspective of these problems and adolescent development, a truth previously learned is re-presented to meet the needs and the curiosity of Catholic youth.

The Church must use this method of instruction because she is a teacher. "And how are they to believe in him, until they listen to him?" (Rom. 10, 14). If you have heard, you have heard something. You have heard a message—the "good news" of the Gospel; consequently the Church will always speak in the catechetical form which I have called positive instruction. The relation of the doctrine to its source is omitted. No attempt is made to construct any disciplined system of thought or any abstract vision of reality from all the doctrines exposed. This is not its purpose. The individuals who receive it are receiving information. The substance of what Christ preached and entrusted to His Church is now handed to all the world. Of course, the Church does this in accordance with the situation and condition of the different people who are to hear the message.

But above and beyond the limits of strictly positive instruction there has always been in the Church, even from earliest times, a disciplined contemplation of the Church's message. We call this contemplative theology. Before our present collegiate system was developed there was little need for the extensive spread of this type of teaching. But now, with the peculiar problems of a college theology in America and the general search for something deeper and more solid, attention has been given to possibilities of introducing this contemplative theology into the college curriculum. Theology is the proper pursuit of the studious confraternity of the theological faculty of the university. There is, of course, the inevitable temptation to teach this contemplative theology by watering it down, by modifying it and by some shrinking of its content.

This produces the *malaise* which is everywhere felt now. Can we fulfill the purpose of sacred doctrine in the college by merely trimming down the treatises which are being discussed and developed in the university's school of divinity? The college, it is felt, has a different function than the faculty of theology. That function is highly relevant to the type of sacred doctrine that ought to be taught in the college of arts, and it actually determines it.

Let us consider the type of college with which we are familiar: the liberal arts college whose whole function is to make the young man or woman pass through a program of humanistic dedication—the dedication to literature, to science and philosophy—not in order to become experts in these fields but rather to see the different ways in which the human being can function on a level other than the pragmatic. It is humanistic. If it is a professional school run in conjunction with a liberal arts college (e.g., engineering, nursing), it nonetheless has certain humanistic ends. The college essays to show to youth the spiritual (not religious) good in human life. Consequently the preoccupation which would be engendered by a strictly scientific course is absent. The student is being taught to know and esteem the good. That is the whole essence of humanism. Needless to say, it will involve some kind of vision; it will involve discourse. But it will not involve any science, as such, for the liberal arts college does not intend to produce a scientist. It wishes to produce a well-rounded human being who can step into any form of human life and can carry the diverse burdens which society and the community will impose on him. Only subsequent graduate training is destined to result in formal scholarship.

Since our college has a purpose differing from that of a school of divinity, it is clear that a cut-down, abbreviated version of what is given in the school of divinity is not going to fulfill the demands of the college. Here theology must have a meaning other than the meaning of the strictly scientific theology proposed in a scientific setting. It must be a college theology. It is theology because it is contemplation; it is more than mere positive instruction, but less than the disciplined contemplation of a man who is looking for the truth in a somewhat detailed and disinterested fashion. Good theology, even when it is scientific, should not and cannot be cold, but the great watchword spelled out above the chair of disciplined theology is *veritas*—truth. It is the good of the intellect rather than the generic good of the total man which it pursues. But theology as a humanistic endeavor is sacred doctrine in so far as it is productive of a penetrating humanistic adhesion to an abiding vision of the meaning of life and work.

The purpose of college theology will make its work quite different from the work being done in a strictly theological school. Great vitality is required. Something must be seen in terms of attraction. It is not mere curiosity which is to be satisfied, but the basic needs which well up in the adolescent and in the grown person. Following the suggestion of Father Jungmann, we must present the Gospel not exclusively as truth but as salvation. As salvation it will answer the needs of the young people. We may prudently assume that the vast majority of our college students will enter into secular life and not into the life of religious contemplation or of priestly activity. Therefore, in the light of the world they are entering, in the light of all the impulses which will be set loose by their contact with that environment, we must offer the Gospel as the ultimate answer to their needs and as the pilot to guide every response the individual makes to all stimuli which will be part and parcel of his post-college life. We must conceive theology on two levels: on the humanistic level, and then it is college theology; on the strictly scientific level, and then it is theology of the university school of divinity. This does not mean that the divinity school is unrelated to the college. There is a definite place for scientific theology with reference to the colleges, but let us understand clearly what that reference will be.

In this country we have obviously broken up the university. Our college is truly a university school, but it is no longer a member of a particular *universitas magistrorum et scholarium.* It is still one small corner of a total university; nevertheless, though the college has been physically separated from the university as a totality, it is still by its nature a small corner of a total university, and belongs in spirit, in function and in destiny to the university.

The universities are intellectually concerned with reality, with being. Their task is to seek to understand it and to help men find the understanding of it through meditation. Clearly, then, the first faculty in order of dignity and importance should be the faculty of scientific theology because the function of scientific theology is to achieve the ultimate vision of total being. Moreover, it has as its data something which cannot be duplicated by the other faculties; namely, the revelation of God. Actually, scientific theology projects into a human stream the highest of all knowledge, God's knowledge. Since it is the function of this knowledge as handled in scientific theology to facilitate an understanding of complete being, the faculty of scientific theology will be the high point in the university.

The faculty of disciplined theology may be related to the college in a more intimate way. We can, if it seems desirable, form a theological college which will not be identical with the faculty of theology. Such theological colleges exist throughout the world, and we call them seminaries. A seminary is not the home of formal theological science. We do not expect from it theological development through rigorous theological method. It is only a theological college wherein men are trained in theology for an extrinsic good to be achieved. Never for a moment does the Church suppose that all her priests will be genuine theologians. That requires a special charism, a particular disposition. Yet the Church demands that all her priests complete seminary training. Why? Because one of the by-products of exposure to theological work is the ability to express the Gospel clearly. The Church uses the former seminarian as her messenger. And his principal teaching function is catechetical work. The Church has found that if he is given some theological training, even though he is no theologian, he will become a better messenger. The Church is not at all blind. She realizes very well that the majority of seminarians have not the slightest inkling of what scientific theology is. But that makes no difference. In pursuing the course of study which has for its by-product an ability to explain Christian doctrine better, the seminarian attains the purpose of the Church. For the Church's purpose in maintaining seminaries is to attain their by-product. Those who want to be scientific theologians find the faculty of theology open to them where work is waiting to be done. Hence in the form of a seminary, we have a theological college. The main consideration to which these young men are exposed is theological lore. The fact that a strictly scientific method is not used does not change the fact that theology is some-how being pursued. With reason we refer to such an institution as a theological college rather than a theological faculty.

Something similar can be done for lay folk. For them a theological college would be a liberal arts college, differentiated from the others because it gives the students an appreciation of life and of the values of life and of the values of humanity in the exclusive light of theology. The curriculum would be primarily theology with the added subjects treated as theological corollaries. Such a college is not difficult to understand, although it may as yet exist nowhere.

The school of divinity is always related to any college theology, no matter how the college is organized. The teacher of college theology actually should have had a course in scientific theology because only on completing such a course is he properly equipped to teach theology anywhere. He will not teach scientific theology, but his training in scientific theology will render him more competent for college-level divinity instruction. We see this paralleled in the requisites for all college teachers. The man or woman ambitious for a career as teacher in an undergraduate school seeks a Ph.D. degree. The colleges want Ph.D.'s to do the teaching. Why? Because a Ph.D. is one who has been through rigorously scientific work, and therefore he is better prepared to handle his subject, even though his classroom treatment is going to be something less than scientific on the undergraduate level. It is then a desideratum that our teachers complete a course of theology in some school of divinity. This desideratum will not be met generally for many years to come.

The faculty of theology in the university also has a direct relationship to the other schools. It should be the ultimate guide of the thinking done in the other faculties, including the faculty of arts, since by supposition and by definition theology has a higher source of knowledge than that acquired merely by man's innate powers. Theology organizes in a human way the knowledge of God. Consequently the faculty of theology should always be exerting some influence upon the other schools of the university.

I am obviously describing an ideal situation—one that does not exist anywhere. It is the situation as Newman conceived it when he spoke of his idea of the university. For Newman the faculty of theology was the defining center of all university life.

Let us now pursue the notion of college theology, or of sacred doctrine in the colleges. It must be productive of a penetrating humanistic understanding which produces an abiding and dynamic vision of the meaning of human life and work. It ought, moreover, to produce a unified vision. It is more than sheer positive atomic instruction. It seeks to find the heart of the Christian message in such a way that it will make one react to all of life in a Christian fashion. It looks for action; it does not look for static truth. If that is the situation, there will be certain qualities which we should expect of it.

The first quality is this: it should be expository. It should present its own findings from its own sources. In other words we should not be controversial. Our attention should not be captive to what the enemy is saying in order to defend ourselves against it. For we do possess a completely positive view of reality. We have something affirmative, not something merely negative. In terms of Catholicism life has a definite meaning which can be ascertained by drawing from our faith a vision to explain life. We cannot do justice to our vision merely by meeting those who deny it. Let us first build into a unity, into a vision of life, what faith unfolds. After this is done, most of the statements of the unbelievers will usually be found to be quite irrelevant. Therefore, we must give less emphasis to the apologetic element of our Faith. We cannot concentrate on making our young people answerers to difficulties. In the past this was certainly the tendency. The students were always being prepared for difficulties against their Faith. When I was in school we prepared arguments against the evolutionists; answers to those favoring artificial birth control; answers to this, and answers to that. This method makes for theological poverty. We must show what Catholic life is in the light of the faith already dwelling within the students. If we were concerned with a group which was without faith, the problem would of course be different.

This introduces the whole question of apologetics as such. Precisely because the old apologetic was essentially polemical and defensive (in the most nervous form of defense), many recent critics have said, "Let us not have apologetics at all." But as a matter of fact theology has an apologetic task and has always had it. But it does not have to be proposed as a polemic against this, that or the other fellow. There is no reason why we should give free advertisement to people like Dr. Marie Stopes or Paul Blanshard. They have sufficient notoriety. By building our apologetics according to the indications of the sources of theology, we find no need to quarrel and bicker with people usually of small concern to our students. Obviously it makes little sense to discuss with today's students the historical questions posed by Adolf von Harnack and his colleagues. The students in class do not know who Harnack was and could not care less. The attitude of mind represented by the historicists was dead before Harnack died. Why should we exhume those ideas? We still drag them out, however, and this is why so many texts of theology are limbos of dead opinions. We can scarcely be surprised if the young men and women are not enthusiastic with such presentations.

A second quality follows from the idea that scientific theology produces a vision of total reality. It ought to be very wide in its investigation. But, since our college men and women are not quite certain what a vision of life is, and do not handle abstractions well, college theology ought to select from the total thesaurus of scientific theology those particular truths which are meaningfully pertinent to these young people. Such truths will later blossom into a fuller vision which they cannot immediately achieve, but to which they ought to aspire.

Both Father Congar and Father John Courtney Murray made a significant point when they insisted that there ought to be an intensely ecclesiological preoccupation in college theology. Ecclesiology gives us the meaning of the Church and of the place in the Church destined for these young men and women. All of theology, every bit of it, can be proposed in terms of the Mystical Body. If it is so done, theology is taught ecclesiologically. It is not necessary that it be so developed, for it can be done in myriad ways.

But the salient fact is that by giving an ecclesiological emphasis, by referring to ecclesiastical relationships, by reflexly selecting materials from the theological corpus, we are meeting the true demands of college theology.

There remains a third and final quality of a solid program in college theology. Since we are conceiving it as humanistic contemplation, rather than scientific or mystical contemplation, it will have to be active. It is essential to humanism that something be done. In the humanities you do not merely read a poem; you must also write one. You do not merely read what the Gospel offers, you must actually do what the Gospel prescribes. It is not enough to know that the Church has this or that activity; you must actually be immersed in Church action. Therefore what I might call the laboratory sessions of college theology are highly important.

It may be that other organizations within the college, such as the Sodality, are performing this function. Still, it would be desirable for such organizations to work hand in hand with the department of college theology. It is paramount for the young people to become immersed in the living expression of theology rather than in the mere study of its data. What are the living data? They are mainly two: Scripture and the liturgical life of the Church. It is consequently very desirable for the college theology professor to guide the students toward the formation of the habit of reading Scripture which is the nurture of saints and is of supreme dignity among all the sources of theology. A similar value is proper to the liturgy. Liturgy is primarily divine service. But it is more than that: it is the preferred means used by the Church for teaching. Icons are placed in churches to serve as the poor man's Bible. Liturgical prayers are not only addressed to God, but also to the human heart, so that it will learn what the Gospel is within the warm environment of prayer itself. Young men and women must learn the Church's whole liturgical action, and they can only learn it by doing it.

Similarly, we should strive to make our youth familiar with contemplative prayer. Mysticism cannot be taught, but students can certainly learn inward prayer using any system approved by the

Church, and there is quite a variety of approved forms. An introduction to these methods of praying should be such that the students will themselves practice such prayer. Only then will they really understand the significance of what is being taught in the lecture halls.

Finally, something always present, but not always as a function of college theology, is our apostolic and service programs. We have always had members of the St. Vincent de Paul Society carrying baskets at Thanksgiving time. Yet these services should be organized and dynamized by the college theology course as laboratory work in college theology. The pupils should do good to their neighbor because that is in strict ecclesiological terms a Christian thing. "When you did it to one of the least of my brethren here, you did it to me" (Mt. 25, 40). Ecclesiologically it will always make sense. Charity is to be exercised, for it is the characteristic action of the Church, part of the work of Christ. The educated Catholic must also give witness, shouting to the world Christ's "good news." Therefore those enrolled in college theology courses should participate in strictly missionary work—giving witness to those who do not believe. This activity can be done through societies which are in a way autonomous, but they should have cooperation and influence from the college theology department.

9.

A New Era in
College Religious Instruction
•
John A. Hardon, S.J.

Religious instruction in the colleges is passing through a phase of development the importance of which cannot be overestimated in the history of American Catholic education.

Symptomatic of the changes taking place was the establishment in 1953 of the Society of Catholic College Teachers of Sacred Doctrine. The ultimate purpose of this group is "to assist teachers in imparting to college students adequate religious instruction well integrated with the rest of the curriculum." [1] At the present writing the organization has 415 members and over 220 member institutions. This indicates how widespread is the desire to revitalize college religion and see to it that it shall no longer be true that "our colleges are imitating the worst features of secular education and neglecting the most important factor in Catholic education. The most important single factor is theology." [2]

In the following study we shall consider some of the main elements which are contributing to the current period of flux and transformation in college religion teaching. No effort will be made to analyze these elements beyond their immediate bearing on the subject, since our purpose is to get as concise and unified an impression of the present changing scene as is possible. The net result should be of some value to educators in appraising the *de*

[1] Cyril Vollert, S.J., "The Origin, Development and Purpose of the Society of Catholic College Teachers of Sacred Doctrine," *Bulletin: National Catholic Educational Association,* LI (Washington, D.C., 1954), 250.

[2] Richard J. Cushing, address delivered before the New England Section of the N.C.E.A., April 26, 1952, at Emmanuel College, Boston, quoted under the title "The Necessity for Theology at the College Level" in *Theology, Philosophy and History as Integrating Disciplines in the Catholic College,* ed. by R. J. Deferrari (Washington: The Catholic University of America Press, 1953), p. 3.

facto situation in their own institutions, and in setting it against the background of the larger issues to be treated in this book.

INCREASE IN STUDENT ENROLLMENT

In the past thirty years, the enrollment in Catholic colleges in the United States has increased by 300 per cent, as summarized in the following table:[3]

COLLEGES FOR MEN

Year	Schools	Men	Women	Total
1926	76	39,370	18,196	57,566
1932	75	59,565	26,507	86,072
1940	76	75,593	37,266	112,859
1948	79	184,359	43,201	227,578
1954	85	142,962	57,266	201,186 (including 958 unspecified)

COLLEGES FOR WOMEN

Year	Schools	Men	Women	Total
1926	78	42	17,241	17,283
1932	97	305	27,281	27,586
1940	117	1,053	47,974	49,027
1948	129	2,701	62,982	65,683
1954	139	3,367	77,446	80,813

It is estimated that the enrollment in Catholic colleges and universities in the school year 1960–1961 will be close to 400,000. Moreover, the expansion of the next decade is only beginning. In 1970 the enrollment should hit a new peak, reflecting the record high birth rate of 2,460 per 100,000 population in 1952.[4]

This increase is substantial not in absolute numbers only. Even comparatively viewed it must be regarded as extraordinary. The national enrollment for all colleges, Catholic and others, showed

[3] Statistics compiled by the Department of Education of the National Catholic Welfare Conference.
[4] Urban H. Fleege, "Expansion of Catholic Education: In the Past Decade and in the Next," *The Catholic Education Review*, LI (Sept., 1953), 439 f.

an increase of 110 per cent from 1920 to 1950. This is roughly one-third of the Catholic increment. In addition the college enrollment has under Catholic auspices grown far beyond that of elementary and high schools, for the over-all increase for the whole system is somewhat over 40 per cent for the three decades since 1920. If the comparison is extended to include enrollment at the turn of the century, the growth in Catholic college education is still more striking. The attendance for 1899–1900 was only 13,450 students, which is less than one-twentieth of the Catholic college enrollment in 1950.[5]

One important aspect of this increased enrollment is the growing number of non-Catholics attending Catholic colleges and universities. Figures are not available to judge how much larger the ratio of non-Catholic to Catholic students is now than it was a generation ago. It is, however, generally agreed that the proportion is greater now than ever before. The largest percentage on record in 1950 was obtained from one institution where only one half of the student body was Catholic and the highest numerically was another school with 2,192 non-Catholic students.[6]

What effect has this phenomenal growth in enrollment had on the character of religious instruction in the colleges? The immediate effect was an increase in the number of students signing up for the courses in religion.

Undergraduates showed differences in their native abilities, previous religious training, spiritual aptitude and vocational needs for their careers after graduation. For example, a recent study of the freshmen classes in sixty Catholic women's colleges showed that about one-fifth of all entering freshmen had had no religious training in Catholic elementary schools, and that a slightly larger number, about one-fourth, had done no previous academic work in religion in a Catholic high school. One small Midwestern college reported that as many as one-half of its 1952–1953 freshman class had never been in a Catholic elementary school, and three-fourths of the class had never been in a Catholic high school, for any part

[5] Louis J. Mercier, "Catholic Higher Education and the American Educational System," *Bulletin: National Catholic Educational Association,* V (Washington: 1908), 189.

[6] Roland G. Simonitsch, C.S.C., *Religious Instruction in Catholic Colleges for Men* (Washington: The Catholic University of America Press, 1952), p. 223.

of their previous education.[7] Homogeneous classification of these varying groups was for the college a practical necessity, provided of course that an adequate number of teachers and classroom space were available.

But even with classification of students based on their previous records or an aptitude test in religion, the size of individual classes generally increased, especially in men's colleges. This was shown by a national survey made in 1950. Out of forty colleges for men, two-thirds reported that their religion classes run to at least fifty students. Several had classes of sixty-five to a hundred. Some poor results were to be expected, as indicated by the complaint that "large classes are very difficult. . . . With sixty to eighty students you have no idea if or what you are getting across." [8] Likewise expected but less predictable in effect was the use of new and improved teaching methods—many of them resulting from pressures of oversized classes. Panel discussions, weekly or daily bulletins, assigned and elective reading lists, visual aids, classroom debates, liturgical exhibits, conducted tours, research projects, essay contests, self-correcting quizzes are some of the techniques which teachers are using to supplement the traditional methods of education.

A more radical effect, however, of the increased enrollment has been the greater amount of specialized training sought by teachers who are now called to devote their full time to instruction in sacred doctrine. In 1931 a study of the catalogues of fifty representative colleges listed only twenty-two persons in these institutions exclusively devoted to the teaching of religion, while ninety-five were given as part-time teachers. Twenty years later forty colleges for men reported that between one-third and one-half of those on the religion staff were full-time instructors. This new state of affairs suggests a marked improvement.

In preparation for this work two types of programs are available, those in faculties of sacred theology in the United States, Canada, and Europe, and those in the graduate departments or graduate

[7] Sisters Ritamary, C.H.M., and Mary Helene, C.H.M., "Religious Education of Catholic College Freshmen," *The Catholic Educational Review*, LI (Nov., 1953), 593 f.

[8] Simonitsch, *op. cit.*, p. 218.

schools of this country where the studies are in theology and Scripture and the degree awarded is the M.A. or Ph.D.[9] As described by one university which offers summer graduate work in theology leading to a Master of Arts degree, "This program is specifically designed to satisfy the desire of religious and laity who seek a scientific training and deeper understanding of sacred truth. Moreover, it is of inestimable value to those who are engaged in the important work of teaching sacred doctrine, for it provides them with a thorough grasp of the deep realities of Catholic theology which is so essential for effective teaching." [10] The core curriculum is in dogmatics, with a philosophy prerequisite, and requires either twenty-four hours of graduate credit with a thesis and reading knowledge of Latin, or thirty hours without a thesis (but with an essay) and no foreign language requirement. A notable and early contributor in this field is St. Mary's College in Notre Dame, Indiana, which opened a permanent School of Sacred Theology for sisters and laywomen in 1944, offering graduate work leading to a Ph.D. in religion.

Not only those who are engaged in the work of religious teaching and formation, charged with the office of initiating Catholic youth into the traditions of the Catholic Faith or of forming young religious in the traditions of the religious life, but all Catholics with a serious desire to participate in various fields of the apostolate, have a right to participate according to their needs and abilities in the treasury of sacred doctrine handed down by the great doctors of the Church. This is in essence the purpose of the School of Sacred Theology or Doctrine.

Saint Mary's School of Theology attempts to give all students a profound understanding of Catholic Doctrine and Morals in its regular courses in Sacred Scripture, Theology, Church History. Special courses and the Reading Seminar seek to prepare students to correlate traditional

[9] Among the latter are Fordham, St. John's (Brooklyn), Notre Dame, The Catholic University of America, and in summer session St. Bonaventure, Xavier (Chicago), Marquette, and Providence. This is an incomplete listing. Two developments not accounted for in the classification above are the Pontifical Institute *Regina Mundi*, founded in 1954, providing theological instruction for religious sisters, and the Institute *Jesus Magister* for religious brothers, inaugurated at Rome in October, 1958. (See, respectively, *Kalendarium in Annum Academicum*, 1957–58, Roma, Via Crescentia 86, and *Circulaire 357*, 29 Juin, 1957, Maison St. Jean-Baptiste de la Salle, 476 Via Aurelia, Roma.)

[10] *A Graduate School Program in Theology*, Marquette University, Summer Session, 1958.

doctrine with modern problems. The Research Problem gives each student an opportunity to develop a truly scientific approach to a problem, which is intimately linked with her special needs and interests.

Prerequisites for the course are a Bachelor or Master of Arts degree with a solid foundation in scholastic philosophy. A reading knowledge of Latin is necessary for admission. A total of eighty-two semester hours of credit is required for graduation as a Ph.D. in religion, a minimum of thirty-five for graduation as a Master. Each candidate must pass an oral comprehensive examination of one and one-half hours for the doctorate, after having pursued a Research Problem and taken a Reading Seminar for four semesters.[11] Pope Pius XII has specifically commended this program of studies.

Many educators believe that the specialized preparation of select teachers is "the crux of the whole problem" of college religion.

Competent teachers of theology would acquire the respect of their colleagues in other departments, of the students, of accrediting agencies; they would arouse the interest of the students; they would settle more quickly the problem of aims, content and approach; they would write the needed textbooks; they would be able to integrate all studies; they would soon make theology dominant not only in their formal courses but in the attitude of all teachers and students alike.[12]

This view requires theological training of a high order and it refuses to agree that a seminary course or its equivalent will suffice for professional competency.

The increased number of non-Catholic students attending Catholic colleges has given rise to significant practical problems. If the school ignores the religious training of non-Catholics it seems to be failing in its duty toward these students, but if it gives them religious instruction in the Catholic faith it might be accused of bigotry, abuse of academic freedom and high-pressure proselytizing. Even now this dilemma has not been resolved in a completely satisfactory way, though different colleges are beginning to adopt one of several policies to meet it. A small number of schools re-

---

[11] *Bulletin of St. Mary's College: School of Sacred Theology, 1958–1960,* pp. 12–14.
[12] Gerald E. Dupont, S.S.E., "Theology and Education," in Deferrari, *op. cit.,* p. 55.

quire of all students, whether Catholic or not, the same minimum credits in the regular religion courses. Most colleges require of non-Catholics an equivalent number of credits, but not in religion. (Courses like philosophy or the social sciences are allowed as substitutes.) A few require religion study which does not assume in students any belief in the truth of Catholic faith.[13] And a fairly large number of institutions have no requirements for non-Catholic students, either in formal religion or in substitute courses. The students are free to attend such classes, and perhaps are invited to do so, but there is no academic obligation binding them.

A typical argument against required religion classes of any kind for non-Catholics declares:

First of all, it is apt to bring odium upon religion. Secondly, it sets up a psychological distaste of its nature, preventing the learning of the subject. Thirdly, if they are well disposed, they will learn from their ethics courses sufficient to urge them on to further investigation. If they are not well disposed, very little good can be done for them.[14]

Those who favor obligatory courses argue that non-Catholics should be given formal religious instruction because "it is the primary reason why they come to our Catholic schools." [15] Moreover, after graduation the non-Catholic alumni "will be representatives of the Catholic college, hence they should be acquainted with what the Catholic college stands for." [16] And most pointedly, "as the spiritual welfare of every student is a responsibility assumed by the institution taking them in, such courses are required." [17] Nevertheless, though Catholic educators advocate some kind of religious instruction for non-Catholics, they generally agree that this should not be the ordinary course given to Catholic students.

[13] E.g., *St. Thomas (College) Bulletin,* LXX, St. Paul, Minn. (Feb., 1955): "Freshman Lectures I, 2 credits, Christianity in general, and specific information regarding the beliefs of Catholics and non-Catholics. A course designed for non-Catholic students" (p. 108).

[14] In Simonitsch, *op. cit.,* p. 233.

[15] *Ibid.,* pp. 230 f.

[16] *Ibid.*

[17] *Ibid.* This is the opinion of A. F. Sokolich, *Canonical Provisions for Universities and Colleges* (Washington: The Catholic University of America Press, 1956), pp. 160–163.

NEW PROBLEMS TO BE SOLVED

Closely related to the new developments in college theology are the special problems which the college graduate has to face in our day. Religious instruction must prepare the student to meet the peculiar challenges of the contemporary scene. Recognition of defects or inadequacies in this regard have prompted Catholic educators to investigate the moral and religious issues of our times and to form their program in accordance with specific needs.

Intellectual Problems: Secularist Philosophy of Life

The basic intellectual issue facing the lay Catholic of today relates to his need, in the face of the prevalent secularist philosophy of life, to achieve a sound understanding of his role in the temporal order. As defined by the American bishops in their statement of November 16, 1947, "Secularism is a view of life that limits itself not to the material in exclusion of the spiritual, but to the human here and now in exclusion of man's relation to God here and hereafter." [18] Another name for this attitude of mind is naturalism, for it denies the existence of any other source of knowledge or order of reality than the purely natural.

Instinctively Catholic educators see that the logical corrective to secularism is the doctrine of supernaturalism. According to Catholic faith, God has supernaturally communicated to the human race a variety of truths naturally knowable but difficult of attainment without divine help, as well as a body of mysteries which transcend the capacity of reason. It is necessary for man to know these truths if he is to possess peace in this life and to attain after death the purpose for which he was made. The unique remedy for naturalist secularism, therefore, is seen to be divine revelation as embodied in the Scriptures and Tradition, and pre-eminently in the Person and teachings of Jesus Christ.

Thus, a growing number of colleges throughout the country are introducing courses in the New Testament and the Life of Christ. The latter are not edifying histories of the Gospel narrative so

[18] *The Catholic Mind*, XLVI (Jan., 1948), 1.

much as inquiries into the precise nature of His saving work. These were altogether exceptional even twenty years ago. Point for point, the tenets of naturalism are neutralized in the solvent of Christian revelation. Where naturalists "regard the universe as self-existing and not created," [19] the students deepen their conviction that "in the beginning was the Word . . . and all things were made by Him, and without Him was made nothing that was made" (Jn. 1, 1–3). In answer to the claim that "the universe depicted by science makes unacceptable any supernatural guarantees of human values," [20] the New Testament shows first that there are supernatural realities, notably the life of grace, and then explains how this life is to be obtained, preserved and increased through faith in Jesus Christ and obedience to His commands. While naturalism identifies the things of God and man, asserting that "the distinction between the sacred and secular can no longer be maintained," [21] the teaching of Christ maintains an abysmal difference between the two, condemning any compromise with mammon and the world. And against the naturalist dogma which "considers the complete realization of human personality to be the end of man's life and seek its development and fulfillment in the here and now," [22] supernatural revelation raises man's hopes to a final destiny beyond himself and this world to the unending happiness of heaven in union with God.

It is significant that the current emphasis on New Testament study as a college discipline coincides with the Church's own insistence on a more earnest study of the Scriptures among the laity as the most effective means of healing "the mortal wounds of the human family." In his Encyclical on the Sacred Scriptures, Pope Pius XII has urged priests and teachers to protect those under their care against the attritions wrought by an unbelieving world and to inspire them with an ardent zeal for its conversion by giving

[19] Roy Wood Sellars, "Naturalistic Humanism," in *Religion in the Twentieth Century*, Vergilius Ferm, ed. (New York: Philosophical Library, 1948), p. 421.
[20] *A Humanist Manifesto* (Salt Lake City: The American Humanist Association, 1933), p. 3.
[21] *Ibid.*
[22] *Ibid.*

them an intimate knowledge and love of Christ. "Men," he explained, "will more fully know, more ardently love and faithfully imitate Christ, the author of salvation, in proportion as they are more assiduously urged to know and meditate the Sacred Letters, especially the New Testament, for, as St. Jerome says, 'Not to know the Scriptures is to be ignorant of Christ.' " [23]

Moral Problems: Divorce and Birth Control

More immediately pressing, however, are the moral problems which have reached an acute stage in America and which place a heavy burden on the religious convictions of the Catholic faithful. No amount of rationalization can minimize the breakdown of family life or the widespread abuse of marital relations. It will never, for instance, help to say that we are only more aware of these evils nowadays, but that really things are no better or worse than they ever were. For to attempt "any estimate of the comparative balance of good and evil between different periods is to undertake a task essentially impossible." [24]

Speaking of the growth of divorce in the States, the present Holy Father complained to the American bishops, ". . . If only your country had come to know from the experience of others rather than from examples at home of the accumulation of evils which derive from the plague of divorce!" [25] He pleaded that "this disease, sadly so widespread, may be cured by being rooted out utterly." [26] How many chancery offices in America are bogged down with matrimonial cases that show a tragic failure on the part of not a few Catholics, including the products of our colleges, to realize that marriage is a sacrament intended by Christ to be a permanent union of man and wife and not an experimental romance.

The case is similar with birth control. A nation-wide poll of American physicians in 1947 showed that 97.8 per cent favored

[23] Pope Pius XII, *Divino Afflante Spiritu* (Washington: National Catholic Welfare Conference, 1944), p. 25.
[24] E. I. Watkin, "The Problem of Evil," in *God and the Supernatural* (London: Longmans, Green, 1936), p. 87.
[25] Pope Pius XII, *Sertum Laetitiae* (New York: The Paulist Press, 1940), p. 14.
[26] *Ibid.*, p. 7.

birth control, while in 1951 magazine publicity reached a new high with 147 articles either wholly or in part concerned with Planned Parenthood.[27]

Catholic college faculties recognize the urgent need for proper instruction about the obligations of Christian marriage and parenthood. Their concern is reflected in the number and range of courses on marriage and marriage problems given in the curriculum. In a national survey of religious teaching in Catholic women's colleges, one of the major conclusions was that

in response to the demands of the times. . . . (there) . . . is increasing attention to marriage instruction. It is evident that preparation for marriage is viewed as highly important and as a responsibility of the religion department. The marriage courses, in general, are not technical, sacramental theology. They deal with problems of choosing a life partner, courtship, responsibilities of parenthood, attitudes toward the sanctity of Christian marriage and toward present-day pagan influences destructive of its sacred purposes. They are designed to meet a contemporary situation, one, moreover, that is particularly crucial in American life.[28]

A corresponding study of men's colleges revealed the same orientation. Representatives of thirty-nine institutions declared, by a ratio of two to one, that "marriage, sex and sex-education" are moral subjects most worthy of special treatment in the religion classes. The nearest competitors were "Justice, honesty and charity." [29]

One aspect of this subject is still in the process of development. It concerns the question whether a satisfactory course on marriage can be given outside the regular religion curriculum—in the philosophy or sociology department, for example. Whatever the arguments pro and con, the final arrangement must take into account the teaching of Popes Pius XI and Pius XII in their pronouncements on marital morality. To resist the prevalent temptations to infidelity and infecundity, Catholics have to know and be trained to use suit-

---

[27] *Birth Control, U.S.A., Highlights of the Program* (New York: Planned Parenthood Federation, 1953), pp. 11 and 13.

[28] Sister Mary Gratia Maher, R.S.M., *The Organization of Religious Instruction in Catholic Colleges for Women* (Washington: The Catholic University of America, 1951), pp. 136 f.

[29] Simonitsch, *op. cit.*, p. 124.

able means for strengthening their wills in conflict with passion. Pius XI urged they be taught to "give themselves to God, continually ask His divine assistance, frequent the Sacraments, and always nourish and preserve a loyal and thoroughly sincere devotion to God." Consequently, he adds,

they are greatly deceived who, along with their underestimate or neglect of these means which rise above nature, think that they can induce men by the use and discovery of the natural sciences, such as those of biology, the science of heredity and the like, to curb their carnal desires. We do not say this in an effort to belittle those natural means not in themselves improper; for God is the Author of nature as well as of grace, and He has disposed the good things of both orders for the use of men in such a way as to profit them. The faithful, therefore, can and ought to be assisted by natural means as well. But they are mistaken who think that these means can establish chastity in the nuptial union, or that they are more effective than supernatural grace.[30]

The necessity for instruction in what Christian revelation interpreted by the Church teaches on the subject of marriage stems, he says, from the fact that God

has constituted the Church the guardian and teacher of the whole truth concerning religion and moral conduct; to her therefore should the faithful show obedience and subject their minds and hearts so as to be kept unharmed and free from error and moral corruption.[31]

RENEWED INTEREST IN ST. THOMAS AQUINAS

Although Thomas Aquinas has for centuries been regarded by the Church as "a model and teacher" of the sacred sciences, the modern Thomistic renascence began just seventy-nine years ago, with the encyclical *Aeterni Patris* of Pope Leo XIII.[32] Seven other Leonine documents on the Angelic Doctor paved the way for an interest in St. Thomas, even outside the Church. This interest has

---

[30] Pope Pius XI, *On Christian Marriage* (Washington: National Catholic Welfare Conference, 1931), p. 36 (adapted).
[31] *Ibid.*, p. 37.
[32] *Aeterni Patris* was published Aug. 4, 1879. In a solemn academy commemorating the 75th anniversary of the encyclical, R. Garrigou-Lagrange declared that the necessity of studying St. Thomas, emphasized by Pope Leo, "is just as great in our own times, and perhaps more now than it was in 1879." *Angelicum*, XXXII (Julii–Sept., 1955), 209.

not been paralleled since the time of Aquinas' death in 1274.[33] Pope Leo's rulings crystallized in the Code of Canon Law which prescribed for seminaries and papally approved institutions that "teachers shall deal with the studies of mental philosophy and theology and the education of their students in such science according to the method, doctrine and principles of the Angelic Doctor and religiously adhere thereunto.[34] Vernon Bourke's Thomistic Bibliography, covering the years 1920–1940, lists five thousand books and articles on St. Thomas published during that short period. In a famous allocution, on the fourth centenary of the Gregorian University, Pope Pius XII explained that the canonical precept has a universal application, placing "St. Thomas as master and guide for all Catholic schools." [35]

Influence on College Religion

Consistent with the Church's mind, the doctrine and method of St. Thomas have notably affected religious instruction in Catholic colleges in the United States. Wilmers' *Handbook of the Christian Religion,* for example, used in America since 1891, leaned heavily on the *Summa Theologica,* often to the extent of lengthy, verbatim quotations. But even where St. Thomas was not explicitly mentioned or his writings directly quoted, his principles were substantially incorporated into the religion curriculum of every Catholic college.

In recent years, however, it was felt that a more systematic

[33] It is impossible to appreciate the modern Thomistic revival without reference to the major documents of Pope Leo in favor of St. Thomas. Following *Aeterni Patris,* in the same year (Oct. 15, 1879) the Pontiff proclaimed his intention to restore the Roman Academy of St. Thomas and to publish the complete works. A year later (Jan. 18, 1880) the Pope ordered a new edition of the complete works of St. Thomas; on March 7 of the same year he proclaimed the necessity of studying the philosophy of St. Thomas. August 4, 1880, in the Brief *Cum Hoc Sit,* the Pope appointed St. Thomas universal patron of Catholic schools. In another brief, *Gravissime Nos,* he invited members of the Society of Jesus to follow the teaching of St. Thomas (Dec. 30, 1892); this invitation he repeated (Nov. 25, 1898) to the Order of Friars Minor. Meantime, May 9, 1895, Leo XIII had approved the new statutes of the Roman Academy of St. Thomas.

[34] Canon 1366, § 2.

[35] *L'Osservatore Romano,* Oct. 19–20, 1953.

teaching of St. Thomas should be made on the undergraduate level. Walter Farrell's four-volume *Companion to the Summa* was the first major attempt in English "to put in popular form St. Thomas' masterly study of God, man and the world" for the use of the educated laity. Soon after, Anton Pegis edited and annotated the *Basic Writings of St. Thomas Aquinas,* "to prepare a useful and reasonably clear English text for students." Both are currently used as textbooks in the religion departments of Catholic colleges.

All the while it was the *Summa* itself which many teachers were using in the classroom, supplementing St. Thomas with private notes and commentaries. Out of these latter has grown a contribution to college religion manuals which appeared between 1955–1957 in four volumes: *A Primer of Theology.* The study represents "an effort to express the basic content and order of the *Summa* in the language that today's students will understand, and in a manner suitable for classroom use." [36] Following the basic order of St. Thomas, the content and development are essentially those of the *Summa,* though necessarily condensed and simplified to appeal to college students. The purpose is to transmit to the student an intellectual *habitus,* the virtue of wisdom. The Thomistic schema makes for solidity and order, and is a determining factor in shaping the "new era" in college doctrine study.

DEVELOPMENT OF CATHOLIC DOCTRINE AND EDUCATION

The elements that enter into the remaking of college programs in religion are often reduced to the simple formula: application of content to practical circumstances. It is assumed in this view that the content itself remains perfectly constant since it represents the invariable teaching of the Catholic Church. The fact is, however, that while the deposit of faith remains unchanged, there is a legitimate development in doctrine and religious discipline. This

[36] Edward L. Hughes, O.P., "Foreword to the Teacher," in *A Primer of Theology,* I (Dubuque: The Priory Press, 1955), ix. Still another series was begun by the same publisher under the general editorship of F. L. B. Cunningham, O.P., *Theology: A Basic Synthesis for the College,* with *Toward Marriage in Christ* (1957) and *God and His Creation* (1958).

development should also be examined in any study of the present trends in the teaching of sacred science.

A simple index to this development is found in the various statements of the Holy See, such as papal encyclicals and addresses, directives and pronouncements of the Roman congregations, from which can be deduced what phase of Catholic doctrine or worship is being specially emphasized, or clarified or applied to modern situations, and in that sense is being developed under the guidance of the Holy Spirit. Without laboring to prove the point, it seems that the doctrine of the Mystical Body, the principles of Catholic action and lay participation in the liturgy are three outstanding examples of dogmatic and disciplinary progress in the Church in the two generations from the accession of St. Pius X until now. Each of these is having a marked influence on the direction in which college religious instruction is going in the United States.

The Mystical Body of Christ

CURRENT EMPHASIS AND DOCTRINAL DEVELOPMENT

Although "the doctrine of the Mystical Body was taught to us by the Redeemer Himself," [37] and while much had been written over the centuries of how the faithful are "one Body in Christ" (Rom. 12, 5), this mystery of the Catholic faith has since the turn of the century reached a degree of clarity and taken on a practical importance that can best be described as revolutionary. "To those who read the history of the Church with a discerning eye," says the Cardinal of Detroit, "it is clear that each succeeding age has seen insistence placed on some application of Christian doctrine which meets the special needs of that age. Our own age . . . is witnessing a providential concentration of Christian thought on the doctrine of the Mystical Body of Christ." [38] Within the doctrine we can further distinguish certain aspects which have a special bearing on religious education.

[37] Pope Pius XII, *Mystici Corporis Christi* (Washington: National Catholic Welfare Conference, 1943), p. 3.
[38] The Most Reverend Edward Mooney, D.D., quoted by Gerald Ellard, S.J., *Christian Life and Worship* (Milwaukee: Bruce Publishing Co., 1945), p. 287.

A study of the sources would show that Christian tradition from apostolic times regarded the Mystical Body as the true Church of Christ. But how far should the identification extend? St. Augustine, for example, speaking of Christ, said:

The Body of which He is Head is the Church, not simply the Church that is in this particular place, but both the Church that is here and the Church which extends over the whole earth; not simply the Church that is living today, but the whole race of saints, from Abel down to all those who will ever be born and will believe in Christ until the end of the world.[39]

Does this mean that all the just of the Old Testament belonged to the Mystical Body; or that non-Catholics in good faith, in all the centuries before and after Augustine, are real members of the Mystical Body of Christ? On the clarification of this point much depends. No small amount of inspiration to labor for the conversion of those outside the Mystical Body is at stake, not to speak of doctrinal motivation for preserving the true Faith lest one be cut off from the grace which flows from Head to members.

As seen in a preliminary draft submitted to the bishops, the Vatican Council intended to define the necessity of the Church for salvation in terms of the Mystical Body. The proposed document read:

Let all understand what a necessary Society the Church is for obtaining salvation. This necessity is as great as that of being joined and united with Christ the Head and with His Mystical Body, outside of which He nourishes and favors no other communion as His Church, which alone He loves and for which He sacrificed Himself.[40]

The Vatican Council had planned to settle the issue by a solemn definition, but circumstances prevented its doing so. Meanwhile the Church's interest developed until it reached a climax in the Encyclical *Mystici Corporis Christi* of Pope Pius XII. In unmistakable terms, the Pope declared:

If we would define and describe the true Church of Jesus Christ—which is the One, Holy, Catholic, Apostolic Roman Church—we shall find

---

[39] *Enarr. in Ps. 90*, PL37, 1159.
[40] *Acta et Decreta Concilii Vaticani*, "*Collectio Lacensis*" (Friburgi Brisgoviae: Herder, 1892), col. 569.

nothing more noble, more sublime, or more divine than the expression "The Mystical Body of Jesus Christ"—an expression which springs from and is, as it were, the fair flowering of the repeated teaching of the Sacred Scriptures and the holy Fathers.[41]

It follows, therefore, that those who are not Catholics, even though baptized and in good faith, are not actual members of the Mystical Body, by reason of their non-profession of the true faith in union with the Vicar of Christ. Hence the plea of the Holy Father, bidding them "withdraw from that state in which they cannot be sure of their salvation." [42]

But if the Mystical Body is the Catholic Church, the converse is also true, the Church is the Mystical Body. This is not a mere platitude but, as the Pope explained, a most consoling and far-reaching truth. In opposition to the concept of a purely invisible Church entertained by some of the early reformers, Catholic apologists had to emphasize the visible side of the society founded by Christ, which they described with Bellarmine as "an assembly of men, as visible and palpable as . . . the Kingdom of France." [43] For three centuries this juridical idea was dominant in Catholic thought and teaching. Only in recent years has there been a notable change, one which pays more attention to the interior life of the Church as a supernatural organism co-extensive with the Mystical Body of Christ. As the present Pontiff says:

The Church is not made up of merely moral and juridical elements and principles. What lifts the Society of Christians far, far above the whole natural order is the Spirit of the Redeemer who until the end of time penetrates every part of the Church's being and is active within it. He is the source of every grace and every gift.[44]

EFFECTS ON THE TEACHING OF COLLEGE RELIGION

Inevitably the Church's modern accent on itself as Mystical Body had its influence on the teaching of college religion. If the classroom manuals of fifty years ago are compared with present-

[41] Pope Pius XII, *op. cit.*, p. 8.
[42] *Ibid.*, p. 39.
[43] St. Robert Bellarmine, "De Ecclesia Militante," *Opera Omnia*, II, cap. 2.
[44] Pope Pius XII, *op. cit.*, pp. 24 f.

day textbooks, the difference is striking. Devivier-Sasia, for instance, went through sixteen editions by 1900 and was used in many colleges in this country. Volume Two of the series gives over 400 pages to a study of the Catholic Church. Every phase of its origin and nature is examined, with scarcely a passing mention of it as Mystical Body. By contrast, a current textbook like Patrick Madgett's *Christian Origins* devotes a full chapter, one out of eight, to "The Church the Mystical Body of Christ." Some educators have been so impressed with the importance of this concept that they are beginning to organize the whole religion curriculum around this central theme. Writes one author and teacher,

We aim to present Catholic Truth in such a way that students will deepen their understanding of it as an organic whole and be impelled to live out intelligently their functions as members of the Mystical Body of Christ. . . . We aim to have the students have the same love for the Mystical Body (which they have for the living Christ), and be overwhelmed with the realization that this same life of Christ has come down to them, the cells of the Body. . . . In this course the student constantly sees himself as a cell of the Mystical Body.[45]

Even when the Mystical Body is not the frame of reference for all studies in a department, it can still serve to integrate otherwise disparate religion courses into an organic synthesis that is pedagogically invaluable. The integration flows naturally from the basic identification of the Mystical Body and the Catholic Church, as clarified by the present Sovereign Pontiff.

The Church. A familiar complaint of priests and teachers is that the faithful too often consider the Church as only a juridical organization, powerful, impersonal and inexorable in its demands on those who belong to it. While extreme, a book like Thomas Sugrue's *A Catholic Speaks His Mind* is illustrative of this attitude.[46] The Church is obeyed, perhaps, at least in major precepts, from fear of punishment and almost under duress. But there is no genuine love, in the personal, abiding sense in which we love a

---

[45] John J. Fernan, S.J., "Catholic Religion Course, LeMoyne College," *Lumen Vitae,* VII (Jan., 1952), 72.

[46] Thomas Sugrue, *A Catholic Speaks His Mind* (New York: Harper and Bros., 1952), 64 pp.

dear friend and are willing to make sacrifices in order to sustain our affection. The perfect corrective, recommended by the Holy Father, is the doctrine of the Mystical Body which provides "an incentive for the heart" to love the Church, "with that ardor of charity which is not confined to thoughts and words but which issues in deeds." The reason, furnished by faith, is obvious,

since nothing more glorious, nothing nobler, nothing surely more honorable can be imagined than to belong to the Holy, Catholic, Apostolic and Roman Church, in which we become members of one Body as venerable as it is unique; are guided by one supreme Head; are filled with one Divine Spirit; are nourished during our earthly exile by one doctrine and one heavenly Bread, until at last we enter into the one, unending blessedness of heaven.[47]

The Incarnation. Correlative with the preceding is the sense of nearness to God through Christ which the dogma of the Mystical Body produces in the believing soul and for which there is no equivalent substitute. The Incarnation is thus removed from its bare historical setting and placed into proper perspective as the eternal union of God with human nature—physically in the person of Christ and mystically in the *totus Christus* of which each member of the Mystical Body is an integral part. Indeed, it is Christ, personally present in the Church, who gives us the highest motive for loving the Body of which He is the living Head. "For it is Christ who lives in His Church, and through her teaches, governs and sanctifies." [48]

The social virtues. From the love of Christ in Himself will follow a love of the members whom His Spirit animates and unites with Himself in the Mystical Body. The radical need in teaching the social virtues of justice and charity, covering every phase of private and public life, is not primarily to make these virtues academically understood. The real need is to convey understanding which will effectively motivate toward the practice of justice and charity in a world that is corrupted by selfishness and greed. This motivation through wisdom and understanding is especially important for

[47] Pope Pius XII, *op. cit.*, p. 35.
[48] *Ibid.*, p. 36.

those whose natural gifts and formal education make them more influential in the society in which they live. Such motivation can be supplied partially by reason, as in special ethics and sociology. But something stronger is needed, indeed in the present supernatural order is absolutely necessary. It is to be found in the mystery of the Mystical Body, which faith accepts and theology contemplates. For if it is a fact that we instinctively love those who are closest to us, who depend most on ourselves and we on them, who are joined to us by the nearest ties of origin, interest and common goal, then the strongest objective motive this side of the beatific vision for loving our fellow men is our union with them as members of the Body of Christ. Those within the Body are loved because we share with them the most cherished possession to which human nature can aspire. Those outside the Body are loved that they may participate more fully in the possession of God's grace, flowing from the Head to the Body and thence to those who are not yet completely one with Him.

The sacraments. The college course on the sacraments can be taught in two ways, as a study of seven visible signs, instituted by Christ in order to give grace, or as a deeper penetration into the seven channels through which the redemptive Blood of Christ flows in a constant stream, like so many arteries, to impart, sustain and increase life of the cells of the Mystical Body. Both methods have their place, but the second is becoming increasingly important for the insights it affords into sacramental theology. Viewed the first way, the sacraments run the risk of being considered quasi-magical rites which automatically benefit any who receive them; viewed the second way they reveal a whole field of implications for the spiritual life. The sacraments are no longer seen as merely administered by the Church, but as being received *within* the Church; not as something extrinsic, like being fed from the outside, but deeply intrinsic, like the nourishment by the mother of an unborn child. It is Christ nourishing Himself, Head to members, by an intussusception that is more vital and more intimate than that of any material body, and no less real. "From Him streams into the body of the Church all the light by which those who believe are divinely illumined, and all the grace by which they are made holy as He is holy." [49] A realization of this union with the life-giving Source of all knowledge and strength will produce sincere gratitude to God for the grace of the Catholic Faith. It will also promote zeal to work in the apostolate for those who "still remain deprived of those many heavenly gifts and helps which can only be enjoyed in the Catholic Church," [50] notably the Eucharist, in which "the very Author of grace is given to us." [51]

Catholic Action

CONCEPT AND MODERN DEVELOPMENT

Comparable to the modern development in the doctrine of the Mystical Body has been theological progress in the concept of Catholic Action, not only as an organized form of the lay apostolate but as an essential part of the Church's work of evangelization. St. Pius X was the first to clarify the term Catholic Action. His encyclical letter *Il Fermo Proposito* is the longest and most detailed papal pronouncement written on the subject. He defines Catholic Action by describing,

the services rendered to the Church by those chosen bands of Catholics who aim to unite all their forces in combating anti-Christian civilization by every just and lawful means. They use every means in repairing the serious disorders caused by it. They seek to restore Jesus Christ to the family, the school and society by re-establishing the principle that human authority represents the authority of God. They take to heart the interests of the people, especially those of the working and agricultural classes, not only by inculcating in the hearts of everybody a true religious spirit . . . but also by endeavoring to dry their tears, to alleviate their sufferings, and to improve their economic condition by wise measures. They strive, in a word, to make public laws conformable to justice and amend or suppress those which are not so. Finally, they defend and support in a true Catholic spirit the rights of God in all things and the no less sacred rights of the Church. All these works, sustained and promoted chiefly by lay Catholics and whose form varies according to the needs of each country, constitute what is generally known by a distinctive and

[49] *Ibid.*, p. 19.
[50] *Ibid.*, p. 39.
[51] *Ibid.*, p. 32.

surely a very noble name: "Catholic Action," or the "Action of Catholics." [52]

As the spirit of the apostolate took deeper root among the laity, Pope Pius XI further refined the concept of Catholic Action by defining it as "the participation of the laity in the apostolate of the Church's Hierarchy." [53] In numerous addresses and written statements, the late Holy Father amplified this definition so that in the late thirties Catholic Action was described as

the general mobilization of all lay people of good will who, being organized amongst themselves, into one and the same Organization, place themselves entirely and unreservedly in dependence upon Diocesan Authority in order that they might assist in the realisation of any aspect whatsoever of its Apostolic Mission.[54]

Pope Pius XII continued the work of his predecessor in promoting the apostolate of the laity, while adding still further refinements on the nature and scope of Catholic Action based on the Church's experience during the previous forty years. Before 1940, Catholic Action was widely understood to mean a unitary organization in the form of a lay society with lay directors and priest assistants, with a mandate received exclusively from the local ordinary. One of the problems that called for solution and was settled by the present Pontiff was the status of societies that were called only auxiliaries of Catholic Action. The Sodality was an outstanding example. In 1948, by an Apostolic Constitution, the Pope declared explicitly in favor of regarding "Sodalities of Our Lady . . . with fullest right, 'Catholic Action under the auspices and inspiration of the Blessed Virgin Mary.'" [55] By analogy with the Sodality, other existing organizations of a similar kind also received Catholic Action status. In this stage of development, therefore, the concrete expression

[52] St. Pius X, "Il Fermo Proposito," in *All Things in Christ,* ed. Vincent A. Yzermans (Westminster, Md.: The Newman Press, 1954), p. 62.
[53] Pope Pius XI, "Discourse to the Catholic Associations of Rome" (April 19, 1931), in P. Lelotte, S.J., *Fundamental Principles of Catholic Action* (Melbourne: Australian Catholic Action, 1943), p. 3.
[54] *Ibid.,* p. 36.
[55] Pope Pius XII, *Apostolic Constitution on the Sodality of Our Lady* (El Paso: Revista Católica Press, 1948), p. 7.

of Catholic Action is not restricted to any one organization or super-organization which alone could claim the title. Moreover, priests are not only permitted as directors but encouraged, as seen from the constitutions of the Sodality; and the mandate, while ultimately coming from the Holy See, may reach the individual conjointly through the local ordinary and the superiors of the Catholic Action society to which the lay person belongs. In his discussion of "The Lay Apostolate" to the Second World Congress of Lay Apostolate in Rome in October, 1957, the Pope made definitive statements widening the concept of Catholic Action, beyond the meaning it had had for his predecessor.[56]

EFFECTS ON COLLEGE RELIGION

By implication, the whole religious program of a Catholic college is a training for the lay apostolate.[57] But specialized Catholic Action, as understood by the popes, looks particularly to the colleges to prepare leaders in the Church's apostolate of the laity; and in this work the religion department has an important role to play. It should give the students what they need if some among them are ever to become the "elite among Catholics" envisioned by the Holy See. Specifically: they must be convinced of the duty and opportunity of working in the lay apostolate, according to the words of Pius XI that "all are bound to collaborate in the work of establishing the reign of Jesus Christ." [58] They must be given adequate motives for generous participation in Catholic Action, based on the teachings of Christ and the exhortations of the Popes. Their faculties and talents must be properly developed, if need be at great sacrifice on the part of student and teacher alike. According to Pius XI, "Catholic Action is an apostolate for which preparation

[56] Pope Pius XII, "The Lay Apostolate," *The Pope Speaks*, IV (Autumn, 1957), 125 f.

[57] See, in this connection, Francis M. Keating, S.J., "The Finality of the College Course in Sacred Doctrine in the Light of the Finality of the Layman," *Second Annual Proceedings, Society of Catholic College Teachers of Sacred Doctrine* (Washington: Dunbarton College of Holy Cross, 1956), 25–39.

[58] Pope Pius XI, "Discourse to the Directors of the Apostleship of Prayer" (Sept. 29, 1927), quoted in Lelotte, *loc. cit.*

must be made by a complete religious, moral and intellectual formation." [59]

Finally, those who are specially suited by nature and grace for working in the lay apostolate should be introduced, early in their college days, to an organized method of doing effective service in Catholic Action, for example, the National Federation of Catholic College Students,[60] the Young Christian Students,[61] the Legion of Mary,[62] the Sodality,[63] the Catholic Students' Mission Crusade,[64]

[59] Pope Pius XI, "Letter to President of A.C.J.B." (Aug. 16, 1927), *ibid.*, p. 45.

[60] The N.F.C.C.S. is a federation of approximately 200 student governments in Catholic colleges and universities in the United States. These are grouped into 20 regional councils distributed throughout the country. Founded in 1937 on student initiative, the Federation has for its purposes: to acquaint Catholic college students with their responsibility to the student community; to contribute to the development of Catholic lay leadership; to promote American Catholic student solidarity; to represent the members on the national and international scene; to act as a center of information on student affairs; to promote democratically elected student governments. Headquarters: 1312 Massachusetts Ave., N.W., Washington 5, D.C.

[61] The Society of Young Christian Students is established in over 70 colleges in the United States, both Catholic and secular. It endeavors to help Christianize the student environment. By working in small groups, students in the Y.C.S. bear responsibility for helping to bring the principles of Christ into the student's relation with his fellow students, with his school, and with the rest of the community. General headquarters for Y.C.S. (college) are at 21 West Superior St., Chicago 10, Ill.

[62] The Legion of Mary was founded in 1921 in Dublin as an association of the Catholic laity whose purpose is to sanctify its members and by personal visitation to intensify Catholic life, reclaim fallen-aways, and seek new converts. The Legion does not concern itself with material relief. About 700 bishops throughout the world have welcomed the Legion into their dioceses. Besides regular members, there are auxiliary members in the Legion, who obligate themselves to certain daily prayers to promote the active apostolate of the Legionnaires. The regional governing bodies in the U.S. are: P.O. Box 918, St. Louis, Missouri; 2901 Ziegle, Cincinnati 8, Ohio; 4205 Willshire Avenue, Baltimore 6, Maryland.

[63] The Sodality of Our Lady is an association founded by the Society of Jesus to help Catholics lead a more perfect Christian life and labor for the spiritual welfare of their neighbor. Since the first formal approval in 1584 by Gregory XIII, the Sodality has been praised and encouraged by numerous pontiffs, including Pope Pius XII, whose Constitution *Bis Saeculari* (1948) definitively established the organization as Catholic Action. The first Marian Congregation in the States after the Revolutionary War was at Georgetown College in 1810. At present there are about 17,000 Sodalities in the country, with more than 200 in Catholic colleges and universities. National Headquarters are at The Queen's Work, 3115 S. Grand Blvd., St. Louis 18, Missouri.

[64] The Catholic Students' Mission Crusade is a national federation of Catholic student mission societies established in 1918 to acquaint Catholic students with

the Confraternity of Christian Doctrine.[65] If we examine what is at present being done in the colleges to prepare the leaders of Catholic Action the picture is encouraging but there is still a great deal of room for development.

Specialized courses. A number of institutions offer specialized courses, on the undergraduate level, in the fundamental principles of Catholic Action. This is sometimes done in conjunction with a treatment of the contemporary social order, as at the Catholic University of America. There a semester-length course for seniors has employed as its textbook Suhard's *The Church Today* and Philips' *The Role of the Laity in the Church.* Other colleges combine the treatment with a course in ascetics. For example, as listed in the catalogues, there is a course in *Catholic Lay Leadership,* which gives "an introduction to the history, principles and methods of Catholic Action. Extensive reading and discussion of recent literature in the field of Catholic Action. An elective for undergraduates." [66] Or on a broader basis, *The Spiritual Formation of Laymen,* in which "Catholic dogmatic truths concerning Christian perfection (are) applied to the life of the laity with the aim of promoting their spiritual life and their participation in the lay apostolate." [67] And along the same lines, a course on *Asceticism*

problems of the missionary Church in the United States and foreign countries. The program includes three principal activities—prayer, study and sacrifice—with particular emphasis on the study of missionary opportunities and problems. Established on a diocesan basis in about 50 dioceses, the Crusade has a total membership of approximately one million students in over 3,000 educational institutions. Publications include *The Shield,* in three editions, as well as books for discussion groups, plays, maps and illustrated lectures. National Center: Crusade Castle, Shattuc Ave., Cincinnati 26, Ohio.

[65] The Confraternity of Christian Doctrine is an organization required to be established by "local Ordinaries, in every parish" (Can. 711, § 2) for the religious instruction of Catholics of every age, but more especially of children (Can. 1373, § 1, 2). A committee composed of members of the national hierarchy directs its operation out of the National Center at 1312 Mass. Ave., N.W., Washington 5, D.C. Approximately 90% of the Catholic colleges have Confraternity units through which religion is taught to the young. Needless to say, the units vary widely in size and effectiveness.

[66] *Bulletin of Information, University of Notre Dame, College of Arts and Letters,* 1954–55, p. 105.

[67] *Bulletin of the University of Detroit, College of Arts and Sciences,* 1953–54, p. 135.

and the Apostolate, treating of "the layman's vocation to Christian perfection . . . The life of prayer: mental and vocal . . . Devotion to the Sacred Heart and our Blessed Mother: the Apostleship of Prayer and the Sodality . . . Catholic Action and the Lay Apostolate: its need and point of application; its method and variety." [68]

Catholic Action and religion majors. Another feature of the current emphasis on the lay apostolate is the effect it has had on the better students in college who are not satisfied with the minimum requirements in religious instruction. Writes one school official:

The development and spread of Catholic Action into the various areas of life has been accompanied by an increased consciousness of students of their responsibilities as Christians toward society. Some of these students began to make demands for something more in Religion than could be expected of the entire student body. The Catholic Action students feel that a more thorough understanding and appreciation of religious values is necessary, if they are to succeed in the work of the apostolate. [69]

The result is that a growing number of institutions is giving a major in religion or theology. Out of thirty-nine colleges for men interrogated, six had already established major programs in religion; eleven others indicated they would do so, if this were possible. The greatest problem is a lack of teachers who are adequately trained to meet the rising needs of the lay apostolate.

Dogmatic training for the lay apostolate. Even where specialized courses in the lay apostolate or religion majors are not offered, the basic principles of Catholic Action are penetrating large sections of the religion curriculum. Since Catholic Action is a necessary corollary to the doctrine of the Mystical Body, with the latter already well integrated into religious instruction, the former is naturally following suit. Many educators, however, feel it is possible to go "all out" for the externals of Catholic Action and forget or at least underestimate the dogmatic principles out of which the lay apostolate is to develop and without which it is ineffective for the lasting good of souls. Frank Sheed writes:

[68] *Catalogue Issue of Fairfield University, College of Arts and Sciences,* 1955–56, p. 78.
[69] Simonitsch, *op. cit.,* p. 46.

One can act as a Catholic only in so far as one thinks as a Catholic. Catholic Action presupposes a Catholic mind; and a Catholic mind— in this sense of a mind from which Catholic action will naturally flow— is not simply one which has the supernatural habit of faith.[70]

Comprehension of Catholic doctrine is also required.

But what is required for comprehension? Nothing is more dangerous than the view that a study of the Church's *social* teaching is sufficient to form a Catholic mind. That social teaching is not a self-sufficient thing, rooted in nothing. Just as it requires to be supported in action by the Church's Sacraments, so it requires to be supported in comprehension by her dogmas. It is simply the application to a particular sphere of human relations of the Church's knowledge of the whole universe of being.[71]

In pursuance of this principle, college religion courses are being consciously geared to a deeper understanding of the mysteries of the Christian faith, joined to a renewed insistence on prayer and the sacraments. Thus, in answer to the question of how college students can be trained for the lay apostolate, one teacher urges:

First of all, let them be conscious of the three divisions of Catholic Action: prayer, study, action. Through prayer and study they must be grounded in solid doctrine. To our mind the true Catholic college should be, as it were, a lay-novitiate wherein the dogmatic and ascetical treatment of the supernatural life and its practical applications to everyday conditions is thoroughly set forth by competent teachers. . . . Then follows action under guidance (through established organs of the lay apostolate).[72]

The Sacred Liturgy

LITURGICAL REVIVAL, FROM ST. PIUS X TO PIUS XII

Like Catholic Action, the modern liturgical movement dates from the pontificate of St. Pius X who, "in the profound vision which he had of the Church as a Society, recognized that it was the

[70] Frank J. Sheed, "Dogma, the Laity and Catholic Action," in *A Call to Catholic Action*, II (New York: Joseph F. Wagner, Inc., 1935), 191.

[71] *Ibid.*, pp. 191 f.

[72] Richard M. McKeon, S.J., "Catholic College Catechists: A Crucial Need," *The Catholic Educator*, XXV (Jan., 1955), 297, 307.

Blessed Sacrament which had the power to nourish its intimate life substantially, and to elevate it high above all other human societies." [73] His legislation in favor of frequent communion and lowering the required age for first communion have led "the Spouse of Christ into a new era of Eucharistic life." [74] Comparable to the Eucharistic renascence was the period of reform in sacred music started by Pius X. In his *Motu proprio* of 1903 he laid down the principles which still guide the faithful "in the common prayer of the Church during the public and solemn liturgical services." [75]

Under Benedict XV the new Code of Canon Law stabilized a whole series of liturgical principles and practices, making them obligatory on those who follow the various Latin-language rites. Under the single heading *Missa*, the index of the Code gives seventy-five detailed references to the time, place, ritual, celebrant and similar aspects of the Holy Sacrifice.

Pope Pius XI in repeated public statements further advanced the liturgical movement by recommending an articulate participation in the Mass by the laity, deploring silent assistance at Mass, praising the divine office as a public prayer of the Church in at least four encyclicals, enjoining Gregorian chant on the faithful of the West, and explaining the concept of the lay priesthood.

During the reign of Pope Pius XII, the liturgical movement has reached its highest stage of development in the Church's recent history. On the doctrinal side, there were the two great encyclicals, *Mystici Corporis Christi* and *Mediator Dei*. In order to have the faithful participate more intelligently in the Church's ceremonies and administration of the sacraments, the Pontiff allowed many prayers of the *Rituale* to be recited in vernacular languages (in English for the United States by decree of the Sacred Congregation of Rites dated 3 June, 1954), and ordered the Psalter of the Roman Breviary to be retranslated for the first time in centuries (*Motu proprio,* 24 March, 1945). To facilitate reception of Holy Communion, he mitigated the Eucharistic fast, hitherto unaltered

---

[73] Pope Pius XII, "Quest'ora di Fulgente," *Acta Apostolicae Sedis,* XXXVI (1954), 311.

[74] *Ibid.*

[75] St. Pius X, "Inter Plurimas Pastoralis," in *All Things in Christ,* p. 199.

since the fourth century (Apostolic constitution *Christus Dominus,* 6 January, 1953; followed by the *Motu proprio Sacram Communionem* of 19 March, 1957). As an aid to more frequent assistance at Mass, and by the above-named constitution, he allowed the Holy Sacrifice to be celebrated in the evening. The restored Holy Week liturgy and Easter Vigil (decree of the S.C.R. *Maxima Redemptionis,* 26 November, 1955), the revision in the rubrics of the Office and the Roman Missal (23 March, 1955), the outspoken condemnation of abuses in sacred art (30 June, 1952), the canonization of St. Pius X, the "Pope of the Eucharist," the numerous public statements of encouragement to liturgists—are further evidence of how sincerely he wants us to "more fully understand and appreciate the most precious treasures which are contained in the Sacred Liturgy." [76]

EFFECTS ON COLLEGE RELIGION

Extrinsic Effects: New Courses and Emphasis on the Liturgy

The zeal of the sovereign Pontiffs for the sacred liturgy has found a ready response among the faithful insofar as it has been brought to their attention. In the United States with its emphasis on education, according to Husslein, "the distinctive characteristic of the American Liturgical Movement came to be the strong appeal made by it to the student body. "School after school, college after college opened wide its doors to give it welcome." [77] On the university level, the immediate result of the liturgical movement was to introduce a variety of new courses or new sections in established courses dealing with some phase of Catholic worship. A recent survey indicates that at least ten different textbooks on the liturgy, besides *Mediator Dei,* are currently used in the colleges. With some, the work is centered around the Mystical Body, so that "while studying the liturgy in order to worship God more perfectly, we (may) come to know at close range, find our places in, and play our sev-

[76] Pope Pius XII, *Mediator Dei* (Washington: National Catholic Welfare Conference, 1948), p. 68.
[77] Joseph Husslein, S.J., Preface to *Christian Life and Worship,* p. vii.

eral roles in, the Mystical Body at Prayer." [78] Others prefer to limit the course to a study of the Mass, historically tracing the present ritual to its original sources,[79] or dogmatically explaining the essence of worship in union with Christ and the ritual progress of the Mass,[80] or combining all these aspects and giving a synthesis which aims directly at a more active participation in the Mass.[81] Along with classroom study, the colleges have elaborated a diversity of liturgical functions and devotions in order to train the students in living out the liturgy in their daily lives. Daily Mass, frequently in dialogue; High Mass weekly or even daily, with congregational singing; Benediction of the Blessed Sacrament; daily, weekly or at least monthly Holy Hour; nocturnal adoration; perpetual adoration in a particular chapel; confessors arranged for daily or several times a week; a special regular confessor from off-campus; Compline as night prayer; the "Family Rosary" in the dormitory or other place chosen by the students; an occasional Solemn Mass, or Mass in an Oriental rite—these are some of the ways of liturgical practice and preparation reported by the colleges.

Intrinsic Effects

CHRIST'S CENTRAL PLACE IN THE RELIGION CURRICULUM. A more evident effect of the liturgical movement has been to put Christ at the center of the religion curriculum, so that He may lead students, both in theological consideration and in prayer, to the Father. This is somewhat parallel to the impact of Catholic Action which has given religious instruction a new apostolic turn. Here the result is a new realization that the Catholic religion means not merely belief in revelation and observance of the Church's laws, but a

[78] Ellard, *ibid.*, p. xiii.

[79] Pius Parsch, *The Liturgy of the Mass*, newly adapted and translated by H. E. Winstone (St. Louis: B. Herder Book Co., 1958).

[80] Joseph Putz, S.J., *My Mass* (Ranchi, India: Catholic Press, 1947); Clifford Howell, S.J., *Of Sacraments and Sacrifice* (Collegeville, Minn.: Liturgical Press, 1952).

[81] Paul Bussard and Felix M. Kirsch, O.F.M. Cap., *The Meaning of the Mass* (New York: P. J. Kenedy and Sons, 1942); A. Chéry, O.P., *What Is the Mass?* (Westminster, Md.: Newman Press, 1952); A.-M. Roguet, O.P., *Holy Mass* (Collegeville, 1953).

personal devotion to the Author of Christianity, in which love and sacrifice are the dominant notes. This bears some explanation, since Christ as the center of instruction has affected every aspect of college religion.

Liturgical worship in the practice of Catholic life is primarily concerned with the Eucharist and the charity which feeds on it. Since the Eucharist contains Christ, true God and true man, the attributes predicable of the Incarnate Word are also applicable to Christ in the Blessed Sacrament. Given the fact that the Incarnate Son of God is sacramentally present in the midst of Christians in all the perfection of His two natures, the Catholic mind needs to learn all it can about the life, work and personality of Christ so that eucharistic offering and reception will be more meaningful to it. The interest here is quite different from that described before, where the doctrines of Christ were recognized as the only effective antidote to modern secularism. Christ Himself is now seen as a worthy object of reverent investigation. Not only must His teaching enlighten every man who comes into this world, but He Himself is deserving of assiduous study and reflection. He is Way, Truth and Life. He is the Light of the World, the One without whom man can do nothing on the road to salvation. He is the Good Shepherd, the Heavenly Bridegroom, the True Vine, Worker of miracles, Fulfillment of all prophecy, Head of that Body which is the Church. Christ in His manifold roles offers scope enough for investigation to occupy many times the four years of college study.

It would be gratuitous to assume that the principal reason for the present-day interest in the Christ of the Scriptures and Catholic Tradition is the liturgical movement. But there has been a transfer, deeper than appears on the surface. At the very least, there was need for explaining in dogmatic and biblical terms the reason for the Church's insistence on frequent, full participation in the Mass. It was impossible for long to emphasize the importance of the Eucharist as sacrament and sacrifice without being forced to give an adequate explanation for this emphasis. To make Catholics appreciate the Holy Eucharist, which is the core of the liturgy, it was necessary to explain it as the living Jesus Christ abiding with us under the sacramental species, who as Priest makes constant intercession for us. The Eucharist came to be seen as important with the importance of Christ—not Christ static or ossified or immobile but Christ active in union with His members. His importance cannot be fully understood, however, without an earnest study of His personality as reflected in the sacred writings. It is in no way surprising that Monsignor W. H. Russell's absorption with the earthly life of Christ was complemented by his attention to Eucharistic sacrifice, praise and nourishment.

RENEWED EMPHASIS ON GRACE AND THE SUPERNATURAL LIFE. By its very nature, the liturgy deals with the instruments of grace in the life of the soul. All the sacraments and sacramentals, liturgical functions and prayers, while ultimately directed to the glory of God, have the proximate purpose of somehow affecting the supernatural life of men. They may be used to obtain the infusion of this life in baptism, or its restoration in penance; to see to its strengthening and sharing in confirmation, its preservation and increase in the Eucharist; to transmit this life to others through matrimony and holy orders and ensure undiminished possession of it despite bodily illness or death, in extreme unction.

The immediate consequence for college religion has been a renewed interest in the sacraments, not primarily as dogmatic entities but as channels of grace for the human soul. Along with this emphasis there was a corresponding accent on the supernatural life in all its phases—again oriented to living this life and not merely having an accurate knowledge of its nature. This is exemplified in typical courses as described in the catalogues:

"*The Sacraments*. Emphasis on their function in the supernatural life of the individual man and modern Christian society." [82]

"*Christian Sacramental Life in the Mystical Body of Christ*. The interior life of the Christian and his supernatural relationship with God. The nature of the Mystical Body of Christ and the spiritual perfection of its members." [83]

"*Spiritual Life and Catholic Worship*. The means of grace and

---

[82] *Bulletin of St. John College of Cleveland*, 1948–49, p. 53.
[83] *Annual Catalog, St. Joseph's College, Collegeville, Indiana*, 1948–49, p. 48.

the ways of personal sanctification. The Sacraments of Penance and the Eucharist. The Sacrifice of the Mass and the liturgy of the Church." [84]

"*Supernatural Life.* Nature of the supernatural life: grace, actual, sanctifying; principal means of preserving and developing the supernatural life; prayer, the Sacraments and the Sacrifice of the Mass." [85]

ASCETICAL ORIENTATION IN COLLEGE RELIGION. In the encyclical *Mediator Dei*, the Holy Father cautioned against an exaggeration in the liturgical movement where the external channels of grace are accentuated to the point of ignoring the so-called "subjective" or "personal" piety of the faithful:

It is an unquestionable fact that the work of our Redemption is continued, and that its fruits are imparted to us, during the celebration of the Liturgy. . . . Sacraments and Sacrifice do possess that "objective" power to make us really and personally sharers in the divine life of Jesus Christ. . . . But if they are to produce their proper effect, it is absolutely necessary that our hearts be rightly disposed to receive it. (Undoubtedly), the Sacraments and Sacrifice of the Altar, being Christ's own actions, must be held capable in themselves of conveying and dispensing grace from the divine Head to the members of the Mystical Body. . . . But observe that these members are alive, endowed and equipped with an intelligence and will of their own. It follows that they are strictly required to put their own lips to the fountain, imbibe and absorb for themselves the life-giving water, and rid themselves personally of anything that might hinder its nutritive effect in their souls.[86]

In the spirit of this admonition, the colleges have recognized the need for proper balance in teaching the liturgy by giving due attention to the response of persons to liturgical life. Courses in asceticism are becoming more common. *Dynamics of Christian Living, Ascetical Theology for Laymen, Christian Spirituality, Spiritual Exercises of St. Ignatius, Ascetics* are typical titles.[87]

[84] *Bulletin, Le Clerc College, Belleville, Illinois,* 1948–49, p. 161.
[85] *Bulletin of the University of Detroit, College of Arts and Sciences,* 1953–54, p. 135.
[86] Pope Pius XII, *Mediator Dei,* pp. 14 f.
[87] Currently taught at Notre Dame, Marquette and Xavier (Cincinnati) universities and Nazareth College, Louisville, respectively.

A fundamental principle of Christian sanctity is involved in this ascetical reorientation. It is not merely a question of supplying the necessary corrective to possible exaggerated sacramentalism. What is accentuated is an insight into the relation between sacraments and Christian morality which an unavoidable fragmentation of religion courses has tended to obscure. This relation is twofold, one on the side of the sacraments, and the other on the side of morality.

On the sacrament side, in teaching the sacramental system the temptation is to overlook the function of asceticism in all its forms: prayer, mortification and the virtues, as requisite means for increasing the efficacy of the sacraments. On the side of morality, there is a risk that in treating the Christian virtues the most effective means for keeping the precepts and counsels of Christ, the sacraments, may be transmitted to another course. The net result can be a dichotomy in the student's mind that he may never fully rectify.

The balanced outlook ensured by the liturgical movement with its careful attention to theological progress is helping the teacher co-ordinate the two foci of Christian morality: the sacraments as coming from God and the ascetical response as made by man. It also serves to "positivize" the system of teaching morals in college by the so-called "method of virtues," which "opens out to the student wider perspectives of Christian living, and lets him see the many opportunities to act in a Christian way that exist in the smallest and most ordinary affairs of daily life." [88] Finally it aids to promote what recent pontiffs have so often emphasized, that perfection is not only for the priesthood and the cloister, but "the law of holiness embraces all men and admits of no exception," [89] since all have

[88] Charles E. Sheedy, C.S.C., *The Christian Virtues* (Notre Dame, Ind.: University of Notre Dame Press, 1949), p. 7. See also Walter Farrell, O.P., and Martin J. Healy, "Part IIB, The Divine Life in Man," *My Way of Life* (Brooklyn: Confraternity of the Precious Blood, 1952), 312–439.

[89] Pope Pius XI's statement on the obligation of perfection for the laity occurs in the encyclical *Rerum Omnium Perturbationem*, commemorating the third centenary of the death of St. Francis de Sales. While directly applicable to the laity, it implies the correlative duty on the part of religion teachers to give their students principles and motivation that go beyond the mediocrity of avoiding sin and lay the foundation for practicing the highest Christian virtue. The pertinent passage reads: "Haec est voluntas Dei, ait Paulus, sanc-

the means of perfection at their disposal in the Catholic liturgy, objectively in the sacraments and the Mass, and subjectively in man's free co-operation with the grace of God.

CONCLUSION

It would be unfair to conclude without briefly qualifying a possible impression left by the foregoing study. Quite consciously, no effort was made to estimate, by praise or blame, the extent to which individual colleges are meeting the exigencies of the times by their programs in sacred doctrine. We have seen the over-all picture after the fashion of a panorama. From this it should be clear that new forces are at work which call for a reappraisal of the whole structure of religious education on the college level. We have also seen that, by and large, the necessary orientation is being made and that theology, which should be the integrating subject of all intellectual life in the college, is gradually assuming some of the prestige it deserves as "the queen of the sciences." The Society of Catholic College Teachers of Sacred Doctrine through its national and regional meetings, its bulletin *Magister*, and its challenge to college educators, has been extremely effective in all this.

But there is still a long road to be traveled before we reach anything near the ideal prescribed by Cardinal Newman, given the adjustments necessary in view of the university structure he had in mind, and the differences between American college populations and those of the university he envisioned. Among "the various branches of knowledge which are the matter of teaching in a University," he writes, it is recognized in theory and in practice that, "theology [is] a branch of knowledge . . . of unutterable importance and of supreme influence" for time and eternity.[90]

---

tificatio vestra; quam quidem cujus generis esse oporteat, Dominus ipse sic declarat: Estote ergo vos perfecti, sicut et pater vester caelestis perfectus est. Nec vero quisquam putet ad paucos quosdam lectissimos id pertinere, ceterisque in quodam gradu licere consistere. Tenentur enim hac lege, ut patet, omnino omnes, nullo excepto." *Acta Apostolicae Sedis*, XV (1923), 50.

[90] John Henry Newman, *The Idea of a University* (Chicago: Loyola University Press, 1927), p. 84.

RELIGIOUS EDUCATION

Practical Considerations

Part III

RELIGIOUS EDUCATION

Practical Considerations

10.

The Formation
Our Catechists Need

•

Johannes Hofinger, S.J.

In the religious instruction of the United States, quality and
quantity do not always tip the scales in the desired proportion.[1]
The chief factor explaining this may be the insufficient training of
the religion teacher for his important but difficult task, for the
quality of religious instruction always depends primarily on the right
selection and proper formation of the teacher.

Certain peculiarities of the American catechetical situation may
account for what seem to be deficiencies both in the present and the
past.

*Far more than in other countries, religious instruction in the
United States is carried on by non-priestly catechists.* A great number of these people are layfolk who give religious instruction only
as a part-time occupation, usually in the impressive army of lay
catechists who instruct as members of the Confraternity of Christian
Doctrine.[2] In the train of the "new catechetical movement" a better
formation was prescribed for all catechists; but, understandably,
since priests are ordained to teach, the primary emphasis was on the
work of priest-catechists. Little, if anything, was done for lay instructors, though a great deal should have been done.

It may be that the parish clergy of the United States are not deeply
concerned with the formation of sisters and lay catechists because

---

[1] An experienced educator has recently compared the relative immaturity
of contemporary Catholic grade school and high school education in the
United States to that of a teen-age adolescent. The educator's findings seem
particularly true in the field of religious instruction. Msgr. William E. McManus,
"How Good Are Catholic Schools?" *America*, 95 (Sept. 8, 1956), 522–27.

[2] Anyone interested in this aspect of religious education should consult the
papers assembled by Joseph B. Collins, S.S., *The Confraternity Comes of Age*
(Paterson, N.J.: Confraternity Publications, 1956).

they themselves give religious instruction only to a limited degree. Quite naturally, they are not affected by the new catechetical movement because they are not immediately associated with it. Another important factor is the time lag between American catechetical needs and knowledge of catechetical developments. But whatever the case, it should be profitable to consider the needs of lay catechists first, in our inquiry into the over-all situation.

THE LAY CATECHISTS OF THE CCD

I. Among Catholics in this country, including the clergy, there is an awareness of the unimpeachable statistical fact that somewhat more than half of the elementary school children attend public schools. Still more meaningful and unfortunate is the percentage of Catholic children in public high schools. About one-third of Catholic students attend Catholic secondary schools. It is more than evident to all concerned that religious instruction must be made available. This task is to a large extent given over to the lay catechists of the CCD. The already overburdened sisters help out generously, but they cannot carry out alone the work that must be done in this area. In most cases bishops are obliged to turn to the magnanimous help of the laity who take on religious instruction in addition to their everyday occupations. It is doubtless one of the signs of the strong religious vitality of American Catholicity that so many virtuous, energetic lay people are ready to undertake this apostolate by enrolling enthusiastically in courses which will train them for it in a special way.

This gratifying fact should not allow us to overlook the problematical character of the catechetical assistance these generous people render. The terms of the problem are obvious in our day. The catechetical mission to be carried out by lay catechists is doubtless a good bit harder than the one encountered in the confines of a Catholic school. Here it is a question of achieving depth of religious comprehension—for mere knowledge does not accomplish much—in students who frequently bring with them from the public school a secularized and distorted idea of life, and who often enough come from broken and non-religious families. For the carrying out of this difficult mission there is only one hour of instruction per week, and that under difficult circumstances of place and time. Obviously, because of the special hardships of the work to be done, qualified teachers are needed. In view of the mission itself, a solid training for the catechists available has to be insisted upon. The question of appropriate training, in our opinion, provides the most difficult and serious challenge in the field of religious education at the present time.

From the point of view of the lay catechists, great self-sacrifice is unquestionably required. Only this spirit will incline a person to undertake a course of some sixty hours and at the end submit himself to examination before beginning his catechetical labors. Grateful acknowledgment must be made of this spirit of sacrifice.

From the viewpoint of the difficulty of the task, however, courses of such length are an absolute minimum for catechetical formation and, indeed, will suffice only under the best of circumstances. Since lay catechists come from the ranks of religiously active Catholics, one should be able to assume in most cases a solid background of religious knowledge. If they attended Catholic colleges or were active Newman Club members, this knowledge is usually assured. Experience shows that the great personal interest they take in the classes promotes the success of the instruction in good part. Still, in sixty hours of training one can expect only a condensed and very elementary introduction.

Out of these sixty hours, at most thirty are used for an examination of Christian doctrine while thirty are devoted to methods of teaching. In thirty hours one can get only a rudimentary treatment of doctrine, even with the best of intentions. This is even truer when one has not only to explore Christian doctrine in such a course but also go into the question of how the basic teachings of Christianity can be presented to the various age groups. Without this necessary tie-in there would be very little usefulness to even the best organized summary of doctrine for religious instructional purposes. It might even hinder it. In the instruction of these adult students what is needed is not a *condensed* summary but one concerned with essentials, that is to say, a well worked-out introduction to certain basic doctrines. There can be no doubt that the training of the lay catechists has come a long way, compared to what it was earlier. Still, an adequate result is to be expected only under the conditions outlined below.

As early as the time of admission to the course, *the necessary selection of candidates* should be made. This selection will be considerably facilitated by the zeal displayed by the laity from the outset, in the sense that as more numerous candidates than are needed show an interest in the work, a better enrollment can be expected. The candidate must have three qualifications to start with if the highly compressed course is to succeed: a solid foundation of religious knowledge, a relatively natural inclination toward the work of religious instruction, and above all the moral stature necessary in a Christian teacher and educator. The least insight into the important and difficult mission of the CCD will suggest that candidates be selected with care before the beginning of the course. This selection is intimately connected with the attainment of the program's purpose.

The course itself must be in complete harmony with the special needs of the lay catechists. Of its very nature, the religious instruction provided by the CCD must be characterized by a deep catechetical concentration, high religious vitality, vivacity, intuition and interest. The matter at stake here is that type of religious instruction which over a short period and under ideal teaching circumstances can best convey the challenging content of Christian knowledge. The student must be won over interiorly to a Christian way of life. Boring, formal instruction will do nothing for the student. In such cases, those few who do come to receive it will not be inwardly formed.

In order for the lay catechists to fulfill all these lofty requirements, the course must be characterized in its treatment of Christian doctrine *by an emphasis on essentials*. Candidates who already have a pretty good religious knowledge often fall down alarmingly when they have to differentiate between essential and accidental, even trivial, elements of Christian doctrine. Formulated, dispensable fragments and devotional hobbies are often overemphasized whereas basic Christian dogmas, although known, are not clearly grasped in their function of molding Christian life. Simply because CCD instruction is geared to catechetical activity, the lay catechists must be told in their training period which elements of the catechetical teaching are essential and why. We may not forget that the candidates are nearly all the products of a religious education which was never intended for catechetical ends.

The same is true of the *power of our Christian message to illumine.* Old-school religious instruction was unquestionably too little concerned with applying the illumining power of Christian teaching to life. Yet the special value of such teaching ought to reside in the demonstration throughout that catechetical instruction really is *evangelium,* "Good Tidings." In the apostolate of the CCD more so than in Catholic schools one can observe a thoroughly vital religious instruction whose mission is to propagate faith. This instruction not only makes Christianity known but also tries to win the student for Christian life. It attempts it in an era when the student has little understanding of Christianity as a life to be lived, either because of the secularism of a public school (though not all are so characterized) or because of a non-religious way of family life. It would be a gross error to assume that large numbers of lay catechists have this insight into the glorious vocation to Christian life. The course must get that across to them for the first time in their lives, or at least make them fully conscious of it for the first time. Out of our own experience, may we just mention the fact that the laity who present themselves for the apostolate of the CCD and take the required training course at great sacrifice are gratefully receptive to a truly kerygmatic presentation of Christian teaching. From it they draw rich benefits for their own religious lives.

It is hard to understand how the demands we have just proposed can be met in a course of some thirty hours. If there are only sixty hours available, the question ought to be considered whether it would not be more appropriate to earmark forty hours for the content of the teaching and twenty for the introduction to catechetical methods. Both are thoroughly important. Yet it seems to be easier to present an initiation into catechetical methods in twenty hours than to fulfill in forty hours of lectures on catechetical teaching the essentials of the task as we have outlined it above.

In the training of lay catechists in methods it is particularly important that they absorb the essence of a well-tried catechesis through practice, rather than mimic something out of a textbook. One method mastered thoroughly helps them much more than five methods they have heard about but which, in the actual instruction process, they cannot use. There is always the danger that after a few vain attempts at new methods which have been described to them they will go back to the easier but sterile device of exegeting the text of the catechism. At least as important as an introduction to the methods of religious instruction is a concise but substantial introduction into the essence, the mode of procedure, and the difficulties of religious education. It must be clear to the lay catechist that the apostolate of the CCD does not consist in mere instruction but also, according to modern catechists, a thorough religious formation of the students entrusted to him. In this context, instruction correctly given is obviously of prime importance.

Next to a solid course in Christian doctrine and methods, lay catechists need for their complete education a corresponding "fidelity of spirit." In our opinion this has unfortunately been given too little attention until now. How important we consider the ascetical training of priest-catechists and school-teaching sisters, and rightly so! There can be no question that they need it. It is equally certain, however, that the lay catechist, who must often work under far more difficult catechetical conditions, is scarcely equipped to carry out his task better if he is denied this important assistance.

Because the training of lay catechists is barely sufficient in the best of cases, pains must be taken to convince them of their goal and to inculcate in them a desire to improve throughout their active apostolate. They, even more than the religion teachers in Catholic schools, need good catechetical material to help them prepare their lessons and projects, and continue to improve in active service. In this connection we should like to refer particularly to the first-rate lessons which some religious in the Far West have prepared under the direction of Sister Maria de la Cruz, H.H.S.[3] These catecheses are to our knowledge the first attempts (and, it may be said parenthetically, highly successful ones) to employ the kerygmatic principles of modern catechetics as early as the first years of instruction. The course which the Mission Helpers of the Sacred Heart have published under the direction of Sister Mary Rosalia, M.H.S.H., also deserves mention here. This series likewise shows familiarity with the fundamental principles of modern catechetics.

Along with works such as these manuals of instruction, lay catechists badly need a solid catechetical periodical geared to their needs. It would bridge the all too numerous gaps in their knowledge; it would present valuable suggestions to help compensate for individual religious shallowness. How eager and grateful thousands of lay apostles would be for such a journal as this.

The work of the CCD in the United States has a pastoral meaning of first importance for the religious practice of millions of Catholic children who attend public schools. It cannot be easily overestimated. The service which the CCD renders to Catholicity in the United States is a shining example of greathearted and widespread lay apostolate. The Confraternity has been indispensable to the Church in America for a long time. However, the acclaim accorded its valuable contribution does not permit us to overlook a serious problem, the solution to which must necessarily be sought through CCD. It is this: Is there not expected from insufficiently trained teachers a task which is at present beyond their resources? The number of Catholic students who attend public schools is bound to increase. These millions of Catholic pupils need a solid religious instruction which will somehow have the same importance in their minds as the other school subjects. Can this be accomplished through the lay catechists of the CCD and their basically sketchy training? A close study of the catechetical situation in the

[3] Sister Maria de la Cruz, H.H.S., *On Our Way* Series (San Francisco: Confraternity of Christian Doctrine, 1957). Only Vol. I, unbound, has appeared.

United States does not permit us to overlook the fact that much less money and effort are spent to ensure religious fidelity in those subject to greater perils than is spent on the religious training of children in Catholic schools. Must we not ask ourselves if the religious instruction of Catholic pupils in public schools can be accomplished only by fully educated, professional catechists? This is especially true in the case of high school students. The professional catechists we speak of should be lay people who have completed a thorough catechetical course theologically based, who are employed chiefly by the Church.

Finally, one might wish for a wider use of the secular clergy in instruction. Anyone familiar with conditions in America knows that the problem cannot be solved by a more intensive priestly catechesis alone. The available strength in no way suffices. However, the more intensive employment of priests in the religious instruction of public school pupils would be a valuable contribution. It would promote a pastoral understanding not only of pressing needs in the realm of technique, but also of the magnitude of the job to be done.

It can be said without fear of exaggeration that the greater part of the parish clergy is so overburdened with administrative work and other secondary tasks that there is serious danger a pastor will overlook the religious training of many of the young people in his parish. At times he will not be actively aware that his public school pupils are in the majority, or that their religious needs have escaped him. Occasional limited attention given to the CCD classes by way of selected catechism quizzing can not convey to him the insights he absolutely requires. More intensive personal attention to this form of religious instruction will not merely serve to fill him with awe for the CCD. It will convince him that his lay catechists need more from him in their difficult apostolate than fatherly supervision and an occasional encouraging word. Their greatest need is clear direction in their catechetical work, and practical guidance toward apostolic holiness. Those two factors alone can provide their religious instruction with the necessary religious impulse and depth.

The preceding leads us directly to the training and guidance needed by lay catechists. In our opinion, this has been dealt with as a secondary factor in religious training up till now. This can not have had a good effect on the whole catechetical situation. Well-regulated organization within a family demands that greater care be taken of those children who are somehow in greater need or danger. We are most solicitous when it is a question, not of one member of the family, but when a number are involved. Care and attention must be given to those in need, even at a serious financial sacrifice. Does not this basic principle hold also for the proper pastoral care of a great religious family, the parish? Naturally the emphasis on the proper discharge of the catechetical task with regard to public school pupils should in no way lead to a neglect of religious instruction in Catholic schools. The former will never be able to get what they could in a well-run Catholic school, no matter what improvements are made. Anyone who knows the history of Catholicity in the United States will realize what undeniable abundance of strength and blessing has flowed through it in virtue of the Catholic schools. The great financial sacrifices made by Catholics for their schools have already made history. American Catholicity is distinguished from that of most countries of present-day Europe by a high religious standard, and this is primarily the fruit of the Catholic schools in this country. The private Catholic school of the United States has on the whole borne much better fruit than the state Catholic schools of Europe.

A closer investigation of how this obvious success has been achieved brings one face to face with a fact which may cause surprise at first. One might expect an especially high grade of religious instruction to be the cause of the great progress. Yet the historical facts seem to be otherwise. It is now generally conceded that religious instruction in this country up until this century left much to be desired in all types of Catholic schools; that on the whole it was much too intellectual and formal; that all too often it consisted of a dry textual exegesis of the official catechism and in the memorization of certain consecrated formulas. Things were no better in this country on this point than in the

European *Lernschule* of the nineteenth century. In the United States the newer catechetical movement has taken several decades longer to take hold than in the countries of Europe north of the Alps. There was so much discussion here of the technicalities of catechetical instruction that an understanding of the more fruitful suggestions of the "new catechetics" has been slow in coming.

How, under these circumstances, can the undoubted success in religious formation (which is a fact) be accounted for? As long as the Christian life of the family remained intact and the disintegrating religious and moral influence of environment could be "sealed out," so to say, the family could pretty well serve as a Christian preserve. This state of affairs was taken for granted, like the language of a country. Under these circumstances, even a religious instruction defective in method and content could perform its duty, provided it were linked firmly to the over-all Christian character of the school. We find this to have been true not only in the United States but also in the Christian Europe of a former day.

Now, however, on both continents the situation of religious pedagogy has been basically and irretrievably changed. Living Christianity is no longer an unbroken, transmitted heritage as it earlier was, a sanctified tradition which is its own self-justification. The "family heritage" means little or nothing to present-day youth, especially if this heritage seems to go against the contemporary stream of satisfactions and pleasures. In most cases the Christian religion can set itself up as a power to mold lives only if it is identified and experienced by the child as the one and only worth-while thing in life. But this personal insight, this attitude rooted in values, cannot be achieved by means of intelligent techniques of instruction alone. A purely intellectual religious instruction cannot lead to this goal: it passes over the essentials, it is blind to values. Religion both signifies values and transmits values. The Good News of Christ must be presented and grasped as the transmission of values that are truly priceless.

This brief look into the religious situation of the present poses a challenge to the catechists of our time, and imposes certain demands with regard to the proper proportioning of time in their education. The catechist of today must be prepared to give his students a correct view of the Christian religion, opening their eyes to the truth and their hearts to the incomparable worth of Christianity. He must transmit to them a whole philosophy of life, a well-rounded unity in which an over-all picture of Christian truth has its part. He must give clear direction to their lives; in conjunction with Christian life as a practice, he must show our religion to be the one and only treasure worth understanding and experiencing. For this end the catechist needs a solid psychological knowledge. He has to come to comprehend somehow the special needs of his pupils. He needs an instructional technique that is the result of successful training. But, above all, he himself requires a fundamental, enlightening insight into the Christian message. He must first grasp the Christian tidings as the joyous *evangelium* to be lived by, as a really basic and close-knit unity which gives proper direction to life. He must think of it as a pearl worth any sacrifice to come by.

The requirements that we have brought out here are in complete harmony with the new catechetics. In its first decades the catechetical movement busied itself with instructional techniques chiefly, but in the past twenty years it has turned toward a deeper understanding of the content of the message we proclaim. Out of the first uncertain attempts at a renewal of catechetical method came an extraordinary kerygmatic resurgence that has brought untold blessings. It was the result of a deeper insight into the catechetical task, and into the special needs of our time.[4]

II. It must now be shown how the basic principles outlined above affect the school sisters and brothers and priestly catechists in their own catechetical training.

[4] More about the goal and development of the modern catechetical movement can be found in Johannes Hofinger, S.J., *The Art of Teaching Christian Doctrine* (University of Notre Dame Press, 1957), pp. 1–9. The masterful presentation of Father Jungmann of the genesis of modern catechetics is available to English readers in the translation of the Rt. Rev. Anthony Fuerst, *Handing on the Faith, A Manual of Catechetics* (New York: Herder and Herder, 1959).

THE CATECHETICAL TRAINING
OF SISTERS AND BROTHERS [5]

In earlier times it was more often than not taken for granted that a sister who had undergone the usual ascetical training of the novitiate, and who had subsequently deepened her spiritual life by daily spiritual reading and meditation, was without further catechetical training *ipso facto* qualified to give religious instruction in grade school. Only the boldest maintained the necessity of a special methodical training. It was expected that in most cases the sister, by the grace of her natural pedagogical gifts and her rich experience gleaned from daily contact with the children, would work out some satisfactory program without too much difficulty. And in fact, not a few sisters and brothers without any catechetical training gave superior or fairly good catechetical instruction on these terms. Their great religious zeal urged them on to a really thorough religious knowledge; their love for God and souls made them inventive; in their catechetical practice they discovered and used many things which the newer catechetics recommended. The motherly sense of the sisters relied increasingly less on the rigid intellectual religious instruction of the old school and thus brought the Christian religion closer to the hearts of the children.

It is a very good sign, considering the brief period of existence of most communities of American school sisters, that the cry has recently arisen from their own ranks for special training for the catechetical apostolate. With characteristic American energy they are seeing to the fulfillment of the needs they feel. Sometimes the attempt is made before an integrated program of special training has been worked out. It should not surprise us, therefore, if the earliest attempts have not always corresponded to the actual need and challenge.

The importance of a basic catechetical training once seen, a deeper initiation into Christian doctrine is rightly recognized as the high point of this training. No one can deny that for school

---

[5] In view of the fact that in some Catholic schools lay teachers teach religion, one has a right to demand of them a special catechetical training corresponding in scope and quality to that of the sisters.

sisters a course in the correct methodology of religious instruction and formation is extraordinarily useful, even necessary.

The greatest danger, in our opinion, is the threat of a superficial imitation of the theological education given in seminaries.[6] The catchword "theology" began to be viewed as though it had some magic power. If one could but master any form of theology, even the theology of the seminary, good results were to be expected. As perfect an imitation as possible of the seminary method and teaching plan should lead to this, it was supposed. One result of this mentality was that the theological training of sisters, modeled on that given to seminarians, could not be rid in the convent of the categories it possessed in its place of origin. That is easy to understand. It is even more to be sympathized with, for the seminary work of today is hardly characterized by a special kerygmatic quality. Seminary education itself demands a thoroughgoing reform with respect to the proper proclamation of the Good Tidings by future priests, as is well known to the most perceptive bishops and seminary faculties.

The question of a solid training for the catechetical apostolate is not one of a few occasional rules appended to a theology course. Although these might be useful in many ways, they transmit no basic, integrated training. It has been our experience that sisters, because of their zeal for religion, derive great profit from courses which have notable shortcomings in planning and execution. Despite this fact, a solid catechetical training can be achieved for sisters only if it features an integral sequence of courses and is taken seriously by the individual teachers and by all members of the faculty.

One of the great difficulties, unquestionably, is that of obtaining teachers of religion who are cut out for the work. The best curriculum does little good when the teacher it is planned for does not

[6] The writer of these lines is completely in sympathy with that goal of the Sister Formation movement which demands a liberal training culminating in a bachelor's degree as the minimum preparation of the young religious for her teaching career. He realizes that philosophy and theology are part of liberal studies, and welcomes their inclusion. His plea is for attention to a professional challenge which neither the ordinary college graduate nor the person who teaches theology is called upon to face.

accept it inwardly, or is actually out of sympathy with it and has
no intention of following it through. To win religion teachers over
and train them solidly, one should be prepared if necessary to make
the greatest sacrifices. Our own estimate of the situation is that
one dedicated teacher who busies herself with the training of sisters,
giving herself exclusively and thoroughly to this task, and devoting
her entire course to the special needs of sisters, is to be encouraged
more than a whole faculty of specialized professors. (We confine
our remarks here to the situation in religious education.) If academic specialists are occupied only part of the time with sisters,
they will be less suitable for meeting the sisters' needs. They will
not know how to fit their particular course into a given study
plan. The best solution with respect to a community of teaching
sisters might be this, that a theologically and pedagogically well-
trained priest and a likewise thoroughly educated sister share the
instruction, give the more important courses themselves, and work
harmoniously toward a goal on which they are equally clear. In
this way the training of sisters would be assured a unity of approach and a realistic proportionment to the actual needs.

This training which is given to all sisters obviously can not be
identical in purpose with the specialized theological training
needed by a few for particular work, such as teaching sacred doctrine in a college for girls. The course which all pursue should
present that deeper introduction into the teachings of Christ and
religious pedagogy which all sisters need for their development as
persons, their educational degree, and their religious lives; in addition it must look to the apostolate which most of them will exercise in grade school. Anyone who is being prepared to teach in
high school should likewise be given a short introduction of the
same sort.

This common course has two extremes to be avoided. It should
not exhaust itself in a simple collection of hints for daily catechetical practice, but must consistently provide a deeper insight into
the teachings of Christianity. A sister is not a mere catechetical
handyman, but a real teacher of the Christian religion. On the other
hand, the course for sisters should be a good bit more than the

theological lectures of a seminary on catechetical practice. In fact, the course should turn out not specialists in theology (presumably a few will go on to become such), but fully equipped and capable catechists. This is no mean role. No pains should be spared to see that sisters play it to perfection.

Among the different sequences presented, the first in importance is that which gives a *systematic initiation into Christian doctrine*. It should bring together in perfect harmony instruction in dogma and morals. Along with this unity, it is absolutely essential that the sisters be presented with a more enlightening insight into the real meaning of the Christian message. The basic course for sisters must be characterized by a consistent condensation of the main points of the scholastic textbooks used in the seminaries, by a stronger emphasis on those things which naturally go together when religious values are the theme, and by a frank sifting out of theological controversy (or at the most a condensation to that minimum which is necessary for a proper understanding of revelation). The chief accent must lie on the positive presentation of Christian teaching, not on theological proof, and most definitely not on any defense against legions of adversaries, old or new.

The sisters have a right to expect from this fundamental course rich fruit and a permanent deepening of their own religious lives. It must transmit to the spouses of Christ who serve as His heralds not only a solid knowledge of His teaching, but above all a holy enthusiasm for His message. It must form their hearts to this message. They must experience within themselves the life-endowing power of the Word of God.

The method of teaching should draw upon certain elements of the scholastic method: for example, clear formulations, systematically presented. As to the rest, the approaches proper to positive theology should be employed. As always in such cases, it is easier to set up the requirements for a kerygmatically oriented course than it is to present it according to these requirements. The difficulty is heightened by the fact that until very recently we have hardly been able to recommend any sources or textbooks for such a course. Understandably, the danger is that in the haste of preparation recourse will be had to the available scholastic textbooks. Without its being noticed progress will be resumed in the old, undesirable direction. Whoever agrees with us on the goal to be achieved ought to agree that for such a course St. Thomas's *Summa Theologica* is hardly the appropriate textbook. So important is the systematic presentation of the message of salvation in this other form that a thoroughgoing presentation of all doctrine with this end in view needs to be produced shortly.

The second place in the curriculum should go to the *course in the methods of religious instruction.* It must deal with religious instruction and religious formation as a unit. Throughout, the role of method in the vital transmission of religious teaching and conversion to Christian life (basically auxiliary) must be demonstrated. Assuming that the basic course in Christian mystery is well given, the methods course can be taken care of in a relatively short time. Hints aimed at the presentation of individual doctrines would be more effective if they were given in connection with the content course, for example specific indications as to when and how the teachings on grace and the Trinity can be handled. Even in the catechetical training of sisters, where a special understanding of pedagogical problems can be assumed, this course should concentrate on the essential points of religious doctrine. If methods of religious instruction have left much to be desired in the past, it has not been because of a lack of knowledge of a highly developed teaching art but from the habitual neglect of basic rules. A learning process overconcerned with details departs easily from the important matter at hand.

Joined to the course in catechetical methods should be some practical exercise of the catechist's art. Good religious instruction demands an ability to do, not merely a capacity to know. This requires both skillful initiation and sustained practice.

All the other courses that may be proposed for the catechetical training period have a secondary role. Moreover, in the training of sisters too many side courses can hinder the necessary concentration of the main task.

Real importance attaches to a course in *Holy Scripture,* needless to say. It is recommended for all the years of catechetical formation. The heralds of Christ need a really practical introduction to Holy Scripture from the outset of their religious training. The Scriptures must be for them an inexhaustible source of their own religious life and apostolate. The sisters must be won to a zealous, personal use of the Bible on its own terms. Certainly in postulancy, novitiate and subsequent college years, special instruction is required. The systematic doctrinal course should draw richly on the Bible, lead to the Bible, and handle Bible questions in connection with the ordered presentation. If that is done, a special theological course in Scripture is of secondary importance. The course suggested must above all lead to a religious understanding of the Scriptures and to their bearing fruit in Christian life.

Regarding a course in *liturgy*, the problem should be faced in the same way. Even more so than the work in Scripture, all depends on proper introduction, then practice. This hinges on a proper introduction and practice even more than the work in Scripture does. A special treatment seems to be of incomparable value if the spiritual life of teachers is to be formed by the liturgy. A basic course showing the place of the liturgy in the work of salvation should be offered, which will demonstrate methodically the strict relationship between religious education and Christian worship.

Even more than a special course in liturgy, however, we might hope for a good course in *Church history*. Sisters need an insight into the interior and exterior development of the kingdom of God on earth in order to gain perspective on Christian teaching as it relates to catechetical practice. This is especially true for those who must teach religion in high school.

Undoubtedly, courses in philosophy and apologetics have their place in the training of those who are pursuing baccalaureate degrees as preparation for their teaching apostolate. Anyone who considers the closest possible approximation to the scholastic curriculum of the seminary to be the ideal will require a basic introduction to scholastic philosophy and a special course in fundamental theology before the presentation of Christian dogma begins. Yet for many sister students the best place to handle relevant philosophical and apologetic questions is in connection with individual revealed truths. Often this will be necessary for a deeper penetration and defense of the mystery under consideration.

The question of the correct organization of catechetical training for sisters is intimately connected with the question of whether the present form of theological training for the priesthood is really fulfilling its task. Even if the answer to this question were to be in the affirmative, it in no way follows that the training of sisters or of brothers should be like it in every detail. Each group should take different things for granted, since each is being trained for a different task. It is well known, however, that training in the seminaries for the catechetical apostolate is in certain respects deficient. Whatever these defects, the attempt should be made to correct them in planning the training of sister and brothers. It should be easier to achieve this in their education since their curriculums at the college level are not so hard and fast as that of the seminary.

THE CATECHETICAL TRAINING OF PRIESTS

We have said that the catechetical situation in the United States is characterized by the strong participation of lay catechists and school sisters in the apostolate. Such assistance is, beyond question, invaluable. A closer look at the situation should make it evident that the priestly part in the apostolate not only leaves much to be desired quantitatively, but even qualitatively. Take for example the none too skillfully executed preaching at divine services. Not only are the sermons unusually short; they frequently give the impression, by their content and presentation, of an insufficient training or at best an insufficient emphasis on this important pastoral duty. Anyone who has much to do with sisters and lay catechists cannot escape hearing complaints about the inadequate understanding pastors have of the principles of modern catechetics. Even the catechetical literature seems to lack the clear priestly guidance one might wish for in a country otherwise so highly developed catechetically. Perhaps the strange silence regarding the long overdue revision of the official catechism can be interpreted as a sign of the insufficient priestly interest in the burning catechetical issues of our time. Have not all the countries of Europe active in this sphere worked out a new and better catechism in the past twenty years? The introduction of a new catechism is obviously the work of the episcopate. The discussion of the questions that go into it are, however, the affair of priestly specialists. This discussion provides the necessary preliminaries and accomplishes a great part of the work of preparation.

In all of this, the heavy burden of administrative work on pastors has been very much a factor, as has the comforting awareness of the American priest that the sisters in the parish school never fail to do their best to teach the children religion. Things seem to be in a static condition, however, which only seminary training can be responsible for. What is lacking there? From time to time the problem is formulated this way: "The difficulties all stem from the same root: the sisters understand the psychology of the children but have too little theological insight, whereas the priests are largely governed by their theological education but lack the necessary psychological knowledge." To us this formulation seems an oversimplification.

It may very well be the case that psychological and pastoral training in seminaries leaves much to be desired. In all seminaries there is a prescribed course in pastoral theology and one in catechetics, but it seems that the importance of this training to the exercise of priesthood is not sufficiently brought home. As a result, future priests are not always convinced of the importance of zealous and solid preaching at divine worship and teaching in the schools. Frequently the proper cooperation between the principal theological subjects and these practical disciplines is lacking. Too often the major theoretical studies are silent on the enlightenment they should bring to Christian life and apostolic activity. The practical disciplines, on the other hand, too often try to get along without theological depth and a solid foundation. They bury themselves under a mass of practical instructions, details, and directions, without projecting themselves deeply enough into fundamentals.

Obviously in these lines we are far from denying that there is much to improve and deepen in the chief branches of practical theology. Nonetheless, it seems to us that the real evil to be identified and eliminated is an exclusively rationalistic treatment of the theological subjects, blind to all values. The priestly herald needs a clear grasp of the religious value of the Good News in order to proclaim it effectively. This can be accomplished best by presenting the future priest with a *kerygmatically directed presentation of dogma and morals* and an introduction to the study of Holy Scripture similarly oriented. Anyone who looks forward to stage one in the catechetical movement, the complete rethinking of religious instruction and methodology, must first come to terms with the catechetical training of priests by providing a few recommendations to improve the study of practical theology. Whoever scrutinizes carefully the uniqueness, core and structure of the Christian Message along the major lines of the contemporary catechetical renewal will require of seminaries a more kerygmatic handling of the chief branches of theology. This in no way means a watering down of scientific theology, but a deepening and religious enrichment. Only by a most unfortunate misunderstanding can the kerygmatic direction called for here be considered out of harmony with the sound scholastic method required by the Church. How the kerygmatic approach can be harmonized with the scholastic is a matter we have dealt with elsewhere.[7] There we describe how the Gregorian University in Rome has but recently acted to apply these reasonable demands correctly to scholastic theology. Seminarians undoubtedly have a right to dedicate themselves to the treasure of Christ in all its incomparable permanency by means of scientific investigation. That, surely, is the true meaning of their study. And how very much they need it for their future apostolate, the essence of which is described as, "to announce the good tidings of the unfathomable riches of Christ" (Eph. 3, 8)!

Furthermore, it seems indispensable to effective catechetical training that it should make clear to seminarians, by means of abundant example, where and why the scientific treatment of theology differs from a good catechetical presentation. Thus, there is absolutely nothing to prohibit beginning the scientific dogma of the

---

[7] Hofinger, *op. cit.*, pp. 234–49.

seminary course with the detailed tract *De Deo Uno et Trino*. But there is much against using it if the seminary graduate later thinks he must begin religious instruction in the lower grades with an abstract treatment of the attributes of God.

The priest is formed in the seminary, after all, for the exercise of his teaching office. It can hardly be insisted on too much that professors of theology should be well informed on the best means of proclaiming the Good News of Christ, and directly conscious of their responsibility to instruct and preach the Word of God. Where this orientation of mind is lacking, theological training remains sterile as regards preaching; theology will be studied with only such zeal as the prescribed examinations demand, and will ever afterwards bear a textbook stamp. The priest with a theology of this sort does not know where to begin in either his spiritual life or his preaching. He draws both from secondary sources of doubtful worth, to the great detriment of his inner life and his apostolate. Is not the recurring lack of dogmatic substance one often meets with in preachers traceable to this cause in particular? That is why a falsely understood "scientific" character of theological teaching in the seminary must unfortunately take the chief blame for the lack of theological content in priestly preaching.

The purely scientific and for that reason rather dead treatment of the chief subjects of study would be more endurable if future priests were nourished in the other subjects; if they were led, in the spiritual direction they receive, to the indispensable sources of Christian teaching: the Bible and the liturgy. Unfortunately there is a grievous lack here as well. It may be that on this point we find one of the reasons why in the United States the catechetical movement is not as advanced as it is in the lands north of the Alps, where it is in tune with biblical and liturgical endeavors. This likewise seems to explain why the preaching of priests at sacred worship is still so unadorned with the spirit and content of the Scriptures and the liturgy.

It would of course be wrong to suggest that the dark side we have described is everywhere prevalent. The United States is a great country. Its greatness as a nation is evident in the meaningful differences which characterize its many up-and-coming seminaries. Under no circumstances may one indulge in a false condemnation of the seminaries of the country; we say this on the basis of the hopes that have been expressed to us everywhere in the interests of the apostolate.

It may well be that a better catechetical training of priests is the most serious need of the catechetical situation in the United States at this time. Such development would turn out to be a blessed fulfillment of all the other hopes in this field of apostolate. Surely a solution of the training of lay catechists and school sisters and brothers would be helped by it.

We have considered in this paper only the training desirable for ordinary catechists. In a land with an army of active catechists there is also need for a great number of first-class, educated *catechetical specialists and thinkers.* The overburdening power of administrative work has proved detrimental to progress in this direction, above all. Almost all available strength is absorbed either in instruction itself or in the administration of programs. There remains, in consequence, much too little time for basic study and planning. The lack of persons sufficiently trained for work of this sort is fairly obvious. Each diocese needs to have at least one priest or other specialist and a number of sisters or brothers who have solid, specialized training and who are left free at least in part for special catechetical studies.

Let us conclude with a brief analogy. Genuine American business methods are characterized by large-scale planning and promotion by specialists. How well, for example, American industry knows the meaning of efficiency studies to pave the way for greater progress. In the catechetical field such foresighted thoroughness of approach has been lacking for a good while now. With the numerous and excellent religious vocations and the financial resources of this country, this lack should be done away with quickly, and forever.

11.

Newman Work
At the College and University

.

J. J. Maguire

"Newman work" is the term generally applied in this country to certain efforts of the Church on behalf of Catholic students attending non-Catholic colleges and universities. That this description should sound vague and ambiguous is not surprising. This apostolate has been and still is a hybrid, grass-roots apostolate. The Newman Club approach does not represent the implementation of advance planning and high-level tactical agreement. Not only the caliber but even the concept of Newman work varies greatly. There is no truly crystallized and uniform technique nor even complete agreement as to immediate objectives.

Part of the reason for this haphazard development has been the fact that the need and the significance of Newman work has been the subject of much controversy. The controversy has been marked and sometimes bitter, even though there is an official mandate for Newman work in what St. Pius X said in 1905 in his encyclical *Acerbo nimis:*

In the larger cities, and especially where universities, colleges and secondary schools are located, let classes in religion be organized to instruct in the truths of faith and in the practice of Christian life the youths who attend such public institutions wherein no mention is made of religion.[1]

In spite of the clarity of the directive, progress at the level of higher education has been slow and circuitous. Only after fifty years has it begun to achieve a minor degree of fulfillment.

[1] Pope Pius X, "Acerbo nimis" (On teaching Christian doctrine), *Acta Sanctae Sedis*, 37:623. Cf. Joseph B. Collins, S.S., *Teaching Religion*, Appendix (Milwaukee: Bruce Publishing Co., 1953), p. 383. Restrictive legislation on this point, including a commentary on present-day prohibition and toleration, is presented by Alexander F. Sokolich, *Canonical Provisions for Universities and Colleges* (Washington: The Catholic University of America Press, 1956).

In this country the Church set for itself a much more ambitious objective. The frequently expressed goal has been "every Catholic student in a Catholic college." This ideal was of course quite in line with the policy of a separate system of lower schools, but for a great many reasons both financial and sociological the erection of a system of Catholic colleges has proved considerably more difficult than the establishment of parochial schools. Faced with harassing problems it was not surprising that Catholic educators should look askance at any effort that might render "impossible the ultimate solution." What Father Wilfred Parsons, S.J., wrote in *America* in 1926 typifies the attitude that was current for decades.

> The evident conclusion is that, admitting the necessity of pastoral work for Catholics at secular colleges, then the prior right of the Catholics at Catholic colleges, and the prior duty of the others to be in Catholic colleges, precludes any extensive program of expansion of that pastoral work until the Catholic colleges have been fully provided for. Let there be pastoral work for those students, but let it be within the limits demanded by the general problem, not subject to the danger of being offered as a substitute for Catholic education or as an excuse for being in a secular college, and not such as will make forever impossible the ultimate solution which is aimed at.[2]

This "ultimate solution" was presumably the hope of absorbing all Catholic students in Catholic colleges. The idea that, except for essential pastoral ministrations, the presence of Catholic students at non-Catholic colleges ought to be tacitly ignored was presumably based on the thesis that the number was relatively small—or that, in any case, it would become smaller if a solid front was maintained. Whatever we may think of this reasoning there can be no doubt that the major obstacle to the development of the Newman apostolate was this fear that an expanded Newman program might be taken as a substitute for a Catholic college education.

Coupled with this expectation of a brighter future there was of course a genuine shortage of personnel and funds, but there was

---

[2] Wilfrid Parsons, S.J., "Chaplaincy, Newman Club or Catholic College?" *America*, XXXV (Sept. 18, 1926), 536. Three papers on the question, of which this is the last, appear in successive numbers of the weekly review.

also a somewhat less apostolic sense of annoyance at seeming disobedience. To be annoyed at the seeming disobedience of Catholics who attend secular colleges is one thing, but to feel that an expanded Newman apostolate is a concession to the disobedient is quite another. The resentment at "concessions" to the wandering sheep (so curiously at variance with the idea of the Good Shepherd) has been a subterranean but important factor. The fact that Newman Clubs could be disposed of in a 1949 issue of *Integrity* with the comment that their function seemed to be that of providing "social activities for nominal Catholics" [3] indicates the prevalence of resentment to any pastoral attempt not stringently intellectual, plus an amazing ignorance of the type of program that had been developed for decades, particularly at Newman centers in the Midwest.

The slow acceptance of the idea of Newman work may also be illustrated by the fact that it was only in 1941 that the National Newman Club Federation was accepted as a member of the Youth Department of the National Catholic Welfare Conference. Yet it was in 1915 that the Federation of College Catholic Clubs (which later took the name National Newman Club Federation) was formed. The National Association of Newman Club Chaplains was organized in 1949 and did not attempt to associate itself with the National Catholic Educational Association until 1955.

This background is not only part of the history of the Newman movement. It is indispensable to the understanding of the Newman Club approach. The somewhat negative attitude of the general Catholic public left the problem of Catholics at non-Catholic colleges squarely in the hands of the pastors of campus towns and their bishops. It was from these that the basic initiative came. This is in fact the key to the understanding of the movement. The basic approach has been pastoral rather than academic.

Such pastors were confronted with the immediate practical problem of caring for the spiritual needs of large numbers of students residing at least temporarily in their parishes. Ordinary pastoral

[3] Peter Michaels, "The Problem of the Newman Club," *Integrity*, III (Sept., 1949), 21.

care demanded that opportunities for hearing Mass and receiving
the sacraments be provided. In some cases this even necessitated
the building of special, non-parochial student chapels. As early as
1897 such a chapel was established at the University of California
at Berkeley.

Even ordinary pastoral care does not however stop with the
preaching of the Gospel and the administration of the sacraments.
This is particularly true in the case of youth. In this area the Church
has always been prodigally generous. Since priests ordinarily devote a seemingly disproportionate amount of their time to youth,
it is not surprising that even otherwise harassed pastors should find
themselves giving rather special attention and service to the college
population. This was a natural and almost inevitable development.
It was equally natural that this special attention should lead to the
formation of special student clubs.

The first student club to invoke John Henry Newman as its patron was one organized in 1893 at the University of Pennsylvania.
The name was suggested by Timothy Harrington, the young med-
ical student who organized the group. Newman was selected as
the patron of the group not only because of all he stood for in
the intellectual world but also because it was he who first conceived the idea of a Catholic student center at Oxford.[4] Incidentally,
though the designation "Newman Club" became increasingly
widespread, it was not until 1938 that the Federation of College
Catholic Clubs took the name National Newman Club Federation.

Though the great cardinal was a singularly appropriate choice
as a patron, Newman's actual influence on the development of the
movement has been relatively slight. Though the National Association of Newman Club Chaplains has recently published a
study guide on Newman by (now Bishop) Paul Hallinan, former
chaplain at Western Reserve in Cleveland and former National
Chaplain, most Newman Clubs do not study the career or ideas
of Newman. Many indeed do not even own a set of his works.

[4] Cf. H. O. Evenett, "Catholics and the Universities, 1850–1950," *The
English Catholics, 1850–1950*, ed. by the Rt. Rev. G. A. Beck (London:
Burns Oates, 1950), pp. 297 ff.

At this point, it may be parenthetically interjected that the designation has not been an unmixed blessing. The name "Newman" means little to most Catholic students, so that for long after they hear it they may make no connection between the organization so designated and their Faith. It is only within the last decade that students have automatically begun to recognize it upon hearing as the official Catholic campus organization. Where most students board on campus and attend a common church or chapel this difficulty has not been so apparent. It has, however, constituted a minor public relations challenge at urban schools at which most students live at home.

A conclusion which would be hard to substantiate but which is equally hard to avoid is that the name "Newman Club" was partially adopted as a disguise. It is interesting to note that other campus religious organizations have adopted similarly veiled designations, whether this be intentional or otherwise. Thus the Missouri Synod Lutheran group is known as "Gamma Delta," the Episcopal group as the "Canterbury Club," the Methodist association as the "Wesley Foundation," and the Jewish students as the "Hillel Foundation." In all of this a curious modesty seems to be involved—perhaps a reluctance to offend secular or other religious ears by seemingly blatant "sectarianism," or possibly a reluctance to assume an official status that was not yet accorded.

In the opinion of the present writer the use of this designation has actually been a drawback. By itself the word "club" seems to indicate something esoteric, or at least intentionally limited in membership. "Newman" seems to make it even more exclusive. Though the name is now consecrated by use and the difficulty partially overcome, the name certainly evokes no special conditioned loyalty in the hearts of the many. That the majority of Catholic students feel no particular responsibility toward joining the Newman Club or even lending it their moral support is a well known fact that will be discussed later in this paper, but it is hard to avoid the conclusion that this designation makes it easier for them to take such a laissez-faire attitude.

Though the Newman Club was originally an extension of the

ordinary parochial ministry, as a campus organization it soon came to embody special features that early distinguished it from the ordinary run of parish societies. The difference lies not merely in the fact that its members were college students, but also in the fact that for the past fifty years American colleges have laid an altogether exceptional emphasis on extracurricular activities. American schools take their extracurricular activities seriously indeed. Participation in one or more student organizations is regarded as an essential part of the student's formation. This is undoubtedly due to the influence of the progressive movement in education. Indeed some educators even give their regular classes a kind of "club" flavor. On the surface, at any rate, they like to give the impression that they are moderators rather than lecturers. Evaluate this as we may, there is no doubt that it certainly has broadened the concept of the learning process. Informality in the supposedly formal part of the educational process readily conditions the students to expect education in the informal extracurricular part.

Because they take their student activities so seriously most large colleges maintain highly trained "student activities" staffs. In many places luxurious "student unions" have been erected. The services of the staff and the resources of the "union" are always at the disposal of the student organization. Attractive meeting rooms, facilities for food service and varied publicity channels are readily available. Since the Newman Club has been, in most cases, an officially recognized student organization it has profited greatly from such services and resources.

Another important aspect of this picture has been the emphasis upon student self-government and student initiative. This again is part of the progressive philosophy of self-expression. The idea is that guidance must not be obtrusive. Faculty advisers must not dominate meetings. The ideal is an exact reversal of the old German proverb that children must be seen and not heard. The faculty adviser must keep his mouth shut and guide the student discussion only in the subtlest way. This laissez-faire attitude can of course be carried to ridiculous lengths, but again there is no doubt that it does have certain beneficial results. It does lead to the development of a greater sense of individual responsibility. The net result of this atmosphere has been the development in the Newman Club of a sense of student leadership and initiative rather more marked than is usual in most American Catholic organizations. Much of the development of Newman work stems directly from this sense of student responsibility—as well as from the less constrained priest-student relationship which it seems to foster.

Though this campus-generated, student momentum has at times made for pastoral headaches, it has also made Newman groups particularly rewarding groups to work with. From the pastoral viewpoint there were, however, several other indispensable advantages. As the adviser of the Newman Club, the pastor gained at least a semiofficial status on campus. In the tightly knit and self-conscious academic world this is no mean advantage. It was the pastor's bridge over the age-old gap between town and gown. To find acceptance merely as an adjunct to a student organization may seem *infra dignitatem,* but anyone who has had any experience of academic clannishness will know that even such a foothold is not to be despised. Put in simple terms, this semiofficial status opens otherwise closed doors to whole areas of apostolic activity.

Discussion of this broader, public-relations aspect of Newman work is, however, better left to a later section. From the pastoral viewpoint the Newman Club was more immediately a way of saving and deepening the faith of Catholic students. How does the Newman Club purport to do this? As currently expressed, the purpose of the Newman Club is to "deepen the spiritual and enrich the temporal lives of its members through a balanced program of religious, cultural and social activities." The most frequently expressed criticism of the Newman Club is that it is too much of a social organization. Though this criticism is both premature and superficial, there is no doubt that there have been many Newman Clubs whose main function seems to have been the promotion of Catholic marriages. However, the fact that many Newman Clubs do not develop beyond this stage is due to the limitation of local resources. Critics have often tended to forget the grass-roots nature of the movement. Newman Clubs were and still are established locally. There is no accrediting agency to pass on programs and grant or withhold a charter. The development of the Newman movement has been based on the principle that any type of Catholic student organization is better than none. There is a genuine value in merely giving Catholic students the opportunity for an informal contact with the priest. Even if Newman Clubs were purely social it would be both unfair and unreal to criticize them on this account.

There is, however, a more pointed answer to this criticism. It lies in that closely knit, intensely centered aspect of campus life to which we have already referred. This is particularly true of the boarding school, but it is also true of the urban one. Campus life is social. In a well-nigh unique way, the university constitutes a world of its own. Its social pressures are comparable only to those of a small town. There is little private life for the college student. Attitudes are more obvious than elsewhere, and the standards of acceptance are more rigid. Students may or may not be influenced by the lectures they hear, but they are certainly influenced by the mores of their fellow students.

In such a milieu even a purely social Newman Club fills an obvious function. It is a valuable countermeasure against other social pressures. To furnish social activities for the Catholic students, nominal or otherwise, is not to offer them a reward, a concession or a luxury item. It is to offer them an escape valve from the pressure of secular conformity. Even the urban college student who lives at home is a displaced person. Entering a new world, he needs to establish a new community of friends. In that new world, incidentally, he has an almost endless variety of social activities offered to him. From the viewpoint of social activities, the campus is definitely a buyers' market. Purely nominal Catholics need not come to Newman for their social activity. Because of the campus atmosphere, even the purely social side of Newman has a necessity and an impact paralleled in few other Catholic organizations.

What more can the Newman Club do besides offer the student a community of friends who share his faith and his outlook? Even with the most meagre resources, Newman Clubs have always offered some form of regular religious education. Regular talks by the chaplain, occasional outside lecturers and discussion groups have always been part of the Newman program. This is still simply the ordinary pastoral ministry.

In all of this, the Church in reality has had no choice. Zealous pastors could hardly do less. The need and the opportunity were there. It was out of the need that the movement grew. Actually, it began to be a movement in 1915 when, as was indicated above, the first "Federation of College Catholic Clubs" was formed. Credit for the continuing development goes largely to Father John Keogh of the Archdiocese of Philadelphia, then chaplain to the University of Pennsylvania Newman Club. With the approval of his superiors but at his own expense he traveled widely promoting the cause. Thus, like the individual clubs, the Federation was a grass-roots development. It was a growth from below and not the studied execution of high level planning.

In discussing the work thus far we have spoken of it from the viewpoint of the *part-time* chaplain. We have spoken not of Newman centers or foundations but of Newman *Clubs*. This was the actual line of development of the work even though, as we have pointed out, special student chapels were in existence from the turn of the century. Even today, full-time Newman chaplains still number less than one hundred for the whole country. Of the seven hundred priests listed in the 1954–1955 Directory of the National Federation, at least six hundred must be considered as part-time chaplains.[5] Some teach in Catholic colleges, some are diocesan chancery officials, some are hospital chaplains, but most are parish priests. By a full-time chaplain we mean a priest whose first responsibility is to the university community—even though many of these will have additional duties. For six out of seven chaplains, Newman work is an adjunct and a side line. Such part-time workers are literally *club chaplains*. Their work on campus is in and through the pattern of club organization. Such work is of necessity limited both in actuality and in conception.

[5] *The National Newman Club Federation Directory of Federated and Non-Federated Newman Clubs* (Washington: Youth Department, National Catholic Welfare Conference, 1955), pp. 60 (privately circulated).

The amazing thing about this part-time grass-roots movement is that out of it a broader and more far reaching conception has been consistently emerging. It has begun to take form as a major apostolate. Re-evaluation of the significance of Newman work has been prompted by the growing suspicion that the percentage of Catholic students attending non-Catholic colleges was much larger than had been supposed. The earlier theory, that except for essential pastoral ministrations no special attention should be paid to Catholic students at non-Catholic colleges, was undoubtedly based on the presumption that the percentage of such students was small. To ignore the mature religious formation of even a small group of potential Catholic leaders is obviously undesirable. However, as long as there was some hope of achieving the "ultimate solution" it did seem to be the lesser evil. On both counts, therefore, the question was one of relative percentages.

Oddly enough, statistics on this problem are not easily obtained. Individual pastors were, of course, long aware of the size of their own student population. However, the first attempt at a complete survey was made in 1949. After consultation with the United States Office of Education, such a survey was undertaken in November, 1949, by Miss Jane Bateman, Assistant First Vice President of the Newman Club Federation. Surveyed were 1,586 non-Catholic colleges and universities. Of these, 1,113, or 70.2 per cent, answered the questionnaire. Of these, 134, or 12 per cent, did not indicate the number of Catholic students enrolled. For the 979 who did give their own Catholic enrollment, the Catholic enrollment was 187,400. This was the Catholic enrollment for 61.7 per cent of the institutions suggested by the United States Office of Education. On these figures alone an estimate of 290,000 Catholic students in non-Catholic schools seems justified.

Actually, there are good reasons for thinking that the figure is much higher. Most schools obtain figures on their own Catholic enrollment from a "religious preference form" included in the material at registration. In tax-supported schools this form is frequently labeled as optional. In other words, the school does not actually demand that the student fill it out. From my own experience at Wayne University and from the experience of other chaplains, I know that many Catholic students do not fill it out. Some do not fill it out because they do not want to be included on Newman Foundation mailing lists; others, regular Newman Club members, do not do so because they feel that they are already on our lists.

Figures on the total enrollment of Catholic schools and colleges are readily available in *The Official Catholic Directory,* published with ecclesiastical approval by P. J. Kenedy and Sons, New York. In the 1950 Directory the total enrollment of Catholic colleges and universities is given as 252,727. By 1958 the figure had risen to 259,251. Included in this is, of course, a certain percentage of non-Catholic students, so that the actual number of Catholic students in Catholic institutions of higher learning is really somewhat smaller.

Such figures speak for themselves. Of all the Catholics attending colleges and universities, roughly 60 per cent were at non-Catholic institutions. In the light of such percentages ostrich tactics become impossible, or at least absurd. Oddly enough, Miss Bateman's survey drew little attention. I drew attention to these percentages in an article in the *Catholic World* for May, 1950, but until recently they have attracted little attention except from other Newman chaplains.

The chaplains and their bishops did not, of course, need this survey to know that there was work to be done. One of the obvious indications of a new attitude toward Newman work was the full-time assignment of priests to urban universities where the majority of students live at home and attend their own parish churches. Here there was no question of merely furnishing necessary opportunities for attending Holy Mass and for the reception of the sacraments. Clearly, the primary work of such a chaplain is in the educational and counseling spheres rather than in the administration of the sacraments. This is a practical and unambiguous recognition of the need of a special program for the Catholic student at the non-Catholic college.

The fact that bishops made such appointments in spite of the continuing shortage of priests shows that the need was recognized as serious. In some cases such chaplains function as members of the college staff and are furnished office space by the college itself. In other cases, however, it has been necessary to erect Catholic student centers, generally separate buildings adjacent to the campus. To attempt a history of the various appointments and foundations would take us quite beyond the scope of the present treatment, but it may be pointed out that such "urban" chaplaincies and installations have been in operation in many places (for example, Columbia, University of Minnesota, University of California at Los Angeles) for over thirty years. A great many more were established in the forties and especially during the post-World War II college boom.

Where the priest's first responsibility is to the university public and where he is, consequently, readily and regularly available, the possibilities of the Newman apostolate become more apparent. In saying this we are not implying that there is any essential difference between the avenues open to the full-time and the avenues open to the part-time chaplain. Obviously many chaplains do a full-time job on a part-time basis. However, Newman work is such that ample time on the part of the chaplain is the indispensable prerequisite for the realization of its potentialities. Criticisms of the effectiveness of Newman work have usually been based upon the shortcomings of the part-time apostolate.

There is no more common or more serious misunderstanding of Newman work than to imagine that the roster of Newman Club membership is the measure of its impact on the campus. This may sometimes be true of the part-time chaplain, but the priest who is readily available becomes a *campus* rather than a *club* chaplain. He is sought out on the most varied matters by Catholic and non-Catholic alike, and by non-members as readily as by members. Exasperatingly enough, to many of the Catholics who seek the chaplain's aid the idea of joining the Newman Club seems never to occur. Needless to say, the chaplain can hardly insist on it.

The standard personal and instructional problems do compose much of what comes to the chaplain, but there are many cases which require some special familiarity with the academic background and atmosphere. That students come to the chaplain with the various difficulties involved in reconciling faith and reason is well known, but what might not be so well known is that Catholics and non-Catholics, faculty and students alike, frequently seek him out for assistance on the religious issues involved in their researches and term papers. From time to time an academically qualified chaplain will be invited to speak in classes and seminars —as well as to other campus organizations. Officially and unofficially he will be a member of various boards and committees.

All of this requires time, not merely time to do these things but time to become recognized enough to be asked to do them. On the campus it is only superficially that the chaplain enjoys the respect which the clergyman receives elsewhere. As a clergyman he gets automatic social respect, but intellectual respect has to be won the hard way, on an individual basis. To explain this would be simply to describe the dominance of secularism. Those who criticize Newman work for its lack of visible progress do not seem to realize the prevalence of a very low estimate of religious thought in general and Catholic thought in particular. If progress seems small in proportion to the time expended, it must be remembered that progress is relative to the starting point.

We have already spoken of the closely knit social pattern of campus life in connection with the Newman social program, but in an even broader way it is the endless sociability of the campus that makes the whole apostolate possible. This is true at both faculty and student levels, for example, the inveterate student habit of sitting for hours over a cup of coffee regularly turns the chaplain's afternoon coffee break into a discussion group. A mere stroll across campus is an apostolic journey. Incidentally, at some Newman Foundations regular cafeteria service is a means of contact and informal religious education.

Though much of the educational work of the Newman Club is carried out in this informal way, there is no lack of formal programs of religious education. As we have already pointed out, even Newman Clubs with the most meager resources have always offered some lecture programs and discussion groups. With the expansion of personnel and facilities such educational offerings have expanded in very many places to full-scale programs comparable to those offered in Catholic colleges. In this as in every other aspect of Newman work there is such absolute variety that we must say with Fathers Welch and Hallinan that "there is no single pattern of Newman Club education in any college or university which is duplicated with exactness in any other Newman Club." [6] It is, however, possible to indicate a broad division into two types: namely, whether the Newman Club offers credit courses or non-credit courses.

In the first category Fathers Welch and Hallinan list the credit offerings in a sampling of seven institutions, Iowa, Illinois, North Dakota, Bradley, Michigan State, New York University and Youngstown College. At Illinois, for example, ten courses are offered: "Fundamentals of Catholic Philosophy," "An Introduction to the Bible and Its Contents," "The Life and Teachings of Christ," "The Church in the World," "The Church in the World of the Reformation," "Christian Morals," "The Spiritual Life," "The Liturgy of the Roman Rite," "Catholic Marriage and Family Life," and "The Christian in the World." At other of the seven schools we find such diverse offerings as "The Catholic Concept of Education," "Morality and Economic Society," "Philosophy of God," "Studies in Thomistic Theological Thought," and "Scripture and Catholic Tradition."

Though temporarily slowed down by the McCollum decision, there has been a steady movement toward accreditation. It is, of course, a complex problem, which is in the last analysis a local one. Much depends upon the courage of the college authorities, the degree of cooperation among Catholic, Protestant and Jewish leaders, the availability of qualified personnel and the actual attitude of the Catholic authorities.

[6] Robert Welch and Paul Hallinan, *The Newman Club in American Education*, National Newman Club Chaplains' Association (Huntington, Ind.: Our Sunday Visitor Press, 1953), p. 9. See also the publication of the same Association, *The Newman Club on the American Campus* (Paterson, N.J.: St. Anthony Guild, 1954), pp. 115.

In the non-credit category the Welch and Hallinan study describes the offerings at Louisiana State University, the University of California, the University of Pennsylvania, Cornell University, Vanderbilt University and Peabody College, Wayne University, and the Intercollegiate Newman Club of Cleveland. At Louisiana State University there are eight offerings, "Introduction to Philosophy," "Epistemology," "Rational Psychology I and II," "Fundamentals of Theology," "Modern Questions in Theology," "The Mass and the Liturgical Life," and "Christian Marriage." As might be expected, the non-credit offerings are generally less technical—though there is much less dependence upon the "problems of courtship" approach than might be expected.

It is unfortunate that more complete statistics and listings are not available. However, the patterns are so fluid and developments are so rapid that it would be hard to keep track of them—even if the Newman Federation were a strongly centralized instead of a grass-roots movement. The interesting thing to note is that a preoccupation with the necessity of a more academic and intellectual approach is evident at every National Convention and at every meeting of the Association of Newman Club Chaplains. A tangible indication is the Chaplains' Institute held annually in connection with the National Convention. The chief purpose of the Institute is to present outstanding scholars who attempt to give the chaplains concentrated briefing in the commoner areas of campus discussion.

At the student level we may mention "The Newman School of Catholic Thought," first sponsored by the Ohio Valley Province of the Newman Federation in 1952 and held on the campus of Notre Dame University. Students attend morning classes in such subjects as scholastic philosophy, Church history and the theology of grace. Afternoons and evenings are devoted to such workshops as those on the lay apostolate, moral problems, political theory, Cardinal Newman's thought, and marriage and the family. An Eastern School was inaugurated at Worcester, Massachusetts, in 1955 and a West Coast School was held in Los Angeles in 1956.

In all of this, it should be clear that no attempt is made to offer

this as a substitute for a Catholic college education. The idea that
the Catholic college is the place for the Catholic student was
clearly reaffirmed by the Association in the "Statement of Principles and Policies" adopted at Atlantic City in April, 1955. This
extension of the Newman apostolate is simply a question of facing
the facts. The simple fact is that the majority of Catholic students
are in non-Catholic colleges. There is no conceivable possibility
of absorbing these students into Catholic colleges in any foreseea-
ble future. Meanwhile, for its own sake, the Church simply cannot afford to neglect the mature religious formation of over 60
per cent of its potential leaders and in any case members. It is not
only a question of saving the faith of these individuals. It is a
question of making some attempt to form future professional men
and women and civic and business leaders into articulate Catholic
spokesmen.

The task is actually gargantuan. The biggest problem is to convince the Catholic students themselves of the necessity of this
training. This is true not only of those who might be classed as
lax Catholics but also of those whose regular reception of the
sacraments entitles them to be classed as devout. A total Newman
Club membership of 20 per cent of the Catholic registration is
unusual. This in spite of vigorous publicity, attractive social programs and every device that students and chaplains can dream of.
A lecture attendance of 10 per cent is regarded as good. In this
connection repeated surveys taken by the author in his own group
at Wayne University surprisingly indicate a higher percentage of
interest in Newman lectures and discussions on the part of those
who have had less than half of their previous training in Catholic
schools. This may indicate that religious instruction at the high
school level leaves the students with the feeling that there is
nothing more that the priest might offer them. However, one also
notes that graduate students who have come from Catholic colleges
seldom feel that they might have a responsibility toward the Newman program, even though they themselves may not experience
any need for it.

Incidentally these statistics are the best answer to the fear that an expanded Newman program might be taken as a substitute for a Catholic education. In many places the Newman program has been thus expanded in the past few decades. Many Newman Foundations now offer religious education programs clearly comparable to those of Catholic colleges. If it were true that any significant number of Catholic students were attracted to secular schools by such programs, where are they when the programs are offered? Or why is it necessary to work so hard to get such relatively meager attendance?

This question is directly related to the question of why there are so many Catholic students in non-Catholic schools. The answer seems to be that beyond the level of basic religious instruction, most Catholics seem to feel that educationally and intellectually the Church does not have much to offer them. In this case Newman work is a good testing laboratory, precisely because of its lack of effective canonical and academic sanctions. When all forms of compulsion are removed, how much zeal for a deeper and more mature religious knowledge does the average Catholic student have? The only way to avoid the patent and disturbing answer to this question would be to object that Newman programs are substandard or that the Catholicity of the students on the secular campus is substandard. The objection is belied by the facts. In any case one cannot say that students have tried the program and found it wanting. They simply have not tried it.

The answer to the second objection lies in relative percentages. Are we prepared to admit that over 60 per cent of our Catholic college students must be placed in the category of indifferent, if not lax and disobedient Catholics? In any case, substandard or not, 60 per cent is a good basis for an indication of the average mentality. In the light of the statistics it would seem that the limited scope of Newman work offers a significant revelation of certain characteristics of the American Catholic mentality. If Newman work is limited in its effect, it would appear to be because average American Catholics do not seem to realize the need for a mature and deepening knowledge of the Faith they profess. If this be so, then it need hardly surprise us to find that they do not grasp the value of a Catholic college education.

To carry the analysis a bit further, it would be helpful to know the real reasons why Catholics go to Catholic colleges. Do they go simply out of blind loyalty? Do they go merely because they regard the Catholic college as a sort of protective ghetto? Or do they go to a Catholic college because they feel that a deeper knowledge of their faith will bring them closer to God? Do Catholics generally feel that deeper understanding is an aid in the spiritual and moral life? If all that the average Catholic sees in a college education is the attainment of religiously neutral skills and techniques, the majority will not make the extra sacrifice that may be demanded merely to gain protection from a danger of which they are not really aware, or merely to get an extra helping of the apologetics and ethics which they feel they learned well enough in their high school religion courses.

Such considerations bring us to roots that lie deep in the whole sociological and intellectual position of American Catholicity. Such problems are not the direct concern of the Newman chaplain, though it is obvious that it is in the light of such problems that the effectiveness of Newman work must be measured. What Newman work does teach us, however, is that the problems will not be solved by a mere emphasis on the corrosiveness of secular education.

In estimating this actual corrosiveness it may be pointed out that the general American intellectual apathy (which is certainly not limited to Catholics) is a saving feature. Actually, the rift between the secular and the religious mind is much deeper than is commonly supposed. Secular education ought to be more corrosive in its effect than it seems to be. (Statistics about the number of Catholic students who lose their faith at secular colleges, it should be noted, are absolutely unreliable because there are simply too many variable factors in the equation.) Oddly enough, the area of least danger is that of the natural sciences. Here the presentation is generally neutral. The area of greatest conflict is in the social sciences, psychology and education. In these subjects, one or the other dominant secular ideology often colors the whole presentation. The saving feature, however, is that the actual impact of classroom teaching is much less than imagined. Students are interested in gaining necessary professional and technical skills. They are interested in passing exams. Beyond this the general intellectual apathy has the effect of neutralizing much of the agnostic approach.

Admittedly this is not a very reassuring picture. Viewed against the whole set of the modern current, Newman work itself is less than reassuring. It is nevertheless a work that needs doing and is badly in need of expansion, both of facilities and personnel. There simply is no other approach that offers any hope of success. The expected increase in college enrollments within the next decade will doubtless fill our Catholic establishments. It should be equally clear that it will also increase the percentage of Catholics attending secular schools.

Meanwhile, whatever the over-all picture, in the Newman apostolate itself a rather happy pattern is slowly emerging. Practical considerations have forced Newman chaplains to develop the very topical, dialectical approach to the teaching of religion to which teachers in Catholic colleges are veering. Lacking sanctions and forced to use every trick in the progressive education bag, Newman chaplains have gained an enviable measure of effectiveness with respect to the students whom they do actually come in touch with. The lack of compulsion, the usually informal setting and the absence of the customary teacher-student constraint make for especially good rapport. When students do come, they come because they like it. They learn because they come to learn and not merely to gain academic credit.

The very *club* technique which is indispensable for promoting attendance and interest is itself a very real training for lay apostleship. In forming a group of devoted and apostolic members, the chaplain is not setting up artificial or peripheral tasks for them to do. There is genuine and necessary work that only the layman can do.

In their small and handicapped way, Newman centers are steadily developing toward the ideal of genuine centers of Catholic learning and culture, centers where Catholics and non-Catholics alike can find Christian warmth and genuine learning in areas that impinge upon religious belief. No one pretends that this is an ultimate answer, but if the results achieved are measured against the actual expenditure of personnel and resources it would be hard to deny that Newman work is a very happy investment indeed.

12.

The Use of Words:
A Problem of Both Content and Method
·
F. H. Drinkwater

"Content" and "Method" are the twin deities who preside over educational thought and divide its empire between them. In the teaching of religion, too, we like to draw the same easy frontier line. "Content" (we say) means what we have to teach, the unchangeable faith and morals taught by the Church. We don't have to worry about that, simply because it *is* unchangeable. It is all there, in Denzinger and the *Code of Canon Law,* and of course Scripture too. It is all boiled down for practical purposes in the various national catechisms. All that is "content." The only aspect of religion-teaching that can be improved (we say) is "method": the various methods of arousing interest or of holding the attention of large groups, and the kinds of equipment—books, pictures and what not—that will be most useful. Method is where modern educational ideas can come in to help; but (and here all of us would agree) all these questions of methods and equipment are of quite secondary importance. None of them matters at all compared with the sincerity and personal religion of the teacher. For the rest, the all-important thing is the content, which is fortunately all there, cut-and-dried, in the catechisms.

It is my purpose to point out how the above view of catechetics is oversimplified. In the first place, content is not such a "fixed quality" as all that, unless we are thinking of the largest headings. To take a simple illustration, the Pater Noster would certainly figure in any list of catechetical contents, and the commentary on it would always include the statement that God is the Father of all men, by creation and by grace. But could such a commentary be called sufficient in these days, in most parts of the world, if it

263

omitted all mention of color bars and color prejudice and the attitude of Catholic doctrine thereto? Oh, you may say, that is
merely the explicit application of a principle that is permanent.
Quite so, but from the syllabus maker's point of view it is an addition to content. Or again, we might consider the campaign which
is now being conducted by all the best catechists on the continent
of Europe for more attention to be given to the great key ideas of
Scripture and liturgy—the Ark, the Pasch, the Vine, and so forth—
in the telling of the Faith, as well as the whole "kerygmatic" urgency of it.[1] This again means a big change in content, the inclusion
(or re-inclusion) of much material that does not figure in the
manuals and catechisms still in use, and in consequence probably
the "including-out" (to borrow Mr. Samuel Goldwyn's useful
phrase) of some of the existing material which has taken up
valuable syllabus space and may be only so much lumber after
all.

But even supposing the present catechetical ferment to have
settled down into a generally accepted syllabus again, so that its
content would once more be a "fixed quantity," even then, we
would suggest, the distinction between content and method will
not be so clear as people like to think. Denzinger itself, after all,
needs some intelligent interpretation and appraisal; the items
chosen by its successive editors for inclusion in that helpful collection of doctrinal utterances of the Church are of very varying
weightiness and all need to be read in their correct background of
historical circumstances; so much so that Denzinger may fairly
be described as a dangerous quagmire for third-rate and fourth-
rate theologians (with whom all theology boils down to a wooden
appeal to extrinsic authority) to flounder about in. But quite apart
from that aspect, even in those points of doctrine where the content
has been clearly and finally stated by the Church, as it has been
in most of the great basic teachings, the sharp distinction between

---

[1] See, for instance, almost any number of the periodical *Catéchistes*, edited
by Frère Vincent Ayel, F.S.C. (78 rue de Sèvres, Paris XIIme). Or the book
by Father J. A. Jungmann, S.J., *Handing on the Faith* (New York: Herder &
Herder, 1959), especially the Appendices.

content and method breaks down, simply because we have to use *words;* and words, and the right choosing of words, are a matter neither of content nor of method precisely, but a bit of both.

We have to use words. I am thinking chiefly of teaching the Faith to our congregations at Mass, though everything said here will have some application to the teaching of school pupils, converts and anybody else. But the congregation at Mass is the final and most severe test of teaching ability, simply because the ordinary congregation is so very mixed, of all ages and sexes and educational levels. And at Mass there is so much that needs to be said, and so short a time to say it. It is rather tragic to think that in some ways the successful invitation of the faithful by St. Pius X to frequent communion almost defeats its own end; if everybody comes to an earlier Mass for communion (for despite the legislative changes, this is still largely the pattern), and so misses the sermon they would have heard at a late Mass, and if communicants are so numerous that the idea of instruction at Mass up to the nine o'clock is abandoned, then what, on a long-term view, is likely to happen when over a lifetime or two the faithful have been fed with the Eucharistic Bread but starved of the Bread of the Word which all authorities tell us is equally necessary? Whatever the correct answer to that may be, the conclusion seems unchallengeable that the Bread of the Word must somehow be broken at Mass, because that is the only time and place when everybody is assembled together.

We have to use words then; and the question I ask is, What sort of words, what kind of language, should we make use of in teaching religion, especially to the ordinary congregation at Mass?

The best preacher I can recall was a little old Franciscan with a long white beard who used to come and help me sometimes at week ends. If you had a good ear for accents you would know that his birthplace was somewhere in Ireland, and I suppose he was a saint. His way of preaching was to stand in the pulpit and let fall rather disconnected sentences in a conversational kind of way, with long pauses in between. The things he said were commonplace enough: but when he said "My dear brethren, God made the world," each word was somehow filled with meaning from inside him. "God created the universe" might have been a more complete statement, but he had no need to strive after verbal completeness. What he would certainly never have said, anyhow, was, "The total framework of creation received its being from Divine Omnipotence."

Everybody admits, of course, that the language we use should be simple, but perhaps we don't always realize *how* simple. A few years ago in England, it occurred to somebody to wonder about the effect of one of the Government's widely circulated pamphlets urging more output, and the Mass-Observation researchers went to work.[2] It was found that many people could not attach any meaning to words like "ultimately" or "resources" or "subordinate." "Formulate" was thought by some to mean "speed up"; "objectives" was understood to mean "obstacles"; "embody" meant "enforce." These are all words in common use, yet the common man cannot ordinarily be counted on to understand them. Intelligence (the psychologists tell us) does not increase after the age of sixteen, and perhaps most adults never reach the teens at all in that respect. Perhaps we shall be safe in thinking of the average intelligence and effective vocabulary of our congregation as less than those of a bright child of ten or eleven; plus some adult experience of life, which however is received *secundum modum recipientis.*

The above caveat must be extended, I fear, to many words which are familiar and deceptively easy-looking. Take for instance the word "divine," which must presumably be called an abstract adjective (if such a term is known to grammarians). The word "divine" occurs frequently, not only in catechisms and sermons but in numberless prayers and hymns. Yet whenever I have tried to get older children to say what they mean by it, I have found that for the majority it holds merely some vague content of holiness or beauty, and it takes a good deal of "eliciting" before some extra-

[2] The Mass-Observation leaflet was by Mr. Tom Harrisson, and details of it were given by Harold Nicholson, "Marginal Comment," *The Spectator* (March 28, 1947), 332.

bright spirit tumbles to the idea that this word in its proper and basic meaning is somehow inseparable from God. Not so long ago some painstaking researchers at the Catholic University of America in Washington (David C. Fullmer and John B. McDowell) conducted separate tests on this very word, amongst others, with elementary-school pupils aged from ten to fourteen.[3] It turned out that over 50 per cent even of the oldest children (and an overwhelming majority of the younger) took the word "divine" to mean "very holy," and were quite prepared to apply it to Our Lady, and also to the angels. I feel sure from my own experience that the same tests would produce the same results in English schools.

The born catechism-maker, if he was statistically convinced of the above facts, would probably sit down quickly and write a new question and answer:

Q. What do you mean by the word "divine"?

A. By the word "divine" I mean whatever pertains to or may be predicated of God.

But would that really get us much further? Wouldn't it still be only the very bright pupil who would use the word with conscious significance?

We are unfortunately much too apt to take for granted that our pupils attach the right meaning to a word simply because it is in constant use. And we people who have studied theology and philosophy and what not are much too apt to take for granted that ordinary folk attach some meaning to abstract terms.

It will be further agreed, moreover, that in our preaching we do not want to reach the mind or intelligence only, but also, and especially, the heart. The *heart*, please; not the emotions. By the emotions we mean, or should mean, the feelings which cause an immediate bodily change in us: the emotion of anger sends the blood into your face; the emotion of fear induces trembling knees or shivers down the spine; the emotion of tenderness brings tears

[3] David C. Fullmer, *The Vocabulary of Religion*, 1943; John B. McDowell, *The Development of the Idea of God in the Catholic Child,* 1952 (both Washington, D.C.: The Catholic University of America Press).

to your eyes or a lump in your throat, and so on. There are preachers who make their appeal to the emotions without scruple, and their bag of tricks has some entertainment value, since they can usually draw a crowd, which is more than you and I can do. Nobody ever walked five yards because *we* were preaching. However, let us at least be clear about the preacher's true target: it is not the emotions, but the heart, which is something much deeper and in surer contact with the will. And the key to the heart is the imagination, in the sense in which Coleridge and Wordsworth used that term. It is the business of the preacher somehow to turn up the lights of the imagination, which is no fantasy, but that *lux vera* in which the eternal truths are seen as more real than the visible world and the light of common day.

Can we arrive at any conclusion about the *kind* of language that is needed to stir the imagination and the heart?

At this point we get some real help from a famous episode in the history of English literature. As we all remember, two young men called Coleridge and Wordsworth published their joint slim vollume of *Lyrical Ballads* in the year 1798, with the declared purpose of starting a revolution in English poetry. They were tired of the artificial phraseology considered *de rigueur* for poets in the eighteenth century (though they could both manage it very well themselves on occasion). Coleridge felt that it left common truth insufficiently illuminated by the higher imagination, and Wordsworth complained that it could not touch the heart. It was Wordsworth who wrote the short preface ("Advertisement," he called it) to the 1798 book, and expanded it into a sort of preface-treatise in the 1800 edition, with further revisions in 1802.[4]

Now thousands of men, millions perhaps, must have felt the touch of nature-ecstasy before William Wordsworth, but he was the first to find out how to communicate the experience itself in suitable words and so perhaps help some to share it who would

---

[4] The early editions of *Lyrical Ballads* have several times been reprinted, even in facsimile, but for anyone interested in Wordsworth's argument much the best book is *The Lyrical Ballads, 1798–1805*, edited with introduction and notes by George Sampson (London: Methuen, 1940), pp. xxxi + 395. This gives all the poems as in the 1805 version, with full variants, and all Wordsworth's different prefaces in full.

not otherwise have done so. Many a writer has done it since, but Wordsworth (yes, not forgetting Traherne either), was the first. When he attempted to explain in plain prose what he was trying to do, he was just as liable to be misunderstood as other theorists. Taken too literally, his theory about the poet's function and language would be no more persuasive than what I may beg leave to call Gerard Manley Hopkins' bit of nonsense about "sprung rhythm." But young Wordsworth's main point, as declared in his preface to the second edition of *Lyrical Ballads*—namely, his revolt against the artificial conventionalities of "poetic diction," his insistence on using "the language of conversation in the middle and lower classes of society"—is worthy of the most serious attention, not least from anybody engaged in teaching religion. No doubt he did let fall some exaggerated phrases, but even these when examined are full of genuine insight. His determination to prefer "humble and rustic language," for instance, is found to be nothing less than a prophetic repudiation of the whole Industrial Revolution and the dominance of the mass mind. Rustic people, he explains, can still use sincere language that comes straight from the heart, whereas with the more educated "a multitude of causes, unknown to former times, are now acting with a combined force to blunt the discriminating powers of the mind, and, unfitting it for all voluntary exertion, to reduce it to a state of almost savage torpor. The most effective of these causes are the great national events which are daily taking place, and the increasing accumulation of men in cities, where the uniformity of their occupations produces a craving for extraordinary incident, which the rapid communication of intelligence hourly gratifies." We can all see what he means now, but it was a pretty bright diagnosis for 1802.

Rustic or not, the Poet's language, according to Wordsworthian theory, must be simple, because it is the Poet's business to speak from his own heart to the heart of his hearers, and only simple language can do this. "The Poet is a man, speaking to men," [5] he said; "Poets do not write for poets alone, but for men." [6] And still more revealingly: "The object of poetry is truth . . . carried alive

[5] *Ibid.*, p. 20.
[6] *Ibid.*, p. 28.

into the heart by passion." It reminds us of Newman's self-chosen epitaph—*Cor ad cor loquitur:* and indeed Newman's distinction between *notional* grasp and *real* grasp of an idea is very relevant. "Truth carried alive into the heart," said Wordsworth. What better description of the catechist's work could we have than that?

Wordsworth's contention was that this could be done only by using the simple language of ordinary life. In the *Lyrical Ballads* (his preface said), "there will be found little of what is usually called poetic diction; as much pains has been taken to avoid it as is ordinarily taken to produce it." By poetic diction he meant the eighteenth century manner which is seen at its best in Gray's "Elegy": poetry most certainly, but of the head rather than the heart, at the receiving end anyhow; a young don musing for undergraduates perhaps, not a man speaking to all men. You may well object that Shakespeare's poetry, or Francis Thompson's, or Wordsworth's own "Immortality" ode, are not written in "the language of conversation in the middle and lower classes of society" (Advertisement to *Lyrical Ballads,* first edition). Wordsworth would reply that the passages in such poems which reach and move the reader's heart are nearly always passages which come nearest to ordinary speech. One rather trembles to think what he would have said about today's ultra-modern school of poetry which, even while using a conversational vocabulary, manages to keep the reader completely in the dark as to what it is all about!

Wordsworth's aim was explained by his friend Coleridge from another angle.[7] Mr. Wordsworth's object, he said, was "to give the charm of novelty to things of every day, and to excite a feeling analogous to the supernatural, by awakening the mind's attention from the lethargy of custom, and directing it to the loveliness and wonders of the world before us," which (he says) we do not feel or understand, on account of "the film of familiarity" which invests them. And isn't that, too, precisely the aim of the good catechist? That his pupils should see the familiar eternal truths with a fresh eye, in their full, compelling reality undimmed by the haze of

[7] Samuel Taylor Coleridge, *Biographia Literaria,* chap. XIV, Everyman's Library (London and New York: J. M. Dent, E. P. Dutton), pp. 160–67.

routine? I suggest that young Mr. Wordsworth knew what he was talking about, and that what he says about language holds good for religious truth as well as poetic truth; that the heart is reached (always supposing we *want* to reach it: one has known professional theologians who disclaimed any such desire quite ostentatiously), by the language of ordinary life and not by academic or scientific or bookish language; that we must indeed employ academic language in religion for the benefit of the head and in the interests of accuracy; but that we must get back from the head to the heart; and *that* means making the transition safely back into ordinary language. Surely we do not do this successfully enough, especially at the secondary-school level. We still tend to use two languages in two separate compartments: the warm simple language accurate enough for practical purposes, which we use for prayers and hymns and missions; and the artificial jargon for the lecture room and textbook and examination questions, and much too often for pulpit instructions too. Can anybody tell me of a secondary-school religion textbook which would fulfill Wordsworth's requirements about language? And please don't anyone say we are asking the teacher to employ language that stirs up the emotions. If people can't see the difference between the emotions and the heart they have not even begun to understand what it is all about. There is a kind of language which can reach to the heart, and another kind of language which seals off the heart as effectually as trouble in the fusebox shuts off the electric current. There are times when you need to shut off the electric current, for repairs or tests or some such reason; but you don't expect any light or heat during these circumstances. It is a question of which kind of language you need for teaching religion, as distinct from "cognate subjects." And the hint from Wordsworth, and from the beneficent revolution he effected in English poetry, can reasonably be borne in mind.

Perhaps this is the place for an illustration, and what could better serve our purpose than the doctrine of Grace which more and more nowadays comes to take a central place in our catechesis, both as the Mystical Body of Christ seen in action and as a new flowering in the Church of devotion to the Holy Spirit? Grace, yes! but how to describe, let alone define, the Grace of God? Somehow when it gets right down into the classroom, not to mention the pulpit, it becomes as matter-of-fact and materialistic as the groceries in the shop round the corner. If the doctrine comes back to us from the lips of our school children as a glib but quite dry-as-dust account of a mechanical soul process supposed to be highly utilitarian but having no special beauty of desirableness about it, it is because the idea of Grace in our own minds has drifted away from the idea of the Holy Ghost and has turned almost into something quantitative and measurable, a quasi-material commodity. For many Christians, says Father Léon de Coninck, Grace seems to be "a thing apart, something that can be isolated in itself; rather like a statue that continues to exist independently of the sculptor. We can get grace as we can get bread or medicine. . . . Grace understood in its relationship with the Holy Spirit is not 'a thing' which one can increase like pennies in a money-box. It loses its impersonal aspect to assume its living vividness in the light of the Holy Spirit." [8] This is profoundly true, and when we can translate such literary expressions as these into the phrases of common speech, as Our Lord did, we shall be getting somewhere with the faithful.

The term Sanctifying Grace is evidently felt to have lost some of its freshness, and to have acquired some of the disadvantages of a technical term; indeed some of the revised catechisms prefer to refer to it more commonly as "the Supernatural Life." The word "life" has the great advantage that it was used by Our Lord. But as soon as you add the word "supernatural" to it you are letting yourself in for lots of definitions, and after a certain number of these you begin to wonder whether all this "plugging" of the idea of Life does not take some of the life *out* of it. Would not the term "New Life" (one wonders) be more handy, vivid and scriptural than the term "Supernatural Life"? Possibly not quite so completely accurate; but is complete scientific accuracy *everything*? "New Life" too is accurate as far as it goes. The word

[8] Léon de Coninck, "The Holy Spirit and the Preaching of Grace," *Lumen Vitae*, VIII (Jan.–March, 1953), 73–76.

"supernatural" is a useful word on occasion, but also a cold-blooded scientific sort of word that you could never use in a prayer or a hymn; a word that Our Lord is not recorded to have used and that He cannot easily be imagined using. And if perfect accuracy is what we are after in catechisms, ought we to use the word "supernatural" as if it necessarily signifies the Divine Life? After all, in itself and by etymological force, the word only means something above one's own nature. You can, for instance, imagine God conferring on a man's soul all the powers of the angelic nature; those gifts would be, in the ordinary understanding of the term by those who use English, supernatural to man, and yet would still have nothing to do with grace and glory. But, you will say, the theologians have supplied us with a word for that, "preternatural." Or again, you say you are using the word "supernatural" in an all-over sense, meaning above *every* nature, above every *created* nature, so that it does signify the Divine Life. All right, but in that case why bother to say "supernatural," why not just say Divine Life, or New Life from God? That word "supernatural," the sap has gone out of it now, but I expect when it was first used it was an inspiring, exciting sort of word, like the word "mystical" when I was young. I suspect that to the Catholic youth of today the word "mystical" is already, or is rapidly becoming, a boresome technical term. Words die and dry away, as the daffodils do.

Sometimes, it seems, the simpler the words are that you use, and the less you explain and define them, the more alive they remain and the more effective in getting as far as the heart. If we just said that God comes to live in our soul, and this New Life is what is meant by "grace"—wouldn't such a statement, keeping close as it does to John 14, 23, be likely to wear as well as the longer or more ambitious words and phrases?

So let us get back to theory, hoping that we will not be considered too theoretical. Let us state our thesis—an elaboration of Wordsworth's, if you like—with brevity and without proof.

It is not just a question between long words and short words, or long sentences and short ones. It is a question of two different ways of *using* language.

There are two main kinds of language, which we may call

Scientific (matter-of-fact, precise, one-dimensional, stripped of ambiguity) and Poetic (in the Wordsworthian sense: meaning not verse, or beautiful choice of words, and certainly not meaning metaphorical as opposed to literal, but simply the language of ordinary life and of literature, full of associations and suggestion, capable of meanings on two or more levels, evocative rather than exact, though it has its own kind of truthfulness and accuracy). Both Scientific and Poetic language may be further divided into difficult and simple. As thus, for examples:

Scientific-difficult: Some formidable sentence out of Einstein or St. Thomas.

Or the usual catechism definitions of Grace.

Scientific-simple: Any easy bit of weather forecast.

A business letter.

Or the statement, "We cannot get to heaven without Grace."

Poetic-difficult: Francis Thompson's "The Hound of Heaven."

Or the following descriptions of Grace:

"Thou who art called the Paraclete, best Gift of God above,

The Living Spring, the Living Fire, Sweet Unction, and true Love."

Poetic-simple: Lincoln's Gettysburg speech.

The catechism answer, "God made me to know Him, love Him, and serve Him in this world and to be happy with Him forever in the next."

Or the statements: "God is living in your soul." "I am the Vine, you are the branches."

The Gettysburg speech is chosen precisely because it is so bleak and bare, and devoid of everything vulgarly understood by imagination or beauty, so much so that the unpsychological might put it into the "Scientific-simple" class. But of course, its choice of words —every one loaded with associations—combined with the circumstances of its delivery to make it overwhelmingly moving, though somewhat by delayed action. However, the Poetic-simple language need not ordinarily be that austere.

My thesis is that the last of the four kinds of language, the Poetic-simple, is the only one that has power to reach the heart. This is what Wordsworth meant to say more or less, though he failed to allow fully for the existence of the Scientific-simple, and for that reason sometimes blundered into the prosaic even in his verses.[9]

The Poetic-difficult has a certain tendency toward reaching the heart: a kind of softening-up process you might call it. But when the time comes to hit the bull's-eye, the poet must get down practically to words of one syllable:

> All which thy childish fears
> Fancied as lost, I have stored for thee at home.
> Rise, clasp my hand, and come.
>
> Good night, sweet prince;
> And flights of angels sing thee to thy rest!

Shakespeare is especially interesting, because the ordinary language of the plays is so very Poetic-difficult, yet when he has to touch our hearts at all costs he always comes down to the simplest

[9] On this point the interested reader may be glad to have one or two further short quotations out of George Sampson's book. In the 1802 edition Wordsworth had seemed to argue that there is no real difference between prose and poetry: "Some of the most interesting parts of the best poems will be found to be strictly the language of prose when prose is well written" (p. 16). Coleridge could not quite swallow this, and about the same time we find him writing in a private letter to W. Sotheby: "In my opinion poetry justifies as poetry, independent of any other passion, some new combinations of language, and *commands* the omission of many others allowable in other compositions." Now Wordsworth, *me saltem judice,* has in his system not sufficiently admitted the former, and in his practice has too frequently sinned against the latter."— *Letters of Samuel Taylor Coleridge,* edited by Ernest Hartley Coleridge, 2 vols. (Boston and New York: Houghton, Mifflin and Co., 1895), 373–75. No doubt it was the force of such criticisms that led Wordsworth to make some changes to the preface in 1805, adding for instance the following footnote: "I here use the word Poetry (though against my own judgment) as opposed to the word Prose, and synonymous with metrical composition. But much confusion has been introduced into criticism by the contradistinction of Poetry and Prose, instead of the more philosophical one of Poetry and Matter of Fact, or Science. The only strict antithesis to Prose is Metre."—Sampson, *op. cit.,* p. 380.

words. This happens in the sonnets too where he was desperately sincere in his efforts to touch one heart at least.

And what of Scientific language? The Scientific-simple often has great usefulness, even in the pulpit. It can play the part of signposts, of strict definition, preventing misunderstanding, or a giant excavator clearing the ground, and so on. Nobody could possibly believe more than I do in definition, in its right place. I hold that if everybody would only define their terms accurately, nearly all controversies would collapse as unnecessary, and many controversialists would discover to their surprise that they were in agreement with each other. Such accuracy can only be achieved by the use of Scientific language even in religion. All I am doing is calling the reader's attention to a fact: namely, that if you want to reach people's *hearts*, Scientific language is not going to do it; even Scientific-*simple* language will not do it, and as for Scientific-difficult it immediately shuts off all approach to the heart, as the dropping of a steel curtain would. Scientific-simple language is often called for in the pulpit, as for instance when we are explaining the Lenten regulations: but at such times we do not expect even the saintliest of people in our congregation to look as if something had lit them up inside.

Nor do I mean (God help us all) that Poetic-simple language will infallibly move people's hearts. Of course not—all sorts of other things are involved; but it is the only kind that has any chance of doing so.

Incidentally, it is right to point out that the Poetic-simple is the only kind of language on record as being ever used by Our Lord, either in the Gospels or in His appearances to the saints. He never defines anything, and certainly not His own terms; never uses Scientific language at all; never uses even Poetic-difficult. Don't ask me why. Phrases like "oriental imagery" are unimpressive here. There is nothing specially oriental about it, any more than about St. Patrick's Breastplate or St. Francis' Canticle of the Sun. It is just human, poetic, non-scientific; by no means plain, but simple, always simple. And concrete, never abstract. (Think of all the things He said about forgiving, yet never once using the abstract word "forgiveness.") St. Paul seems to use Scientific-difficult language sometimes, as about justification and all that, but perhaps one should call it rather Poetic-difficult: elaborate metaphors, and so on. I suppose one permanent complication about the science of theology is that it must erect a lofty structure of truth expressed in scientific language upon a basis of truth expressed in non-scientific language. It is like building a mighty bridge not on solid ground, but across some wide river bed. This can be done to last, but not by any second-rate engineers in a hurry. And how wise the Church is to insist that the "Bible and Bible only" is not enough.

But let us turn away from these deep and perilous waters, and concentrate on our practical problem of the right language for communicating the Word of God. Evidently, the Poetic-simple must be the kind to be mainly used, since it is the only kind which can be relied on to touch the imagination and reach the heart. But on the other hand it is the only kind which is *not* used when, in our seminaries and our pre-seminary schooling, we are taught the religion which we are going to teach to others. The aim of the theologian (and we may add of the canon lawyer, since theology mostly seems to be learned in terms of canon law nowadays) is to *eliminate* all imagination from his intellectual process and reduce his language to the purely scientific—more often than not the Scientific-difficult, full of analysis, abstractions, divisions, generalization, technical terminology. Even when we escape from the Latin, or the Latinized Scientific language of the manuals (which also colors the school textbooks and catechisms), what we escape *into* is likely to be not the Poetic-simple but the Poetic-difficult literary kind of vocabulary which can doubtless be a help to the educated reading public, but is without meaning to ordinary folk. Not for worlds would I disparage those thoughtful, philosophic sorts of books, the Maritains and Berdayevs and Guardinis, and their numerous counterparts who write in English. To people at university level who think in that kind of language, especially to the adolescent imagination which delights in broad sweeps and novel vistas, such writing can be very stimulating, though I doubt whether it gets as far as the heart by itself. But for our ordinary listeners, the Poetic-difficult is no more helpful than the Scientific; phrases like "vibrance of infused charity," "contemporary Messianic hope," "the mysterious economy of salvation," which I cull at random from any page of my favorite authors, would pass like a chilly breeze over the heads of our congregation, just as much as this one from a secondary-school textbook: "Confession should be complete and integral: there are two kinds of integrity, material and formal." This would presumably fall into the category of Scientific-difficult. And finally there is the language of the encyclicals, the *stylus curiae*. I don't know what class it would fit into exactly, but I'm afraid it would not be the Poetic-simple.

What is the consequence of all this for the teacher of religion? The consequence is that preaching and catechizing become primarily a work of translation. We clergy learn our religion in one language (I don't mean Latin—that's another complication—I mean Scientific-difficult English), and have to preach it in another. *Most of us think it is enough to translate the Scientific-difficult into Scientific-simple, and that is where we are mistaken. If we want to have some chance of reaching people's hearts, we have to translate it into Poetic-simple—the language of ordinary life.*

Some readers, I am sure, will be up in arms against the idea that there is any such difference between Scientific-simple and Poetic-simple. "He loved me and delivered Himself for me." That statement certainly goes to the heart; and is it not the literal truth, is it not a scientific theological fact? To be really scientific, the sort of statement that a pernickety *censor librorum* would pass if you or I had written it, instead of St. Paul, would have to run something like this: He loved me, as He loved all the other millions of mankind: He offered His death to atone for my sins amongst others, and I may reasonably hope that He would have done the same even if there had been no other sinners in the world." By the time you have said all that, the temperature is perceptibly cooler, isn't it? I am not saying that these qualifications ought not to be made somehow, somewhere. All I say is that while you stop to make them, while you strive for complete accuracy of statement, your arrow is less likely to fly straight to the heart.

On the other hand it may be possible that just as some of us are without any ear for music, so there may be others of us who are so literal and matter-of-fact and flat-minded that we are capable only of Scientific-simple language and not of ordinary everyday human language at all. If so, possibly we ought not to preach, since it is certain we cannot get any further than people's intelligence, except perhaps by some miracle, or psychological back door, for there are probably more things in heaven and earth than your philosophy and mine have dreamed of.

But it is a real question whether the dull and unimaginative should be set on teaching religion, or indeed become teachers at all.

In any case it is very much to be desired that schools should put the best teachers, not the weakest ones, on to the teaching of religion. This has not been the general custom by any means on the side of the Atlantic where this article comes from, and its writer would be edified but surprised if the tradition on the other side of that ocean were different. There are usually so many urgent reasons, especially in schools run by religious orders, for putting all the best teachers on to the secular subjects, as if mere piety were enough in the religious teacher. But in the long run it is rather a disastrous policy. If only it could be changed, especially in the higher reaches of education such as teacher-training colleges and the upper forms of high schools! If only the Good News could be taught by the imaginative and inspiring teachers who can see something of what it means and know how to light up its relevance to the whole of life! No other reform in catechetics could have such an immense effect as the changing of this bad tradition.

This was one of the points rightly urged by Mr. Frank Sheed in a recent pamphlet which I hope drew as much attention in the United States as it did in England and in Ireland.[10] The point is closely connected in practice with his other demand for a richer and deeper teaching of the great central doctrines. Teachers with pious but second-rate minds, faced with the task of teaching the

[10] F. J. Sheed, *Are We Really Teaching Religion?* (New York: Sheed & Ward, 1953), pp. 35.

Scientific-difficult jargon of seminary theology and catechisms, prove quite unequal to the task of translating it even into Scientific-simple language, much less the Poetic-simple. They do not in fact even perceive any need of doing so, and just end by teaching the stuff, and their superficial "explanations" of it, in the parrot-fashion way they were probably taught themselves when young. Yes, it is a *very* bad self-perpetuating tradition of bad teaching. Monsignor Russell was himself a conspicuous example of the better way of doing things, and spent his life in spreading it. It would be a happy result of this volume if Catholic high-ups became convinced that religion in the classroom is not less important than other subjects but far more important, and needs first-rate teaching, the beneficent effects of which would certainly not be confined to religion but would overflow into the whole life and teaching of a school.

A few other practical conclusions might follow, once we were all agreed on the desirableness of such large simplifications as are suggested here. Catechetics would need to be taught in seminaries, and the teaching of theology would need to be re-orientated in a pastoral direction. Conferences and collaboration would be needed, not only between theologians and catechists, but between all those active in teaching, including somehow parents (who always get left out of everything, don't they?). Catechetical exhibitions and libraries would be needed in every locality. All these suggestions have already been put forward urgently and officially by the first International Congress of Catechetics which met in Rome in 1950.[11] There is much hope, too, in the Higher Catechetical Centers which have begun to operate in countries like France and Holland, and which aim—as I am sure Monsignor Russell aimed in his lifetime—at sending forth the future key teachers of the coming catechetical blossom time. I shall, I imagine, not live to see all this; but let us hope it will be soon, for the world's need of it is even more urgent than ever before. *Veni, et noli tardare!*

[11] *Acta Congressus Catechistici Internationalis*, MCML (Roma: Typis Polyglottis Vaticanis, 1953), pp. 565.

13.

Confirmation at the Age of Reason
·
Georges Delcuve, S.J.

THE DEVELOPMENT OF FAITH,
AIM OF RELIGIOUS EDUCATION

Catechists and professors of religion are frequently divided about the aim of religious education. One group struggles almost exclusively with the transmission of a precise knowledge; its members profess themselves satisfied if pupils know the letter of the catechism. At the opposite extreme are those who make too weak a case not only for memorization but for intellectual effort as well. Their sole objectives seem to be the encouragement of religious practice and the implantation of virtuous habits.

Both groups are concerned with certain aspects of the total goal, but the exclusive outlook of each—be it strict intellectualism or pragmatism—hinders one as well as the other from grasping the full reality, namely the development of faith on which our salvation depends. "The heart has only to believe, if we are to be justified," St. Paul wrote to the Romans; "the lips have only to make confession, if we are to be saved." (Rom. 10, 10) And he added: "See how faith comes from hearing; and hearing through Christ's word." (Rom. 10, 17) The aim of the catechist, of the professor of religion, of the preacher, is to work with grace in the awakening or the increase of that faith which justifies us.

Now, this disposition of soul is a complex one. We become aware of its richness only in studying successively the principal elements that go to make it up. Following St. Thomas, Canon Mouroux has designated them by the three lapidary formulas: *Credo Deum, Credo Deo, Credo in Deum.*[1]

Credo Deum: "I believe about God." Our faith has an object, a

---

[1] *Je crois en Toi* (Paris: Editions de la Revue des Jeunes, 1949).

content. At first glance it seems to deal with a multiplicity of things and with abstractions. Do we not speak of "the twelve articles of the Creed"? Actually, under this apparent variety of abstractions, we find the triune unity of God. The content of our religious teaching can be reduced to one fundamental reality: "God present to humanity in order to save it."

The role of the professor of religion is not limited therefore to arousing a certain sentiment or eliciting a religious practice. He has a message to communicate in its objectivity and integrity. However, his task is not to reproduce a compelling demonstration but rather to prepare for the reception of a witness.

Credo Deo: "I believe God." Revelation has come to us, the fact is, by means of testimony or witness. "No man has ever seen God; but now his only-begotten Son, who abides in the bosom of the Father, has himself brought us a clear message." (Jn. 1, 18) "We speak of what is known to us," Jesus declares to Nicodemus, "and *testify* of what our eyes have seen, and still you will not accept our *testimony*." (Jn. 3, 11) Later he will add, addressing the Pharisees who refuse His testimony, "My Father who sent me testifies on my behalf too." (Jn. 8, 18)

The "Good News" of salvation was introduced into the world by two witnesses: the external witness—deeds and words—of Jesus Christ, and the internal witness—an intimate attraction—of the Father. "No one can come to me," says the Lord, "unless he has received the gift from my Father." (Jn. 6, 66)

Ever since the Ascension the Christian message continues to be transmitted by means of a twofold witness: the external witness of Christians, both personal and in community, and the internal witness of the Holy Spirit. "When the truth-giving Spirit, who proceeds from the Father, has come to befriend you, he whom I will send you from the Father's side, he will bear witness of what I was; and you too are to be my witnesses, you who from the first have been in my company." (Jn. 15, 26 f.)

The acceptance of any testimony depends largely on our dispositions with regard to the witness. If he is sympathetic toward us we trust him. If the contrary is the case we raise objections and manage to escape him somehow. It will suffice here to recall the conduct of the Pharisees.

More basically still, the acceptance of a sublime act of witness depends on our moral dispositions and our human experience. How difficult this acceptance is for the man who is not genuine, who lives in the midst of a deceitful and seductive world.

Under these conditions it will not suffice for the teacher of religion to address himself exclusively to the reason of his pupils. He must contribute something of himself toward bringing them close to the Savior. In his own person he is a modest and subordinate witness; but he gives true testimony nonetheless. He must merit the confidence of pupils. He must be able to build on their experience of loyalty developed through personal conduct and contacts.

Credo in Deum: "I believe in God." God is not only the object of revelation and its authorized witness, He is also the beatific End. Him we shall enjoy fully in the life to come; toward Him we are oriented in this life, in a sense possessing Him already. Faith is an intellectual adherence and a trust and also a commitment of the whole person. That is to say, our task remains unachieved if having elicited the immense love of God we do not seek the means to promote an ever more generous response to it.

This simple analysis of faith enables us to recognize its two aspects, the *intellectual* and the *vital,* which certain educators dissociate and isolate from each other.

Faith is an *intellectual adherence* to the message of salvation proclaimed publicly in the Church. It is an intimate acceptance as well, since it is a response to that attraction whereby God gives testimony in our hearts. The principal object of this adherence as we have pointed out is "God the Savior," or more precisely, the Paschal Mystery, the Mystery of Christ. Does not St. Paul center his whole missionary preaching on Christ risen? "If Christ has not risen, then our preaching is groundless, and your faith, too, is groundless." (I Cor., 15, 14.)

Faith is also a commitment, a lifelong gift of self. In the case of the conversion of an adult this may even be called its most striking aspect. Up until this decisive act, the individual had thought himself the shaper of his destiny. He looked upon the world as the framework in which the issues were joined. He was forcing himself to solve problems according to the potentialities of a human universe. Then it was that God intervened as the Living God and Friend to man, the one whom man must accept as his Master and the Guide of his destiny if he wishes to find a life which encompasses and surpasses by an infinity that of his own efforts. This life will vanquish death itself and every limit to the condition of this mortal body. Man says "yes" not through weakness or fear but because God is stronger and more alive than he.[2]

If, in order to appreciate better the steps of the believer, we have seen fit to distinguish the various aspects, let us recall that they are closely joined to one another. The order in which they have been presented must not lead us into error. Actually, the full knowledge of adherence is sustained by that force which carries us on toward God. In the first response to the divine invitation, these various aspects comprise but a single one. Faith is the encounter of the human person with divine Persons.

From the time of conversion onward, or with the first stirrings of consciousness in the baptized, this encounter must normally turn into intimacy. That supposes a progressive purification: his love more disinterested, his knowledge less sensual. Faith becomes interiorized and the believer comes to have a certain experience of the world of faith, a fruit of the presence of the Spirit of Christ. "It is by acknowledging the Son that we lay claim to the Father too. . . . The influence of his anointing lives on in you, so that you have no need of teaching; . . . according as this anointing has taught you, live on in him." (I Jn., 2, 23–27)

The increase of faith is manifested also by its spread. More and more it inspires all the activity of the Christian, who thereby takes on the aspect of a witness to Christ and apostle.

Such is that faith which it is the whole object of the catechist or

[2] The treatment here follows the thought and at times the phrasing of Fr. A. Liégé, O.P., "Faith," in *The Virtues and States of Life*, The Theology Library, IV (Chicago: Fides, 1957), 1–59.

the professor of religion to develop. Helping others to give themselves over to God or to remain faithful to the first commitment is his real task, along with encouraging an increasingly interior adherence and promoting the spread of faith. He will go about these tasks zealously, knowing that "faith comes through preaching," but above all with a deep-seated humility, for he is only the instrument of the interior Master whom the liturgy calls the "Light of hearts." He will also have a particular esteem for "the sacrament which gives the Holy Spirit."

This leads us to a consideration of the significance of confirmation.

THE SIGNIFICANCE OF CONFIRMATION

For about thirty years now the sacrament of confirmation has been the object of a particular interest. Theologians are engaged in determining its specific character and distinguishing it from baptism. Following their lead, we shall open the Scriptures, contemplate the liturgy, and consult the documents of the *magisterium*. It is a long road but it leads to enlightenment.

Scripture

1. *The Gospels.* Just as the baptism of the Christian receives its full meaning only in the light of Christ's baptism, so also it seems to us that our confirmation will be better understood with reference to the anointing or "confirmation" of the Savior.

"Then Jesus," we read in St. Matthew, "came from Galilee and stood before John at the Jordan, to be baptized by Him . . . and as he came straight up out of the water, suddenly heaven was opened, and he saw the Spirit of God coming down like a dove and resting upon him. And with that, a voice came from heaven which said, 'This is my beloved Son, in whom I am well pleased.'" (Mt. 3, 13–17)

According to the Fathers and scholastics, the baptism of the Christian reproduces in some way the baptism of Jesus in the water;

confirmation is a participation in His anointing, that fullness of the Spirit manifested by the descent of the Spirit.[3]

Quite frankly, these comparisons are surprising at first glance. Those who institute them hold that by baptism the Spirit takes up His abode within us, and that the sacrament of confirmation merely develops the spiritual energies infused in the water of baptism. According to them, "It corresponds to the *progressive setting to work of these energies,* by which the baptized person, a child in Christ, attains his full stature as a perfect man."[4] Neither the spiritual (or "pneumatic") aspect of baptism nor the dynamic character of confirmation is obvious from the baptism narrative, thus interpreted. Consequently, those commentaries which discover in the account of the baptism of Christ the heralding of the baptism *and* the confirmation of the Christian seem somewhat arbitrary, even though they may have their justification.

It is quite another matter, we think, if instead of limiting our gaze to certain verses about baptism (Mt. 3, 13–17), we consider the whole "wilderness pericope" (Mt. 3, 1–4, 11):

In those days John the Baptist appeared, preaching in the wilderness of Judea: Repent, he said, the kingdom of heaven is at hand. . . . Come, then, yield the acceptable fruit of repentance; do not presume to say in your hearts, We have Abraham for our father; I tell you, God has power to raise up children to Abraham out of these very stones. . . . As for me, I am baptizing you with water, for your repentance, but one is to come after me. . . . He will baptize you with the Holy Ghost and with fire. He holds his winnowing-fan ready to sweep his threshing-floor clean;

---

[3] Cf., J. Daniélou, S.J., "Confirmation," *The Bible and the Liturgy* (University of Notre Dame Press, 1956), pp. 114–26. The baptism of Christ and that of the Christian are not identical but analogous. From the time of its conception, Christ's humanity was filled with grace and truth. According to St. Thomas, the sacrament is a sign of three things: it is a memorial of the past, the Savior's Passion; it is a sign of a present reality, grace; it prefigures the future, eternal life. As to Christ's baptism, that also can be called a sign of three things: it is the sign of the accomplishment of a prophecy, namely, the prediction of the suffering Servant; it is the sign of the initial realization of this destination to the Redemption; and lastly, it is the sign of full accomplishment to come, the Cross. (Cf., P. Henry, S.J., "Het sacramentalisme van het Doopsel," *Bijdragen,* XI [1950], 42. Also I. de la Potterie, S.J., "L'onction de Christ," *Nouvelle Revue Théologique,* 80 [Mar., 1958], 225–52.)

[4] *Op. cit.,* p. 126. Italics mine.

he will gather the wheat into his barn, but the chaff he will consume with fire that can never be quenched. [Mt. 3, 1–12. Here the baptism narrative begins, followed immediately by the "temptation" episode.]

The preaching of John the Baptist gives us the meaning of baptism: entrance into the kingdom of heaven, a penitential rite, an intervention of God capable of raising up a progeny to Abraham, a judgment like that rendered by God in Egypt. Is it not the heralding of Christian baptism, which is new birth in God's image?

On the other hand, stating it briefly, the "temptation" narrative gives us the meaning of confirmation or at least makes it explicit. Cyril of Jerusalem recognized this when he said:

Lastly you have been anointed on the breast so that, clothed with the breastplate of justice you may resist the demon's attacks. Indeed, just as Christ after his baptism and the coming on him of the Holy Spirit went out and triumphed over the Adversary, so you after holy baptism and sacramental anointing, having put on all the armor of the Holy Spirit, will resist the hostile power.[5]

A reading of the Gospel thus leaves two positions open to us. We may either see in the baptism narrative a relation to the baptism *and* the confirmation of the Christian, a relation prepared for (in the case of baptism) by John the Baptist's preaching, and made explicit (in the case of confirmation) by the "temptation" episode.[6] Or, we may recognize in the baptism of Christ the prototype of our baptism only, and compare confirmation to the temptation of Christ which was brought to an end by the dispatching of angels as bearers of the divine presence.

Plausible arguments can be put forth to support both positions. It matters little to our purpose, however, to decide whether the significance of confirmation is conveyed in the "temptation" narrative for the first time or if it is only found there more explicitly. The fact is that we can never neglect this narrative in a study of confirmation. The two passages of the Gospel—baptism and temptation—

---

[5] Cited by Daniélou, *op. cit.*, p. 121.
[6] We said above that in general this was the tendency of the Fathers and scholastics; namely, to find in the one account of the baptism of Jesus the prototype of the two sacraments.

are closely associated, as the ceremonies of baptism and confirmation were to be in the early Church. The "wilderness pericope" serves as a model for the Christian initiation: catechumenate, baptism, confirmation.

Baptism. "The baptism of Christ in the Jordan," writes Father Henry, "is a solemn ritual act by which Christ is consecrated preparatory to his death and resurrection." [7] The actions and words of the baptism recall the figures and preparations of the Old Testament and announce the Paschal Mystery, the realization of which is already begun. Let us examine it.

After having eaten the paschal lamb at the time of the "passing over" of the avenging angel, Israel had "passed through" the Red Sea, sojourned in the desert, crossed the Jordan (which the renewed miracles had, so to speak, identified with the Red Sea), and finally entered into the Promised Land. Similarly Christ "passes through" the Jordan before repairing to the desert and entering into the Promised Land. John baptizes him. The Spirit descends on Jesus and "the consecratory voice coming from heaven declares: 'Thou art my beloved Son; in thee I am well pleased.'" (Mk. 1, 11) It is an echo of the "Servant songs," of the Passion of Our Lord Jesus Christ according to Isaiah," as the last song has been called. (Is. 53, 1) [8] These "songs" are evoked by the utterance of the Father, to be sure, but also by the coming of the Spirit and the words of John the Baptist: "Look, this is the Lamb of God; look, this is he who takes away the sin of the world." (Jn. 1, 29; Is. 53, 7)

Thus it appears that Jesus comes to the Jordan to accomplish the prophecy of Isaiah. Now, in what sense was that prophecy evocative of the Messiah? First, it speaks of him as the messenger and renewer of justice (42, 1); then as a man humiliated unto death and exalted in a true resurrection. "Exaltation is linked to death in a cause-and-effect relation. Redress is achieved in virtue

---

[7] Henry, *op. cit.*, p. 49.

[8] Cf., F. X. Durrwell, C.Ss.R., *La résurrection de Jésus, mystère de salut* (Le Puy: Mappus, 1950), p. 16. Isaiah had written: "And now, here is my servant . . . the man of my choice, greatly beloved. My spirit rests upon him." (Is. 42, 1) And further on (53, 7): "Sheep led away to the slaughter-house . . . no word from him."

of abasement." (Cf. 53, 10–12) The Passion of the Servant now contributes to a redemptive purpose. The Sufferer expiates crimes he is not guilty of, the crimes of his many brothers, and just as his humiliations touch him in his own person insofar as he is a substitute for sinners, so also the personal glory which these humiliations win for him redounds to the profit of his brothers. "If he offers his life in expiation he shall see a posterity; long shall he live, and what pleases Yahweh shall be accomplished by his hands." (53, 10) We already know from other songs of the Servant what that purpose is; namely, establishing justice among the nations (42, 1–4), leading Jacob, making light to shine among the Gentiles and bringing salvation to the ends of the earth. (49, 5 ff.) Because he bears their guilt on his shoulders, God will assign to the Servant "multitudes, and with the mighty shall he divide the spoil." (53 12) "God will exercise dominion over them in whose favor He has offered his expiatory sacrifice. This Lordship exercised by the humble Servant is the stroke which consummates the previous intuitions of this fascinating text." [9]

The Servant is the messenger who proclaims judgment on the nations. He offers Himself as an expiatory sacrifice and rises again. Thus does he become Master. Are not the three missions of Christ, prophetic, priestly and kingly, thereby prefigured?

It can be seen from this how the baptism of Christ sketches out beforehand the Paschal Mystery to come. Now, He passes through the Jordan on His way to the Promised Land; then, the hour will have come for Him "to pass from this world to the Father" (Jn. 13, 1), and He will eat the paschal lamb with His disciples. Now, He is designated the Servant of Yahweh; then, He will accomplish this prophecy: He will render the supreme witness which shall lead to His condemnation, He will offer the redemptive sacrifice, He will rise and be proclaimed Lord of creation. Thus is His baptism the dawn of the passion and the resurrection.

Is it surprising then that the Lord Himself should have spoken of His Passion as a baptism? "Have you strength to drink of the cup I am to drink of, to be baptized with the baptism I am to be

[9] Durrwell, *op. cit.*, pp. 16 ff.

baptized with?" (Mk. 10, 38) "There is a baptism I must needs
be baptized with, and how impatient am I for its accomplishment." (Lk. 12, 50)

Is it surprising that in the conversation with Nicodemus (Jn. 3,
2–15), where He expounds the necessity of baptism for His disciples, He announces His own crucifixion and ascension? In His
"raising up" (cf. Jn. 8, 28 and 12, 32; also Numbers 21, 8), He will
"draw all things to Himself," a drawing realized when the Christian
by his baptism finds himself associated with the "baptism" of
Christ.[10] Later St. Paul will see in baptism a being made like to
Christ dead and risen again, a certain consecration to the death
and resurrection of Christ.[11]

Thus, as Henry writes,

The life of Jesus unfolds as one great sacrament, between a *beginning*
(His baptism) which is primarily *rite and symbol,* and an *end* (the
passion) which is primarily *deed and effect;* between a *sacrament-sign*
which inaugurates and consecrates, and a *sacrament-reality* which consummates and achieves.[12]

The anointing or "confirmation" of the Lord. According to the
majority of authors, as we have already seen, Christ was "anointed"
spiritually when the Spirit descended upon Him; He was "confirmed" and His strength manifested in the dialogue with Satan.
Henry prefers to relate the confirmation of the Christian to the
ministrations which the Savior received at angels' hands after the
threefold temptation. He writes:

In the interval (between the baptism and the passion), all the solemn
moments in the life of Christ, those in which the action of the Father is
manifested sensibly and ritually, so to say, are sacramental moments in
the strict sense, that is, they signify and effect death and resurrection.[13]

[10] Henry, *op. cit.,* p. 49.
[11] Rom. 6, 2–11. Cf. also what L. de Grandmaison has written concerning
Christ's baptism (*Jesus Christ,* Sheed and Ward, New York, 1934, II, 11):
"The best commentary on these facts, and the key to the way in which Christianity interpreted them from the beginning, is to be found in the final commandment of the Saviour, and in the Trinitarian baptismal liturgy which followed from it: 'Going, therefore, teach ye all nations, baptizing them in the
name of the Father, and of the Son, and of the Holy Ghost.' (Mt. 28, 19)"
[12] Henry, *op. cit.,* p. 49.
[13] *Ibid.*

In either hypothesis we are invited to search for some light on confirmation in the temptation narrative.

This is the perspective in which we should like to reread the narrative. Jesus is "led into the desert by the Spirit" to be tempted by the devil. The Tempter suggests to Him that He use to His advantage some of His marvelous power and change stones into bread. Jesus answers him with the Scriptural phrase which recalls to every Israelite the primacy of the spiritual in life. "Man cannot live by bread only; there is life for him in all the words which proceed from the mouth of God." Then Jesus is brought to the pinnacle of the Temple, before all the people of Israel. "If thou art the Son of God," the challenge comes, "cast thyself down to earth." In other words, do that deed which those who look for the Messiah expect. Give the sign from heaven so ardently anticipated. What have you to fear? Is it not written, "He has given charge to his angels concerning thee, and they will hold thee up with their hands, lest thou shouldst chance to trip on a stone." "But it is further written," Jesus said to him, "Thou shalt not put the Lord thy God to the proof."

Staking everything on his last throw so as to gain all, the Tempter brings before the eye of the Nazarene as if on some lofty summit the vision of the empires of the world and all earthly glory. Then, aggressive and terribly sure of himself, he offers to share with his impenetrable Adversary this empire and this glory, if he will but do homage to him—for "they have been made over to me, and I may give them to whomsoever I please." But Jesus puts the brazen one to flight: "Away with thee, Satan; it is written, Thou shalt worship the Lord thy God, and serve none but him." Defeated, the Strong One armed disappears, at least for a time.

Father de Grandmaison, from whom we have borrowed this paragraph,[14] says by way of conclusion: "What we have to remember concerning these very significant events . . . is that from then on the question of the Messiahship and the Kingdom of God was prominently before the Master, and formed the framework for the temptations which were to assail him."[15]

---

[14] *Op. cit.*, pp. 13 f.
[15] *Op. cit.*, p. 14.

It does not seem out of place to go further and put the three temptations parallel on the one hand with the three great phases or aspects of the life of Christ, on the other with His three missions, prophetic, priestly and kingly.

Jesus prefers the word of God to bread; He will preach the Good Tidings of salvation and will reproach the multitude with looking for bread other than His "words which are spirit and life" (Jn. 6, 63 and 68); for He is a *prophet*.

Jesus does not cast Himself down from the pinnacle of the Temple. He will not conquer spirits and hearts by "signs from heaven"; He will act as a "Servant" throughout His life, but especially on Calvary. He will not come down from the cross to triumph over the incredulity of the chief priests by a dramatic exploit. He is our victim and our *priest*.[16]

Jesus does not sacrifice his soul to the cause of dominating the whole world. He will be *king*, yes, but his reign will begin when he is lifted up on the cross.[17]

Put briefly, in the desert episode as in the Servant Song recalled by His baptism there is an allusion to the three missions of the

---

[16] This interpretation of the second temptation is suggested by a comparison with two other Gospel texts. The word of Satan is spoken through the sarcastic taunts of the chief priests on Calvary. "If thou art the Son of God," said Satan, "throw thyself down, for it is written, He has given charge to his angels concerning thee. . . ." (Mt. 4, 6). The chief priests: "He has but to come down from the cross, here and now, and we will believe in him. He trusted in God; let God, if he favors him, succour him now; he told us, I am the Son of God." (Mt. 27, 42 f.)

Another passage brings to mind the second and third temptations. Peter has just acknowledged Jesus as "the Christ, the Son of the Living God." (Mt. 16, 16) Jesus commends him, and follows through with the prophecy of his Passion. "Whereupon Peter, drawing him to his side, began remonstrating with him. . . ." Jesus turned around and said to him: "Back, Satan; thou art a stone in my path; for these thoughts of thine are man's, not God's." Then follows Christ's promised reward of a life of renunciation and the cross, in which the Son of Man would return in His Father's glory surrounded by angels to make recompense. (Mt. 16, 22–27)

[17] Cf. the end of the preceding note. On the cross, Jesus begins to dispose of the Kingdom of God. "Lord, remember me when thou comest into thy kingdom," begs the thief. And Jesus answers, "I promise thee, this day thou shalt be with me in Paradise." (Lk. 23, 42 f.) Cf. also the texts on the attraction which Jesus will exercise after his "being lifted up" on the cross. (Jn. 8, 28 and 12, 32; also Num. 21, 8)

Savior and to the three phases or principal aspects of the redemptive work.[18]

From this moment, Jesus accepts his three missions in the light of the Paschal Mystery. During his public life he will fulfill especially that of prophet or herald of salvation. (Lk. 4, 18; Is. 61, 1) That, however, will not hinder his remitting sins or working miracles at the same time, the signs of a dominion which extends to the material universe. Even so, if in his passion Christ is primarily a priest he is nonetheless a prophetic witness and king as well.

Let us conclude the Gospel account. Jesus has come out into the desert impelled by the Spirit to be tempted there. Once the demon is worsted the angels who are bearers of the divine presence intervene. According to Henry, they make of this moment a ritual thing: "Christ is fortified in his destiny as suffering Servant; we have here a *confirmation*." [19] If one recognizes the *anointing* of Jesus in the baptism narrative, it will be easy to see here the renewed assurance of the good pleasure of heaven.

The common elements in the Savior's baptism and his "confirmation" are the active intervention of the Holy Spirit, orientation toward the Paschal Mystery (indicated in the baptism by the circumstance and the words, in the confirmation by the struggle with Satan for fidelity to the Father which only the Savior's victory will terminate), and references to the prophetic, priestly and kingly missions (clear in the baptism if one consults the Servant songs, probable but less clearly identifiable in the other case).

---

[18] There is no need, however, to depend too heavily on the chronological sequence; St. Luke reverses the order of the second and third temptations.

[19] There is a striking parallelism between the episode in the desert and that in the Garden of Gethsemani. (Mt. 26, 36–46) In each case there is struggle (the word "agony" means "struggle"). Three times waves of distress roll in on the soul of Jesus. Three times he comes to find his apostles. "Watch and pray," he says to them the second time, "that you may not enter into temptation." (v. 41) Just as in the desert, Jesus receives aid from heaven: "And he had sight of an angel from heaven, encouraging him." (Lk. 22, 43) The "confirmation" of the Lord was the consecration of his action; the succor or anointing during the agony will be the consecration of his passion and death. If, as Henry thinks, the succor brought from heaven to Gethsemani is the prototype of extreme unction, it would be plausible to regard the intervention of the angels in the desert as a "confirmation."

In the transition from the baptism of Christ to His "confirmation," He is seen to be in general more active in the latter, very clearly aware of His destiny (the meaning of His life), determined upon an encounter in which He will struggle victoriously with Satan, who departed from Him "for a while." [20] To this deepening there was probably joined a greater extension. At the Jordan, Jesus presents himself as an individual among others who come to confess their sins and ask for baptism. In the desert, He combats an adversary over a conception of the Kingdom of God.

We shall not tarry long over the *Acts of the Apostles*. Two passages in Acts speak explicitly and without any possible confusion of the rite of laying on of hands, that is to say confirmation insofar as it is distinct from the baptismal rite. (Acts 8, 14–17 and 19, 1–7) The first deals with the mission of Peter and John to Samaria, where the two apostles go to complete the work of the deacon Philip; it is followed by the meeting at Ephesus of Paul and the disciples of John the Baptist. It should be remarked that in the first of these texts especially, the Spirit's coming is linked to the rite of the laying on of hands.[21] Certainly the Spirit is already present in the baptized. But by a literary ellipsis the author of Acts signifies to us that for him, as for the first generation of Christians, confirmation is the "sacrament which gives the Spirit," the sacrament of the Spirit. At Ephesus, after Paul had laid his hands on twelve men, "the Holy Spirit came down on them, and they spoke with tongues, and prophesied." (Acts 19, 6)

Since confirmation is, par excellence, the sacrament which gives the Spirit, we are invited to see what the effects of the descent of the Holy Spirit were on Pentecost day, even though this has to do with a special case, that of the Apostles.[22] Upon reading the second chapter of Acts, one sees there the following effects.

First, there is the fullness of the Holy Spirit, the Spirit sent by

[20] Cf. Lk. 4, 13 and 22, 53.

[21] I borrow these lines from a study of the late M. l'Abbé Lucien de Bontridder, to appear in *Lumen Vitae;* his work has inspired several passages in this paragraph concerned with the significance of confirmation.

[22] This enlarged treatment is all the more legitimate as the effects of St. Paul's intervention at Ephesus recall in a striking manner the events of Pentecost.

the risen Christ: "They were all filled with the Holy Spirit." (Acts 2, 4) The apostles receive an understanding of Scripture, a grasp of the history of salvation, in particular of the Paschal Mystery and the Eucharist. Peter, who had grown indignant at the thought of the Passion some weeks before, has comprehended the design of God. According to St. Thomas, Pentecost was also "the time when the Holy Spirit initiated the hearts of the disciples into the full knowledge of the mystery of the Eucharist." [23]

The disciples are caught up in this "story of salvation." Their first activity is preaching—"prophecy," witness. But the "breaking of bread," the Eucharist, is called for directly afterward. Under the impulse of the Spirit and the direction of the Apostles, the Church grows in strictest unity. The Acts describe this spread, beginning with Jerusalem to the very ends of the earth.

To sum up: Under the influence of the Spirit sent by the risen Christ, the Apostles receive some understanding of the Paschal Mystery and of the Eucharist. They engage, in turn, in the history of salvation itself as heralds and priests for the extension of the Kingdom of God.

The Liturgy

In the life of the Savior, His baptism and "confirmation" are preparatory steps toward the redemptive passion. The descent of the Holy Ghost on Pentecost unites the minds as well as the hearts of the Apostles in the mystery of our salvation. It is accomplished by the Father who sends His Son, by the Son who dies and rises again, by the Spirit who is sent by Christ in glory.

Even though baptism and confirmation (at least as made manifest or more explicit in the desert), are both oriented toward the passion, there is nonetheless a progress from the one to the other. At the Jordan, the entry into public life is like a birth, a recognition: "Thou art my Son," says the Father to Jesus who appears in the role of "Servant of Yahweh." In the desert, without any change in perspective, it is a matter of personal choice and a pledging of self to establish the Kingdom of God.

---

[23] Sermon for the feast of Corpus Christi, *Opusculum* 57.

This ordering in the direction of the Paschal Mystery, these relations, are things we shall see represented in an impressive way in the early liturgy.

1. *The early liturgy.* In the Paschal Vigil and Mass the Christian community accomplished a complete Eucharistic rite, a great act of thanksgiving memorializing the Savior's Resurrection. Before the offering of the sacrifice, both baptism and confirmation were conferred. It is in this context that confirmation, ordained toward the Eucharist, reveals if not its entire significance at least one of its chief roles:

The whole community took part actively and hierarchically in preparing for and celebrating this feast.

Laymen, that is to say men "provided with the sacred character common to the entire 'royal priesthood,' have presented and then instructed the candidate for baptism; in this vigil they were the first to lay hands on him." After that, a *deacon* descended with him into the piscina and with a second imposition of hands immersed him in the baptismal waters. When he had come forth a *priest* began to anoint him with holy oil, saying to him the while: "I anoint you with holy oil in the name of Jesus." Finally, they brought him to the *bishop* who laid hands on him once more, saying almost to the letter that prayer which is still used to conclude the confirmation ceremony; then he completed the anointing in the name of the entire Trinity. After the kiss given by the bishop, the candidate took his place in the ranks of the faithful.

"The new Christians pray with their brothers [as they were not able to do before, Hippolytus carefully points out], and exchange the kiss of peace with them. They all proceed immediately to the offering where they likewise take part for the first time. Then the bishop pronounces the consecratory prayer when the deacons have brought him what has been offered. All is brought to a close by the communion of the neophytes in company with the rest." [24]

In the ceremony reserved to the bishop, let us observe more attentively on the one hand the rites and their effects, and on the other the person of the minister and his role.

---

[24] L. Bouyer, of the Oratory, "Que signifie la Confirmation?" *Paroisse et Liturgie,* 34 (1952), 8. The author high-lights—unfortunately in somewhat too exclusive a fashion—the relations obtaining between confirmation and the Eucharist.

Even in the Old Testament the laying on of hands by a man of God had as its effect the gift of wisdom.[25] When Samuel anointed Saul and then David, the Spirit of God rested on them and transformed their hearts in view of the mission which these elect of God would have to fulfill.[26] In the New Covenant, "God anointed Jesus of Nazareth with the Holy Spirit and with power." (Acts 10, 38; see also Lk. 4, 18 f. which reproduces the Septuagint text of Is. 61, 1 f.) Those confirmed are made to participate in this grace when they receive from the bishop a palpable anointing. "It is God who gives both us and you our certainty in Christ; it is he who has *anointed* us, just as it is he who has put his seal on us, and given us the foretaste of his Spirit in our hearts." (II Cor., 1, 21 f.) Thus we have received in our measure the same Spirit as Christ. We are put in harmonious union with the Head of the Mystical Body, prepared to participate actively in offering His sacrifice.

The *minister* of this imposition of hands and this anointing is the bishop. Ruler, shepherd, teacher, pontiff, he receives us into the community as Christians who by the grace of the Holy Spirit reach adulthood and become capable of participating maturely in the Eucharistic oblation which the Church makes.

In the context of the primitive Paschal Vigil, confirmation thus presents itself to us as a day of twofold significance: it completes baptism and associates us more intimately with the priestly office of Christ; administered by the bishop, it introduces us as adults into the community of Holy Church.

Before long, however, the Church had been extended from country to country and conversions had multiplied. It grew impossible to lead all the neophytes before the bishop immediately following their baptism. Consequently the liturgy evolved in two directions. In the Eastern Church care was taken to preserve the strict unity of the three sacraments of Christian initiation, and confirmation was

---

[25] "Now Josue, son of Nun, was filled with the spirit of wisdom, since Moses had laid his hands upon him." (Deut. 34, 9)

[26] "Then the spirit of Yahweh will descend upon you, you will enter into ecstasy with them and be changed into another man," Samuel had announced to Saul (I Sam. 10, 6); the prophecy was realized (*ibid.*, 10, 10). "Samuel took the horn of oil and anointed him in the midst of his brothers. The spirit of the Lord took possession of David from that time onward." (*Ibid.*, 16, 13)

conferred by every priest. In the Latin Church reasons for re-
serving confirmation and the reception of adult Christians into the
community of the Church to the bishop prevailed. The sacraments
were separated from one another, with the unfortunate effect that
the connections between confirmation and baptism and the Eucharist largely escaped notice. Despite all this, however, the Church
in general came to abide by the order: baptism, confirmation,
Eucharist.

2. *Historical sketch: the order of the sacraments.* I shall limit my-
self here to reproducing the conclusions of a study done recently
by Father Levet, professor in the Major Seminary at Arras. These
serve to strengthen the positions of his predecessors.[27]

This order in the conferring of the sacraments is a matter of
tradition, one may say. Levet writes:

The Church has always considered it normal for the baptized, adults
as well as children, to receive confirmation before the Eucharist.

To our knowledge there is no Roman text which foresees the possibility
of adopting the reverse order habitually and in principle.

Rather is it the case that the letter of Leo XIII (1897), the latest
edition of the Roman Ritual (1952), and the instruction of the Sacred
Congregation of the Sacraments (1932), show that the Church still
thinks in the same terms. These documents require observance of this
rule except in cases of impossibility. With adults this impossibility is realized whenever a bishop is not present at the time and place of their
baptism. In the case of children, from the fourth to the twelfth century
there was often an equal impossibility deriving from a bishop's absence;
from the twelfth century to the Decree "Quam Singulari" (1910), the
impossibility practically never existed, confirmation being given several
years before first communion. Since *"Quam Singulari"* there may sometimes be an impossibility arising from the coincidence of the ages for
reception of the two sacraments and the urgency of the precept to receive communion at the age of reason. That brings to mind the concluding part of the response of the Sacred Congregation of the Sacraments
to the Spanish-speaking countries. But bad arranging must not render
such an impossibility habitual.[28]

---

[27] R. Levet, "L'âge de la confirmation," in A. Chanson, *Pour mieux ad-
ministrer Baptême, Confirmation, Eucharistie, Extrême-Onction,* 2ième éd.
(Arras: Brunet, 1953), 437–46.

[28] *Ibid.,* p. 444.

Over the centuries the Church remained faithful to the order of the sacraments. This practice is not incompatible with fluctuations in the matter of age. It should not be superfluous to record the history of practice here. If, in this regard, historical study does not yield a decisive argument for reception at the age of reason, it will at least no longer justify us in considering the ages of eleven, twelve or thirteen as "traditional"; quite the contrary.

3. *Historical sketch: age of confirmation.* The age at which confirmation has been administered has varied greatly in the course of centuries and in the law nothing hinders that it vary even today. The following summation is from Levet:

a) Up to the IV Lateran Council (1215), no distinction was made in the manner of conferring Christian initiation on adults and children. To both, baptism, confirmation and the Eucharist were given equally.

b) From the twelfth century the tendency grew not to give communion to children "before the age of reason."

Furthermore, shortly after the IV Lateran Council, even though the usage of confirming babies continued (Council of Arles, 1260), there likewise began to arise the custom of putting off confirmation until the ages of one, three, seven and even twelve—but in any case, before communion.[29]

c) The Roman Catechism (1566), catechism of the Council of Trent, canonized in that year the custom of putting confirmation off to the age of reason. It therefore played the same role in the history of confirmation

---

[29] "Why this delay? There were numerous reasons: neglect to receive a sacrament which is not strictly necessary for salvation; infrequent appearances by bishops. Most of all, around 1215 the Gloss interpreted a text of the Council of Orléans reproduced by the decree of Gratian in favor of confirmation at twelve years: *'ut jejuni ad confirmationem veniant perfectae aetatis'*—'let them approach confirmation fasting, at a mature age.' This *'perfectae aetatis'* made an impression; but as Suarez remarks the text is speaking of adults to be confirmed and it does not speak as if it were only necessary to confirm adults. Doubtless too there was a tendency from 1215 on to wish that confirmation be received with personal dispositions like those for the Eucharist. Certain particular councils tried to struggle against the idea, but in vain. Others recognized the custom (Cologne, 1280, which said 'seven years and more'). On the eve of the Council of Trent we find a Council of Cologne (1536) citing both usages: confirmation administered to the very young and in other cases deferred until the age of reason; no absolute decision was made in favor of the one or the other." (Levet, *op. cit.*, p. 441).

that the IV Lateran Council had played in that of the age of first communion.[30]

d) From the beginning of the nineteenth century to the decree "*Quam Singulari*" (1910), in the Latin Church in general no change in discipline, except that starting with the mid-nineteenth century one sees a reaction set off by Rome against conciliar or synodal prescriptions which contemplate too late an age for first communion.

But first in France and later in Austria-Hungary the custom of putting off confirmation even until after first communion became widespread.[31]

Nevertheless, a return to the general usage of the Latin Church took shape after an intervention of the Sacred Congregation of the Council which demanded modification of the acts of the provincial council of Algiers in 1875.

e) The decree "*Quam singulari*" (1910) on communion at the age of seven constitutes the authentic commentary on the decree of the IV Lateran Council of 1215. . . . Generally only its eucharistic consequences are observed. It does seem that even outside of France it is not realized how modification of the point of view on the age of communion was meant to render the obligation of early confirmation much stricter.

In France the anomaly of the nineteenth century was aggravated in most dioceses.

In 1917 the *Code of Canon Law* was promulgated. In canon 788 the prescriptions given by the Roman Catechism for the age of confirmation were reverted to. But since the catechism was not a legislative text, this

[30] The text of the Roman Catechism is susceptible of two interpretations: 1) "That is why (= given that) it does not seem good (= lawful) to wait until the age of twelve, though it is mandatory not to confirm before seven;" 2) "that is why, if (for such a child) it is not considered obligatory to wait the age of twelve (though lawfully one might do so), it is at least ('*certe*') required to wait until the age of seven." Since internal criteria are not clear recourse is necessary to external criteria; namely, seeing how this text was understood by subsequent provincial councils. According to Levet (*op. cit.*, pp. 440 f.), two points seem established: 1) by examining *all* the councils of the second half of the sixteenth century, it can be seen that confirmation was generally given *around the age of seven;* 2) *lesser psychological conditions* were being required for confirmation than for communion, and in fact *confirmation was preceding communion.*

[31] "Why this new deferment? The reasons for it are expounded in pastoral letters, diocesan statutes, and canons of provincial councils. Many children had not been able to be confirmed during the Revolution, and the bishops who signed the concordat found themselves faced with multitudes to be confirmed, beginning with adults. Further, by putting off the age of confirmation they could be surer that children would continue with the cycle of catechetical instruction up until first communion time." (Levet, *op. cit.*, p. 442)

was the first time that a law was made on the age of confirmation: "Licet sacramenti confirmationis administratio convenienter in Ecclesia Latina differatur ad septimum circiter aetatis annum, nihilominus etiam antea conferri potest, si infans in mortis periculo sit constitutus, vel ministro id expedire ob iustas et graves causas videatur."

An *Instruction of the Sacred Congregation on the Sacraments* (1932) authorized the Spanish-speaking countries to retain the custom of administering confirmation shortly after baptism, while at the same time declaring it preferable to follow canon 788 so as to be able to precede the reception of confirmation with a *"catechesis instructio."* [32] It contained another directive as well for other countries: "Certainly it is opportune and more in conformity with the nature and effects of the sacrament of confirmation that children should not come to the Holy Table for the first time until they have received confirmation, which is like the complement of baptism and in which the Holy Spirit is given (*S. Th.* III, q. 72, a. 2, c., where *'robur spirituale'* is described as befitting *'perfectae aetati'*); however children must not be forbidden access to the Holy Table if they have come to the age of reason without having been able (*non potuerunt*) previously to receive the sacrament of confirmation." Briefly, the Church intends to remain faithful to the order in which the sacraments should be received, but the practical impossibility of receiving confirmation will not necessarily retard first communion.

f) Since its Instruction of 1932 the Sacred Congregation on the Sacraments has promulgated two decrees relative to confirmation.

The Instruction of May 20, 1934 says apropos of age: "Besides the custom already cited (that of Spanish-speaking countries), there can also be, according to the view approved by several theologians, other legitimate causes for giving confirmation before the age of seven, especially when the prolonged non-appearance of the bishop is foreseen."

The Decree of Sept. 14, 1946 concedes to certain priests the power to give confirmation to persons—whether children or adults—in danger of death. One clause seems to us to put an end to debate on the *"catechesis instructio"* mentioned in the document of 1932: "The common law of the Latin Church, codified in canon 788, stipulates that the ad-

---

[32] The Sacred Congregation does not specify what this *"catechesis instructio"* must be. According to Fr. Galtier ("L'âge de la confirmation," in *Nouvelle Revue Théologique*, LX [1933], 675–86), it must be more advanced than that for first communion. Fr. Jungmann adopts their opinion (*Katechetik*, 2nd ed., Freiburg, Herder, 1955, p. 262). This interpretation has difficulty in harmonizing with the rest of the instruction (as Fr. Jungmann recognizes, *ibid.*, p. 262, n. 99), and with later decrees of the same Congregation. It has not yet been received by the French hierarchy (see R. Levet, *op. cit.*, pp. 443 and 443 bis, n. 20).

ministration of this sacrament be deferred until the seventh year, so that, after a fitting (or appropriate) instruction, the children may derive from it more abundant fruit."

"31. The Church desires that confirmation be given at about the age of reason (the age, that is, of the so-called "private communion"). Should anyone say that "confirmation is the sacrament of adulthood," the answer is that the phrase must be understood in the domain of spiritual and supernatural life, not physical and social life on the natural level.

"32. Just as it is legitimate to delay certain of the engagement ceremonies, so would it be contrary to the intention of the Church to delay confirmation. The faculties granted to pastors to confer confirmation on the sick illustrate this point well."

4. *Conclusions from historical research.* We repeat at the close of this résumé of liturgy and ecclesiastical history that one fact is certain: the Church has always considered it normal for the baptized to receive confirmation before the Eucharist.

At times the reverse order has obtained, as in the case of the rare appearance of the bishop or (following a period of persecution, for example) when there were excessive numbers of candidates for confirmation. In these instances the children were required to await their turn until after the adults.

We prescind from these accidental modifications resulting from circumstance, however. More profound reasons came along to delay confirmation and even to put it after first communion, especially when the latter became obligatory at the age of seven.

First of all, there was the idea that it is not a sacrament necessary for salvation.[33] From this it follows that there is no urgency to confer it and that, for serious reasons, it may be delayed. The nineteenth century, which was prone to identify religious formation with the study of a systematic, abstract catechism, would be disposed to defer confirmation in the hope of guaranteeing catechism study more surely, or would at least be disposed to over-

---

[33] Levet points to this to explain the custom of delaying confirmation which was established shortly after the IV Lateran Council (*op. cit.*, p. 441). Similarly, Jungmann notes it as a consideration invoked in favor of waiting until adolescence (*op. cit.*, p. 261).

estimate the intellectual demands made of the "confirmand."[34]
The twentieth century, more solicitous for morality than faith, and
justifiably shaken by the dangers to which adolescents are exposed—likewise answering the rallying cry of Catholic Action—
chooses to see in confirmation a help in the difficulties of puberty,
a means of resistance to the influences of a dechristianized culture,
and the defensive armor of a knight of Christ. It wishes to see
entrance to adult life marked by the consecration of a sacrament.[35]

But do not these pedagogic, moralistic and apostolic concerns
run the risk of deflecting the sacrament of confirmation from its
profound significance intended by the Savior? After the study of
confirmation in Scripture and the liturgy, the question is certainly
in order. If such is the case we shall not really be serving the causes
so important to us.

Acts of the Magisterium

According to the documents of the *magisterium,* confirmation is
a sacrament which gives us the Holy Spirit.[36]

In relation to baptism, it marks an increase of grace (*"augmen-
tum," "augemur in gratia"*); [37] a making firm in faith (*"roboremur
in fide," "roborati," "robur"*); [38] it has as its effect the communication
of a power to profess the faith (*"ut Christianus audacter Christi
confiteatur nomen"*); [39] it is a balm which enables us to give off in
every direction the good odor of Christ.[40]

In the enumeration of the sacraments it almost always follows the
first, baptism, and comes immediately before the Eucharist.[41] The
decree for the Armenians (1439) likewise indicates clearly the inter-

---

[34] See Franz Arnold's article, "Renouveau de la prédication dogmatique et
de la catéchèse," in *Lumen Vitae,* III (1948), 496–99.

[35] Jungmann has expanded upon these motives admirably, *op. cit.,* p. 261.

[36] Denzinger, Bannwart, Umberg, Rahner, *Enchiridion Symbolorum,* 30th
ed. (Freiburg: Herder, 1954), 98, 419, 450, 697.

[37] *Ibid.,* 695, 697.

[38] *Ibid.,* 419, 695, 697.

[39] *Ibid.,* 697.

[40] *Ibid.,* 697.

[41] *Ibid.,* 424, 695, 852, 996; in 465, penance is inserted between confirmation
and the Eucharist.

connection of the three sacraments of Christian initiation: "By baptism we are reborn spiritually; by confirmation we grow in grace and are fortified in faith; then, born anew and strengthened, we are nourished with the divine food of the Eucharist." [42] When the reference is to character, confirmation is cited after baptism and before order.[43]

In other contexts, the *magisterium* notes several times that confirmation must be conferred by the bishop, the successor to the apostles who gave the Holy Spirit by laying on of hands; [44] if a priest is delegated he must use chrism blessed by the bishop,[45] whose action he prolongs.

A Theological Reflection on the Meaning of Confirmation

If we reflect on the data of Scripture, the liturgy, and the *magisterium,* we see in confirmation a new intervention of the Spirit which has as its effect an interior change and a participation in the missions of the Savior.

The three divine Persons are at work in all the sacraments. Consequently, the new relations which we contract with each of them are the essence of these santifying interventions on their part; these relations constitute our Christian personalities.[46] By baptism the Holy Spirit unites us with Christ in His death and resurrection. We become adoptive sons in the only Son on the occasion of this rebirth, *filii in Filio.* The spiritual energies transmitted in the baptistry, however, lie dormant in the one who is baptized. In Christ he is as yet only a child. But it is not God's will that we remain minors forever. He invites us not only to achieve our salvation with Him but to collaborate in the salvation of the world.

How does one become a collaborator with the creative and re-

---

[42] *Ibid.,* 695.
[43] *Ibid.,* 852.
[44] *Ibid.,* 98, 419, 424, 450, 465, 697, 873, 960, 2147a.
[45] *Ibid.,* 697.
[46] See the profound treatments of P. Ranwez, S.J., "The Sacrament of Confirmation, Builder of the Personality for Service in the Mystical Body of Christ," in *Lumen Vitae,* IX (1954), 17–34; "Confirmation et vie chrétienne," in *Catéchistes,* 19 (1954), 169–82.

demptive Word, a little bit like the human Christ? It is quite impossible without a new intervention of the Spirit. He alone, sent by the Father and the Son, can carry on the creative work begun at baptism and make the baptized person participate in that *anointing of Christ* which transforms him into another Christ. By confirmation the Spirit extends to each of us who is baptized all the influence He exerted in the Incarnation and Redemption, bringing us close together and making us like the Person of the Word who creates and redeems. It makes us capable of working with the Spirit for the increase of Christ in ourselves and others. Endowed thus with the power of the Father whose instrument he has become, the Christian is ready to participate in the Savior's Eucharistic sacrifice as one responsible for himself, for his neighbor and for the whole world.

This influence of the Christian is possible only in view of the inner transformation which he undergoes. He becomes more closely configured to Christ in intelligence, will and entire being. His confirmation is an illumination. He understands the "wonders of God" (cf. Acts 2, 14–36), which are chiefly the events of the Paschal Mystery. The Christian is guided by the Holy Spirit unto all truth (Jn. 16, 13), but in a way so persuasive that His teaching is a "witness" in the full force of that term (Jn. 15, 26). Confirmation also gives the Christian strength, the strength of a magnanimous love and a devotedness docile before the Spirit. To have "the same mind which Christ Jesus showed" (Phil. 2, 5) is a thing not accomplished in a Christian save by confirmation. So much is this the case that the Church prescribes the confirmation of children in danger of death that they may achieve in Christ their full stature as adults.

The transformation of the baptized is not accomplished immediately, however, through confirmation. The Holy Spirit continues His work in docile hearts through a progressive purification of the concepts and the affections of carnal man.

In the New as in the Old Testament, when the Spirit plummets down upon someone and transforms him into a new man this is done with the purpose of investing him with a mission. The sacraments of baptism, confirmation and order incorporate man into the

Christian community, and confer on him a particular mission in the Church. They comprise a consecration in man analogous to that of Jesus who by His union with the Word is constituted Mediator between God and men. One can see why the bishop, the pontiff, teacher and shepherd of the diocese should be the ordinary minister of confirmation, for this sacrament confers on men an adult participation in the priestly, prophetic and royal missions of Christ.

By confirmation we men become capable of taking part actively —as mature individuals responsible in a spirit of solidarity for the good of the community—in the Mass, wherein the Paschal Mystery is presented anew. This is the highest function for which confirmation prepares us, given the fact that "the character deputes a man to the worship of God in accordance with the Christian religion." [47] In general, this is insisted on far too little with the consequence that the theocentric character of confirmation goes undeveloped.

When we participate actively in the celebration of the Eucharist which by means of union with God and neighbor builds up the Mystical Body, when we observe in every detail of life the new commandment of charity whose source is Christ, when we prepare for the appearance of new heavens and a new earth in an ever closer union with the creating and redeeming Word, then shall we be collaborating in the extension of the Reign of God, the gathering into one of a whole race of men redeemed, and in a sense, of a Universe made holy in trinitarian Unity, in accord with Christ's vow, "That they all may be one." (Jn. 17, 21)

Confirmation does not have as its purpose to confine the life and effort of a Christian within the limits of the works of piety, nor even works described as "charitable." It looks to all the human activity of this son of God. For the life of grace must be introduced into every field of human effort, into all the trades and all the professions. Only at this price will the world undergo a reconstruction in Christ.[48]

Confirmation is a participation in the three missions of Christ. It is not only the sacrament of the apostolate, however, but also and

[47] St. Thomas, *S. Th.* III, q. 63, a. 3, ad 2.
[48] François Taymans d'Eypernon, S.J., *La Sainte Trinité et les sacrements* (Bruxelles: Edition Universelle, 1949), pp. 68 f.

primarily of personal commitment and spiritual progress. It brings about a development of faith, refining spiritual sensibilities.

The question is frequently posed, Does confirmation destine us for any one of the three missions of Christ more than the others? Ordinarily one speaks of the prophetic mission in this connection, that of bearing witness. In Christ, we have observed, the missions are very closely joined, though at various times in His life He seemed to exercise one mission somewhat more than another. In one who is confirmed the functions of Christ are intimately conjoined. Assistance at Mass is for him a sharing in the priesthood, a profession of faith, and an active collaboration in establishing the Reign of God.

The proper role of confirmation is not to orient us toward one function of Christ in preference to another. What it does do is render us able throughout life to participate in the missions of Christ as adults responsible for their own salvation and that of the world.

Confirmation accomplishes in us for our earthly existence what extreme unction will achieve in the perspective of passing from this world to the Father. There is in fact a strict parallelism between the various sacraments of initiation, baptism, confirmation and the Eucharist, and the last sacraments, penance, extreme unction and Viaticum.[49] Confirmation unites us more to Christ's public life which was principally but not exclusively revelation and testimony. Extreme unction consecrates our passing and prepares us for revelation face to face. In a comprehensive sense, it can be said that the sacrament of confirmation is conferred on us with testimony to truth in view. It enables us to be other Christs, witnesses to the Savior.

In saying this we must not forget that the highest function it renders us capable of, the most efficacious for ourselves and the Mystical Body, is the new participation in the Eucharist, which is the sacrament of charity. The principal gift of the Holy Spirit is, in

[49] See above the parallelism between the Temptation narrative and that of the Agony. Early liturgical discipline permitted the administration of extreme unction before Viaticum. In 1948, the Week at Vanves expressed the hope of a return to the former custom. It is so done in the bilingual German ritual.

fact, the charity which unites us intimately with God and neighbor. He distributes other gifts in all sorts of ways for the upbuilding of the Body of Christ.

If one had to include all these data in a single formula perhaps it could be put thus: "In the sacrament of confirmation the glorified Savior gives us, through the imposing of the bishop's hands and anointing with chrism, his Holy Spirit, who transforms us into strong and conscious Christians; he stamps our hearts with a new seal of the cross and gives us an active share in the work of Christ."

CONFIRMATION AT THE AGE OF REASON: A NECESSITY FOR THE EFFICACY OF RELIGIOUS TEACHING

We said at the very outset that the purpose of religious instruction is the development of faith. That means an intellectual adherence to the Paschal Mystery, the message of salvation brought by "the Witness." It is an adherence which is characterized by the orientation of one's entire person, in a word by commitment. Hence the mission of the catechist or the professor of religion is broken down into three tasks: helping others either to give themselves to God or else to remain faithful to their earlier personal commitment, assisting them in an adherence which is increasingly more conscious, and promoting the spread of the Faith through the sacramental and the interior life just as much as through the witness borne by a man's whole conduct of life.

All research done on the role of confirmation has concluded that this sacrament enlightens us as to the meaning of the Paschal Mystery and the history of salvation, and gives us the strength to take on, on our own account, the obligations assumed by our godparents. It thus marks a stage in the growth of that faith which must animate the interior life and active participation in the Eucharist, not to speak of all Christian conduct and witness. This simple collocation of argument proves sufficiently that for the normal efficacy of religious formation confirmation at the age of reason—if not sooner—is a necessity. Left to himself, the catechist or the professor of religion will necessarily be unequal to the three tasks incumbent upon him. If, on the contrary, he discharges them with children who have received confirmation or are preparing for it, he sees himself in the lofty position of humble co-worker of the interior Master. In the pages that follow I should like to show how much the early reception of confirmation would facilitate personal commitment, an increased religious awareness and the burgeoning of faith in every aspect of life.

Confirmation and Personal Commitment

The light of faith shed upon the data of experience yields two conclusions as to the role of confirmation in the religious life of children. They are these:

Confirmation is very useful, indeed necessary, for the child to attain the use of reason in a true sense (that is, to prefer God to himself) and recognize sufficiently the God to whom his self-offering is directed as he stands at the threshold of life.

The influence of confirmation is by no means least in the matter of perseverance.

1. *Confirmation and one's earliest personal choice.* Let us begin by studying the role of confirmation in the initial option or self-determination. What does that consist in? How much is at stake here? Father Claeys Bouüaert writes:

Everyone knows that the beginnings of moral life in man coincide with the onset of what is correctly termed the age of reason. This is the time when he discerns good and evil and deliberates inwardly, is "oriented personally" in St. Thomas's phrase, toward some final end, and ceases to depend entirely on his instinct and his surroundings. He really takes hold of himself and becomes in actual fact a reasonable being. To reach the age of reason is to enter into moral life. Again, once it is understood in its full and only coherent meaning, the moral life cannot be conceived without the notion of strict obligation. This in turn implies and supposes the notion of the true God. Therefore we can make the following identification: the age of reason is the age of moral life and also the age of knowledge of God. All three terms signify the same thing.[50]

These equations sufficiently indicate the importance of this age.

[50] Paul Claeys Bouüaert, S.J., "Tous les athées sont-ils coupables?" in *La Nouvelle Revue Théologique,* 48 (1921), 171 f.

It is then that the child becomes capable of either following freely or resisting the natural impulse of his intelligence which, divinely elevated, carries the creature toward the Creator. Such is the drama of the age of reason. But notice that the self-determination is by no means so simple as it may appear.

a. First of all, it may either never take place, or else the soul may not arrive at the age of reason for a good while. The reader needs only to recall various unfortunate cases of abnormalcy to concur on this point. These cases are not the most tragic ones, as Claeys de Bouüaert points out:

> Let us imagine, for example, disastrous moral conditions in thoroughly civilized countries in which children are obliged to develop in coarse and even thoroughly corrupt surroundings, where their souls must be formed for life; where they never hear God spoken of nor conscience, duty, or any ideal whatsoever, save in terms of hate and derision as the invention of priests and the rich. Out of these surroundings they finally escape, by that time unreservedly given over to their instincts and without any other aim in life than money and pleasure. If we try to estimate the effect of such an education on the souls of the young and if we recall that the Vatican Council authorizes us to believe, even in the matter of knowledge of God, in the power of social influences, it will doubtless be hard to continue affirming calmly that in the soul of every human being who enjoys the gift of intellect the notions of obligation and of God must necessarily develop early; and this, mind you, with all the certainty required to engage the conscience, that is, to set the alternatives of mortal sin and perfect love in opposition, as a result of which the soul will reject or accept anything that conduces toward its last end.
>
> We have been speaking only of children raised in the crudities of a milieu which knows neither faith nor law. Evidently that comprises but one set of cases. Other situations can produce the same effects. May not, for example, the spirit and the understanding grow embittered in the most refined surroundings just as surely as in the crudest? Do not science and culture have it in their power as well as a defect of education to lead the spirit astray and close it to a higher world of truth? [51]

There should be no need to apply these considerations to our own time. We witness the material suffering of millions of children and the spiritual distress of all who are subject to rationalizing influences much too early. Given these material and cultural conditions it is

[51] *Op. cit.,* pp. 176 f.

to be feared that many human beings do not arrive at the level of personal choice for a long time. Thereby the ranks of unbelievers who are without responsibility in their amoral condition are swollen. What results is a partial bankruptcy of religion, of morality, or of humanity.

b. The same causes outlined above will incline some of those oriented toward a final end to *prefer self to God.* Perhaps this choice will have been prepared for by an egoistic childhood in which parents were eager to satisfy the youngster's every whim. From two to four the child chooses between his "I" and others. He thus acquires a disposition which will be influential when the moment of decision comes in which he must prefer either the great Other or himself. Appearances can deceive us. The recitation of prayers is no sure index of virtuous choice. It has to be determined whether the child's religion is purely self-interested or whether sacrifice plays any part in it. Depending on which is the case, formalism will continue to be accentuated or, contrariwise, the purification of love.

If we cease to credit outward appearances overmuch and judge as Christians, we will acknowledge how much strength and light is needed by the child at the age of reason to make the personal act of choice that prefers God to himself. He needs both gifts to recognize sufficiently the God whom he is being called on to offer himself to at the dawn of conscious life.

2. *Confirmation and persevering at one's commitment.* Important though this election of the child may be, it is not that of an angel. It can undergo revision, whence comes the problem of persevering in the initial declaration in favor of the good.

The child needs to be guided in the business of remaining on the right path. The modern world puts him off the track by a whole series of deceits: lies, commercial huckstering, nationalist or party propaganda. His moral resolve needs strengthening because the climate is debilitating in the extreme. Even on the supposition that without the aid of confirmation the first personal election would have been excellent, the sacrament would still be very useful and even necessary for perseverance.

Certain psychologists speak of the "psychological optimum" in discussing the teaching of some matter or an educational proposal of some sort. If a thing is tried too late it can come to nothing, for by that time the subject has a taste for something else.

The effects of a tardy administration of confirmation make themselves felt. Deprived—I underline the point—deprived of confirmation from the age of reason to the age of eleven or twelve, the soul has been spiritually put to severe strain. It can have lost if not the understanding of God at least the taste for Him. In the most favorable cases, the child has mastered a religious knowledge which is the pride of priest or catechist. Could not this knowledge have been checked on anywhere along the line? It is a well known fact that even the non-Catholic youngster sometimes comes out first in religion-study competitions. My point is that normally, if confirmation is what we believe it to be, the adolescent of twelve will present himself to the bishop less well disposed than the child of seven. He will have lost in resiliency of spirit what he might have gained in the realm of a knowledge that can be checked by questioning.

Confirmation and Conscious Adherence

Catechetical instruction is faced with an antinomy in our day. In various countries the courses in religion are too challenging and the manuals too substantial for children malformed by their surroundings and spiritually anemic. But on the other hand, the necessity for solider religious formation presents itself as secular culture grows and the pattern of life is divorced from the sacred. A solution to the problem presupposes the concurrence of several factors, among them the early reception of confirmation. Since I cannot enter into all the details, I should like to highlight three points.

1. Contemporary philosophy has brought to the fore the roles of freedom and love in any progress in knowledge. Blondel's labors have been completed by the observations of the existentialists. Thanks to them we understand better today that knowledge of God progresses variously according as we have acted for Him or against Him. Similarly, on the supernatural plane, the believer animated by divine charity will discover God in a different fashion from the believer who does not live in God's friendship. Writes Father de La Taille:

The light of faith, although in the mind, has not entered into man through the mind but through the heart. There is its gate of entry. There is the aperture through which God pours it more or less abundantly, more or less alive, according as love itself is alive within us beyond all other affection or, conversely, as self-love dominates the love of God and overwhelms it.[52]

As has been said above, confirmation has a great influence on the most personal area of choice and on fidelity to this first commitment. It increases our love of God. On this count it enjoys a considerable role in the progress of religious knowledge.

2. Passing from the child's faculties to his program of religion study, we can testify to a happy evolution in our day. All teaching that savors of rationalism is at least theoretically proscribed and in its place the message of the Good News is addressed simultaneously to intellect and will. It is being presented as the story of salvation or, better still, the mystery of salvation. Well and good. But this divine sense of history which needs to be communicated to children was not grasped by the apostles before Pentecost day. Is it out of place to believe that the introduction of a kerygmatic program requires the special assistance of the *Lumen cordium,* a preparation of hearts and spirits?

3. Finally, there is the problem of methods. In this area too, great progress is reported. But there are pitfalls to avoid. Professor Arnold fears that priests and catechists skilled in these methods may exaggerate their helpfulness and forget the role of the interior Master.

Activity methods rouse the pupil from torpor, but they also run the risk of occupying him with superficial tasks to the detriment of interior growth. We have to plead today for "more soul" in catechetics as Bergson pleaded for it to a world whose spiritual development had not been on a par with its technical prowess. The progress of methods and techniques might delude us if the action of the "interior Master" were not taken advantage of.[53]

[52] Maurice de La Taille, S.J., "L'oraison contemplative," in *Recherches des Sciences Religeuses,* IX (1919), 283.

[53] F. Coudreau, P.S.S., "The Holy Ghost and Individualised Teaching," *Lumen Vitae,* VIII (1953), 77–85; also Suzanne-Marie Durand, "The Holy Spirit and Active Methods," *loc. cit.,* 86–93.

The task of religious education is far more than a matter of reproducing slavishly the conduct of Christ. It has to do with continuing—I had almost said "devising"—Him anew in His earthly existence. We can do a thing like that only by docility to the Spirit who led Jesus. This is the condition on which we shall be sons of God. "Those who follow the leading of God's Spirit are all God's sons." (Rom. 8, 14)

Our religious instruction has become Christ-centered once more, an incontestable sign of progress. But it is still not "spiritual" enough or sufficiently "pneumatic" in the term of the Fathers. How necessary it is that the Spirit descend upon our children in His fullness very early, and that they come to think of Him habitually as "another Friend"; come to need Him and to act with Him!

When we consider today's children, many of them cut off from religion or thoroughly disoriented by war and its effects, by family mobility and divorce, we are dismayed at the weight of their obligation if they are baptized and wish to live as Catholics. They themselves have to struggle for perseverance; no one can do it for them. They can only do it by working to alter their surroundings, their study, their leisure.

Mankind in our day has great hopes for youth. It has learned that on the education of today's youth depends tomorrow's peace. The efforts made are remarkable, but in all likelihood much too short-sighted. The spread of knowledge and uniformity in teaching cannot make up for moral and religious education. Without the latter, children will never become fashioners of the kind of universe we hope for. Without it, international alignments can not look to the Mystical Body of Christ to sustain them. The Holy Spirit is the Soul of the Body. Were He to animate youth in all the forms its vigor takes, nations and races could grow in unity without detriment to their diversity.

We work against Him, we who have the power to transmit Him sacramentally, if we keep Him from the young in the years they most need Him.

Index

Abelard, 27
Abraham: act of faith, 147-148
Abstractions: catechism as summary of theology, 117
  children and, 126
  premature teaching of, 122-123
Acceptance of faith, 144-146
Adults: catechetical instruction of, 173
Affiliations (Saint Sulpice), 110
Age of reason, 309ff.
Albi, Synod of, 40
Alcuin of York, 23-26
Ambrose, St., 16-17
Anointing in confirmation. *See* Confirmation
Antony the Hermit, St., 50
Apollos, 5
Apologetics: college theology, 179
  task of theology, 180
Apostles: Pentecost, 295
Apostles' Creed:
  Niceta of Remesiana on, 14
  tradition of composition, 15
Apostolate: Catholic colleges, 205
  dogmatic training for, 208
  Newman Club technique, 261
Apostolic Council, 4
Apothecaries, 49
Art, religious, 211
Asceticism: function, 216
  orientation in college religion, 215
Associations (Saint Sulpice), 109-110
Augustine, St.
  on the ages of man, 20
  on catechetics, 17ff.
  Christocentric, 19
  good and evil and, 19
  method and insight, 18
  the number seven, 30
  predestination and, 29
  on sacred history, 22
  typology, 20
Avitus, St., 21

Baker, Dom Augustine, 75

Baptism:
  see also Catechumenate
    Infant baptism
    Neophytes
  catechetical instruction of the child, 122
  Christian initiation, 121
  confirmation and, 286
  death and resurrection with Christ, 289ff.
  devoted family life, 124-125
  Easter Vigil liturgy, 19
  efficacy, 140
  generation, St. Ambrose on, 17
  generation of supernatural life, 142
  Hornyold on, 79
  medieval regard for, 43-44
  preaching of John the Baptist, 287
  religious instruction related to, 140-141
  as soon as possible, 161
  Trinity and, 304
  Vaux's catechism, 74
Baptismal name: history of practice, 43-44
Bateman, Jane, 252
Baüyn, Father, 95
Beggars: law of 1476, 40
Belief: *see also* Faith
  dedication of life, 135
  definition, 146
  divine witnesses, 282-283
  "reply" to God, 147
Benedict XV, Pope, 210
Benet of Canfield, 75
Bible: Alcuin of York on, 24-25
  Augustine and, 18
  Augustine's interpretation of, 20
  curriculum in religious education, 237
  early and medieval catechesis, 3-37 *passim*
  living data of theology, 181
  Old Latin version, 15
  oldest catechetical assumption, 16
  publication in Penal England, 67

315